EFFECTIVE WRITING FOR BUSINESS

ISABELLE A. KREY
Kingsborough Community College

BERNADETTE V. METZLER
Hunter College

EFFECTIVE

WRITING FOR BUSINESS

In consultation with
ESTELLE L. POPHAM
Hunter College

HARCOURT, BRACE & WORLD, INC.
New York / Chicago / San Francisco / Atlanta

Foreword

COMMUNICATION, especially in its written forms, is basic to business life. The young person aspiring to a successful business career must, therefore, master the techniques of effective writing. Professors Krey and Metzler have written a concise and lucid book that shows the reader, step by step, how to achieve that mastery.

In their long experience as teachers of business communications, the authors have learned what points are especially difficult for students, and they have been able to develop and test fresh, imaginative ways of teaching those points. *Effective Writing for Business* is a result of their experience. In it, they discard the pedestrian, prescriptive approach of earlier books on business writing in favor of a direct, informal style and numerous examples. Instead of merely giving the student a finished letter, they show him how to put the letter together and how to correct (and eventually avoid) the common mistakes. This technique enables the authors to anticipate the student's problems and to enlist his active participation in finding solutions.

Effective Writing for Business should, then, make the study of business communications an interesting and rewarding experience.

ESTELLE L. POPHAM

Preface

EFFECTIVE WRITING FOR BUSINESS is a basic textbook on business writing. It provides an introduction to the general principles of effective communication as well as instruction in the techniques pertinent to specific types of business correspondence.

We have adopted a modified case approach and a direct, informal style so as to involve the student directly in the writing process — to develop his skills as he is being informed. Therefore, each chapter builds upon the skills and information gained from the preceding material, and the examples show the step-by-step procedure by which a given problem can be solved.

The book is divided into three parts. The first is a thorough discussion of general principles, including sections on how to put a letter together, how to choose the appropriate style, and, most important, how to create a message that will reach the reader. In this last connection, we have emphasized such fundamentals as keeping the reader in mind, tailoring the message to fit its purpose, and using clear, effective language. These principles are then used and reiterated throughout the book.

In Part II, we discuss social- and personal-business communications, beginning with the simple request and working up to the application series. We have attempted to use the student's own needs and experiences to give him an introduction to basic business procedures and to illustrate the importance of written communication in the business world.

We then analyze the various types of on-the-job correspondence in Part III. While continuing to build upon the elements common to all letters, we have stressed in this final section the unique purpose of each type of letter and the way language is utilized to achieve that purpose.

Because we feel that language skills and styles are central to effective writing, we have used side glosses to highlight points of grammar, spelling, vocabulary, and usage and have treated each point more than once. The student can make the best use of these glosses by noting them as they occur and then reviewing them after he has finished reading the chapter. We would further recommend frequent use of the dictionary to determine the precise meanings of unfamiliar words.

At the conclusion of each chapter, an exercise section provides an opportunity for practical application of the techniques we have introduced in the chapter as well as those learned in preceding chapters. In addition, the exercises contain grammar and punctuation drills (each preceded by the relevant rules and explanations) and a test on the chapter's spelling and vocabulary words. The exercises are designed so that the student can type the answers on separate sheets of paper and thus get useful practice in form and style.

Our sincere thanks go to Dr. Estelle L. Popham, chairman of the Department of Business Education, Hunter College of the City University of New York, for her interest, encouragement, and counsel. Her expertise and acumen contributed greatly to the development of this book.

ISABELLE A. KREY

BERNADETTE V. METZLER

Contents

EFFECTIVE WRITING FOR BUSINESS

I

ELEMENTS OF EFFECTIVE WRITING

1 | Why Write Business Communications?

EVERY business firm, government office, and service organization is deluged with typed and duplicated materials — house organs, bulletins, government reports, handbooks, instruction leaflets, letters, interoffice memorandums, manuals, minutes of meetings, and proposals. Higher and higher builds the paper mountain! However, through these materials flows the life blood of business. Without written communication, orders would not be filled, supplies would not be received, credit would not be established, new techniques would not be devised, research would be slow and plodding, and management's decisions would be based on inadequate information. Without written communication, our economy could not have expanded so rapidly. Over the past two decades our gross national product (the total value of all final goods and services produced in the economy in one year) has nearly quadrupled.

 The quality of communications can speed up the service you or your company gives or receives. Your ability to communicate in writing will enable you to run your own business life more efficiently, and it is a

deluged

received

3

skill that business firms need in their personnel, from clerks to top executives. Do you know how much it costs to write a business letter? A recent survey by a **management** team of management consultants showed that today's letters cost anywhere from $1.37 to $3.18. The good letter costs no more than the poor one, but it gets better results. Management seeks results.

WHY WRITE IT DOWN?

Why write that letter? Why not communicate directly **it's** over the telephone or by a personal visit? It's faster, *(contraction of "it is"; not the possessive "its")* and you get the answer right away. True, but face-to-face conversation is not always feasible, practical, or **feasible** the most efficient means of contacting another person.

Economy

Distance, with the resulting expense of a toll call, is **deterrent** one deterrent to telephone conversation. It is less expensive to write to someone in another state or in another country than to telephone and to wait for an answer while the minutes tick away on that toll call. And you may save only a little time, since the answer may not be available at once and may have to be sent through the mails anyway. It is also more economical to write when hundreds, thousands, or tens of thousands of people must receive the same information — think of the letters inviting charge customers to a private sale at a leading department store.

Efficiency

It is impractical in today's business world to interrupt a customer by telephoning him to thank him for his order and to tell him when he will receive shipment. Just as annoying would be the department-store call to your home in the middle of a luncheon or a bridge game to tell you that delivery of the rug you had ordered will be delayed until the end of the month. A **suffice** card would suffice.

```
November 19, 1968

Dear Mrs. Jones

The trucking strike is over, and your
9 x 12 foot Karastan rug will be de-
livered on Monday, November 25.

We are sorry for the delay.

Sincerely

GROSS DEPARTMENT STORE
```

In determining the most efficient means of communicating, the letter writer must think not only of himself but of the person to whom he is writing.

Accuracy

The major determinant of the method of communication is, of course, the type of information to be transmitted or requested. Detailed, intricate information requires the written word to ensure accuracy and correct understanding. Would you call your salesman to make ten changes in a price list? How would you get the proposal for a new program of in-service training before the personnel manager? Can you rely on a telephone conversation to get the breakdown of individual item charges for your automobile insurance? What about that yearly schedule of club activities? How would you like to take the information in this letter over the telephone?

determinant

schedule

```
Your automobile-insurance policy No.
01-GA24-3234 includes coverage for:
bodily injury of $100/300,000 for a
premium of $103; property damage of
$25,000 for $33; comprehensive fire
and theft, according to value, for
$21; collision, with $50 deductible,
for $68; towing up to $25 for $2.
```

collision; deductible

These items must be in written form. Word-of-mouth communication can often result in error, such as a transposed figure, an incorrect date or address, or a misheard phrase; but a carefully written communication ensures accuracy.

Official Record

Finally, a written communication becomes part of the record — it becomes official. You will find that corporations, prior to their annual meetings, send out written proxies for their stockholders' signatures. You will find that the pressured executive asks you to "write it up" when you offer a proposal for a change in office procedure, for a change in letter style, or for an office bowling competition or picnic. Giving your supervisor a good written proposal can win a promotion for you; mentioning it to him in passing can consign your idea to oblivion.

The mail clerk who wrote this memorandum got a promotion in a growing advertising agency:

proxies

competition
consign

```
Date:    August 9, 1968

  To:    Mr. Matthew Peters
         Office Manager

From:    I. Smart
         Chief Messenger

Subject:    Handling Incoming Mail

When the mail comes into the office
each morning, it is delivered un-
opened to the departmental secretary,
who must then process it.

I propose that the following proce-
dure be considered for all depart-
mental offices.
```

```
The mail clerk:

    Opens all pieces of mail.
    Time stamps each individual
        communication.
    Checks for enclosures.
    Indicates on letter special
        envelope notations such as
        airmail, special delivery,
        certified mail, registry.
    Sorts by departments.
    Has delivered by office mes-
        sengers.

This procedure would necessitate the
purchase of this equipment:

    mail-opening machine
    date-and-time stamping device

Because our mail volume has now in-
creased to over a thousand letters
daily, this procedure would effect a
more rapid and efficient handling of
incoming mail.
```

necessitate

efficient

The man with ideas who has the ability to put them in writing scores. The worker who generates ideas for others to "write up" under their own names remains obscure.

Most businessmen will also request an official invitation instead of a telephone call. You may call the vice president of a department store in your community to ask him to speak at your retailing club's annual dinner the following month. "I'd be glad to be your guest speaker next month," he says, "but will you write me a note on it? And please be sure to include your suggestions for a topic." In your personal-business life, you write notes for the record — for example, when you write that you have already paid a bill for which you have just received a dunning letter.

dunning

PURPOSES OF BUSINESS WRITING

Business firms use written communication for these same reasons of economy, efficiency, accuracy, and record-keeping. At least 85 percent of business is conducted either completely or partially by mail. The more than 30 billion first-class letters mailed annually in the United States alone attest to the importance of written communication. These letters are written for a variety of purposes: to get information or materials; to answer a request; to volunteer information; to remember the amenities with such communications as thank-you notes, congratulatory messages, and condolences — and thus to build goodwill.

attest

amenities

Requesting and Furnishing Information and Materials

If you had lived several centuries ago, you, as the sole owner of your business, would have supervised all your work and would have been in touch with your suppliers and customers personally. Except for keeping records, you would have had little need for the written word. However, today's improved methods of transportation enable businessmen to operate farther from their markets and from their sources of supply. Letters assist business in bridging these distances. Airmail is so rapid today that your letter with vital information can be received in an office across the country the next morning; your request for information can be answered and received the following business day.

farther

    These letters sped across the country within two days, enabling the distributor in Boston to get the answer to his request for information:

enabling

```
Gentlemen:

Please quote your terms on 100 red-
wood picnic sets (table and four
chairs), No. 5522, for delivery by
March 15.
```

We are considering featuring these sets in the opening of our outdoor furniture department at the end of March.

Sincerely,

J. J. Greenwood

J. J. Greenwood
Manager

Mr. Greenwood received his answer from the supplier as follows:

supplier

Dear Mr. Greenwood:

The 100 redwood picnic sets, No. 5522, can be delivered by March 12 at the cost of:

Quantity	Item	Unit	Total
100	Redwood picnic set #5522	$20	$2,000

Our terms are 2/10, n/30.

As soon as we hear from you, we will ship your order.

We are pleased that you are considering the California redwood picnic sets as a feature in the opening of your outdoor furniture department.

Thank you.

Sincerely yours,

That is, the buyer may take a 2 percent discount within 10 days or pay the full amount within 30 days.

Building Goodwill

You buy in Smith's market rather than in Brown's. Why? One reason could be that Smith's clerks greet you with a friendly "Good morning. How are you today?" and a "Thank you." Smith's employees create goodwill for his business, so when you need something you think of Smith's.

While a businessman may do many other things to build goodwill and to hold it, he realizes that his letters also should create a favorable image of his company. Every letter — of sales, adjustment, credit, request — presents an opportunity to develop this tre-

intangible

mendously important intangible asset. Many people to whom you write never see you, never talk to you. Their firsthand impressions of you and of your business and their attitudes toward you are formed entirely through the letters they receive. When you direct your writing to the reader's viewpoint, you build goodwill for your business. For this, you must have an understanding not only of business operations but of human nature. The importance of letters as goodwill ambassadors or

exaggerated

human-relations tools cannot be exaggerated.

Consider the action taken in this following situation. A client of an auto-rental company had parked his rented car on an out-of-town city street while he called upon a customer. When he returned to the car, there was a dent in the rear fender. The client reported the damage to the rental agency immediately and was told that there would be no problem in handling the case because he was not at fault. He was further told

further

that the rental agency's insurance would cover the damage. A few days after he returned to his home office, he received the following letter:

Cincinnati

```
Re the damage to our rented car in
Cincinnati (Rental Number 64325) on
July 6:
```

```
According to the scant information
you supplied us at the time of the
accident, you are completely at fault,
and we will not accept any responsi-
```

negligence

```
bility for your negligence, which
obviously caused the damage to said
car.
```

```
Under the terms of the insurance cov-
ering the car, Contract 105558, you
must pay the entire bill. Please send
your check for $89.38 immediately.

Should you have anything further to
say on this subject, you can write to
Mr. Sidney Martinson in our Cincin-
nati office.
```

What is your reaction to the letter? Should the client have requested a release from the rental agency? Did this letter create goodwill? Would you write a letter like this? What would you do if you received it?

SUMMARY

In your personal-business life as well as in your business career, you will write letters that request or furnish information. You will find that written communication is more effective than verbal communication in terms of economy, efficiency, and accuracy and that it provides a necessary permanent record. But, no matter what the purpose of a letter may be, the way it is written can either build or destroy goodwill. It is important, therefore, that you learn to use written communication effectively.

permanent

[1] SPELLING

Can you discover the misspellings in the following paragraph? What is the correct spelling for each of these words?

Its said that he recieves several offers of employment each week. Although we know that he is a responsible, eficient worker and that compitition for such employees is keen, we believe he has exagerrated his importance. He says it would not be feasible for him to accept an offer in Cincinati because his scedule will not allow him to travel further than 20 miles each day. But managment wants him to accept, for they feel his refusal will necesitate a switch in supplyers. They are offering him a large salary increase, a consinement of top quality merchandise, and a permenant position on the staff. And, of course, his added expenses would be deductable.

[2] VOCABULARY

Here are the vocabulary words that were spotlighted in the chapter you have just read. Make them part of your everyday vocabulary.

feasible	intangible	proxies
dunning	negligence	attest
amenities	determinant	suffice
deterrent	enabling	deluged
collision		

a. Choose eight of these words, and use each in a sentence that illustrates its meaning.

b. Do you know the difference between *further* and *farther*? If you aren't sure, check your dictionary; then fill in the blanks in these sentences:

She _further_ told me that I had walked _farther_ than all the others.

We had _further_ information, which confirmed that we had traveled _farther_ than was necessary.

c. Write a sentence that shows you know the difference between *it's* and *its*.

[handwritten margin notes:]
deluged
recieved
management
it's
schedule
deductible
competition
consign
necessitate
efficient
farther
supplier
exaggerated
further
Cincinnati
permanent

2 | Appearance Counts

AFTER a long walk down a well-polished corridor, the young job applicant finally found the room to which she had been referred by the college placement director. She introduced herself to the gentleman who had been watching her through the open door. She had the job the moment she walked into the office — his appraisal had been made during that long walk. Yes, appearance does count. Think of the many times you have become interested in someone because of the way that person looks. Think, too, of the millions of dollars business spends in packaging its products, and the importance of outward appearance assumes even greater proportions.

The same is true of the letters you write. From the address on the envelope to the last initial on the letter itself, it's you the reader sees. Be sure the impression you make is a good one.

LETTER STYLES

Style, of course, is important. It characterizes you as an up-to-date, behind-the-times, or avant-garde individual.

well-polished
(Hyphenate compound adjectives.)
only preceding the noun

appraisal

up-to-date; behind-the-times; avant-garde

13

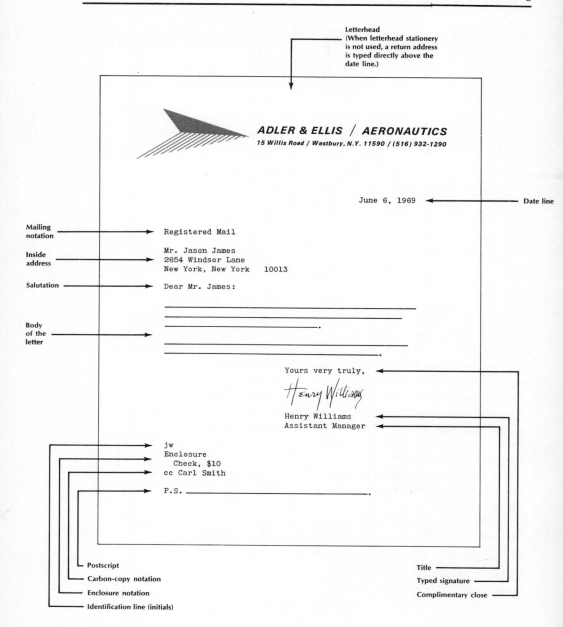

Figure 2 – 1
Parts of the Letter

But before we can proceed to discuss style, you must be able to identify the parts of a letter. Figure 2 – 1 shows what these parts are called and where they are usually placed.

proceed
(but procedure)

Now let's look at four of the business styles currently in use so that you can get an idea of the style you would choose. Remember, however, that the office in which you work will probably make that decision for you until you achieve the kind of position that gives you the authority and responsibility to choose the style you prefer. The office manager, the executive secretary or administrative assistant, or sometimes the employer himself makes that decision.

Hint for good human relations in the office.

The four main business-letter styles we will discuss are the *semiblock*, the *modified block*, the *full block* and the *simplified*.

The Modified-Block and Semiblock Styles

The two most popular business-letter styles today are the modified block (Figure 2 – 2) and the semiblock (Figure 2 – 3). Of the two, the modified block is the more clean cut, and it is gradually replacing the semiblock. Every part of the letter in the modified-block style begins at the left margin except the date and the closing. Notice the type of punctuation used in both styles. It is *mixed punctuation*: colon after the salutation and comma after the complimentary closing.

clean cut
(Don't hyphenate predicate adjectives.)

Mixed punctuation.

complimentary

The semiblock differs in only one way — the paragraphs are indented, usually five spaces.

The Full-Block Style

The up-and-coming advertising executive, the publicity director, the business educator, the business publisher probably would select the next style — the full block (Figure 2 – 4). More and more business firms are adopting it, too. Every part of the letter begins at the left margin, which saves time, offers less opportunity for error, and is therefore more efficient. Of course, this

adopting

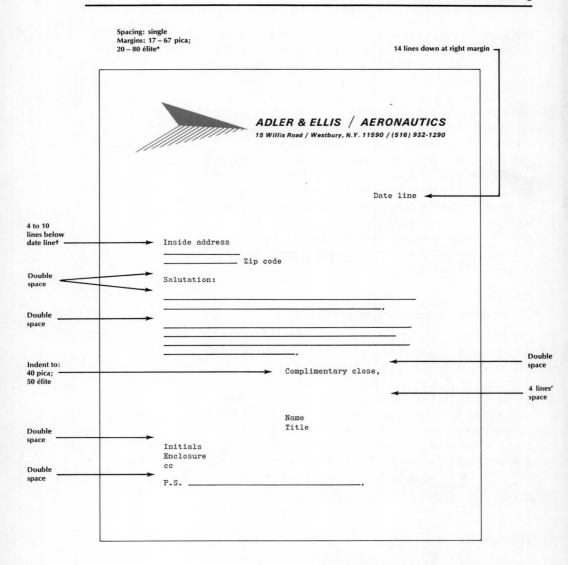

Spacing: single
Margins: 17 – 67 pica;
20 – 80 élite*

14 lines down at right margin

ADLER & ELLIS / AERONAUTICS
15 Willis Road / Westbury, N.Y. 11590 / (516) 932-1290

Date line

4 to 10
lines below
date line†

Inside address

Zip code

Double
space

Salutation:

Double
space

Indent to:
40 pica;
50 élite

Complimentary close,

Double
space

4 lines'
space

Name
Title

Double
space

Initials
Enclosure
cc

Double
space

P.S.

* Margins given (for all styles) are for medium-sized letter (100 – 200 words); they can be adjusted somewhat for longer or shorter letters.

† Space above inside address depends on length of letter.

Figure 2 – 2
The Modified-Block Style

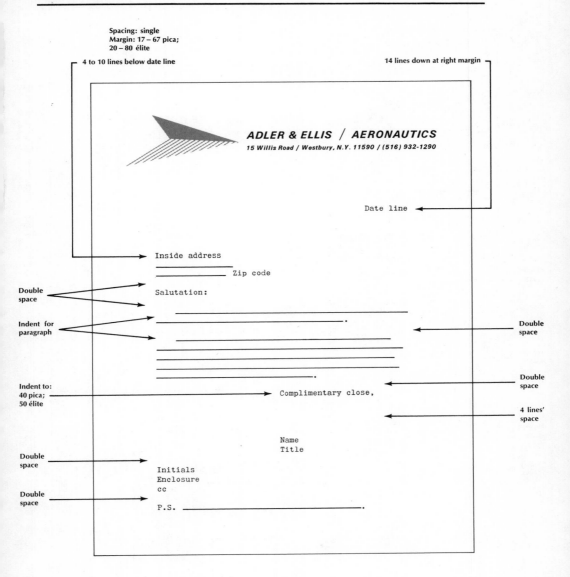

Figure 2 – 3
The Semiblock Style

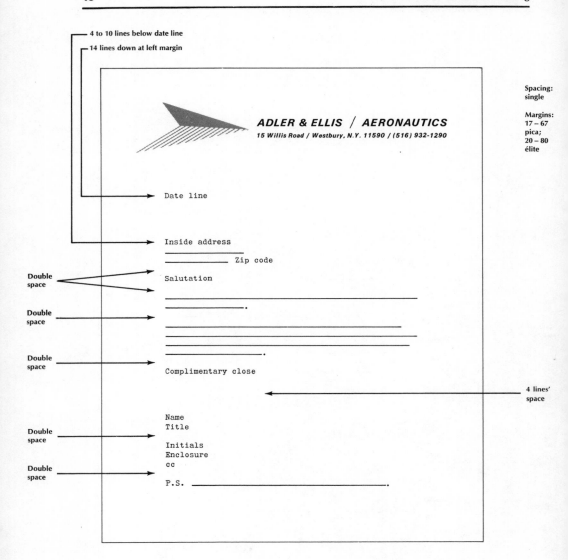

Figure 2 – 4
The Full-Block Style

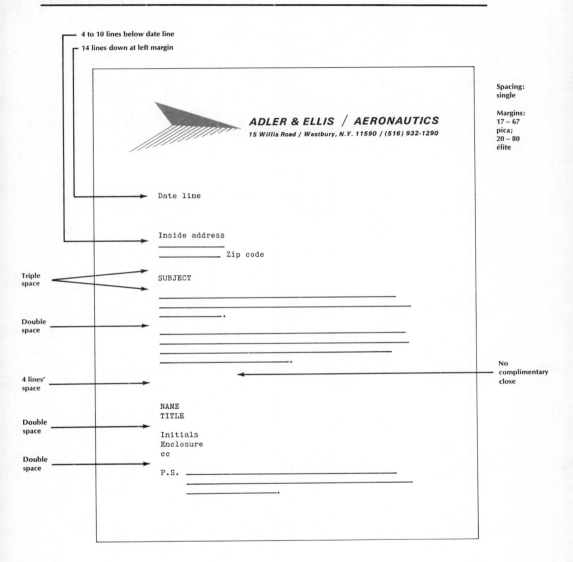

4 to 10 lines below date line
14 lines down at left margin

Spacing: single

Margins: 17 – 67 pica; 20 – 80 élite

ADLER & ELLIS / AERONAUTICS
15 Willis Road / Westbury, N.Y. 11590 / (516) 932-1290

Date line

Inside address
Zip code

Triple space   SUBJECT

Double space

4 lines' space

No complimentary close

Double space   NAME
TITLE
Initials
Enclosure
cc

Double space   P.S.

Figure 2 – 5
The Simplified Style

style cannot be used if it does not blend with the company's letterhead.

Open punctuation.

omission

Do you notice the innovation in punctuation used in this style? This is *open punctuation*: omission of the colon after the salutation and of the comma after the closing. Open punctuation is modern, too, to conform with the modern full-block style.

The Simplified Style

Next is the simplified stye (Figure 2 – 5). Contrast it to the full block. The differences are obvious: although all items begin at the left margin here, too, the simplified style omits the salutation and closing and includes a *subject line* in capital letters. After all, our letters are coming closer to normal conversation. No one greets you with "Dear Sir" or ends his conversation with "Sincerely yours." The Administrative Management Society has endorsed this style, but business has not yet popularized it

Other Styles

THE OFFICIAL-BUSINESS STYLE

occasion

You may have to write to the president of the local Rotary Club, the pastor of your church, the rabbi of your synagogue, or a city, state, or federal official, requesting him to speak or to lend his support to an activity or thanking him for his assistance. This type of letter requires a more formal style than those we have been discussing. Figure 2 – 6 illustrates the proper style for such an occasion. (Notice that mailing notations — airmail, special delivery, and the like — are omitted, as are typist's initials. Note, too, the placement of the inside address.)

interoffice
(Many common prefixes, such as inter, non, pro, *and* semi, *are joined to the following word without a hyphen. When in doubt, check your dictionary.)*

THE INTEROFFICE MEMORANDUM

When you write to another employee in your office, the proper form is the interoffice memorandum (Figure

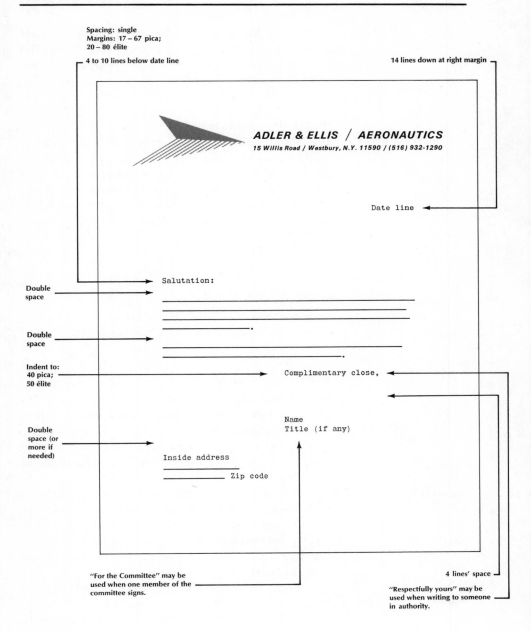

Spacing: single
Margins: 17 – 67 pica;
20 – 80 élite

4 to 10 lines below date line   14 lines down at right margin

ADLER & ELLIS / AERONAUTICS
15 Willis Road / Westbury, N.Y. 11590 / (516) 932-1290

Date line

Double
space

Salutation:

Double
space

Indent to:
40 pica;
50 élite

Complimentary close,

Double
space (or
more if
needed)

Name
Title (if any)

Inside address

Zip code

"For the Committee" may be
used when one member of the
committee signs.

4 lines' space

"Respectfully yours" may be
used when writing to someone
in authority.

Figure 2 – 6
The Official-Business Style

2 – 7). You save time and effort by omitting an inside address, a salutation, and a complimentary closing. The heading includes these essentials, as well as a subject line.

THE PERSONAL-BUSINESS LETTER

The letters you type for a business firm and those you type for yourself differ slightly in style. Since you usually do not have personal letterhead paper and must use plain bond paper, you have to include your return address. And it is assumed that the typist is the writer, so initials are not typed after the closing. (See Figure 2 – 8.)

PARTS OF THE LETTER

Now that you have seen the picture of the letter as a whole, let's examine the individual parts separately.

separately

Stationery and Letterhead

Standard-size paper for most business letters measures 8½ by 11 inches. Smaller sizes (baronial and executive) lose themselves in the files and cost extra money in time wasted locating them when they are needed. While there is a trend toward color in paper, white is generally used.

watermarked

Letters should be typed on a good quality, watermarked, rag-content paper of 20-pound weight. It has a clean, crisp feel, and your typing stands out more clearly. Furthermore, and you will agree that this is important, it is easiest to make neat corrections on paper of good quality.

imperative

Every business has a printed letterhead. In good letterhead design, simplicity is imperative. Important information must be supplied within the top fifth of the page. This information includes the company name, address, telephone number, and (if there is one) cable

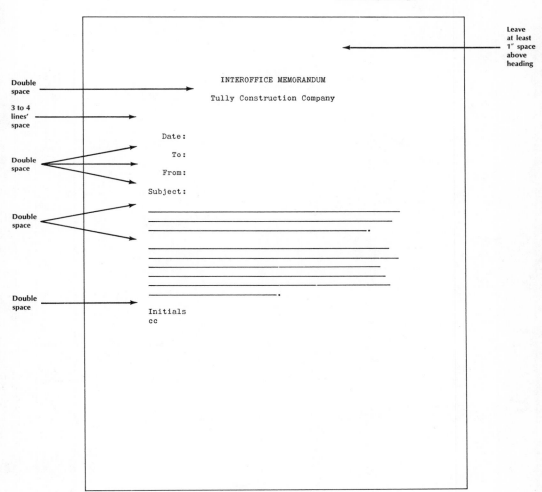

Figure 2 – 7
The Interoffice Memorandum

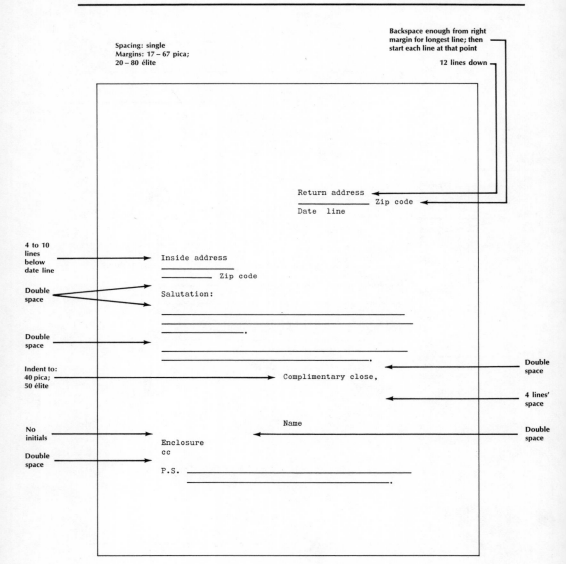

Figure 2 – 8
The Personal-Business Letter

address. To indicate the nature of the firm, an emblem
or trade mark is often incorporated in the design. That
design must reflect the company image forcefully. See
Figure 2 – 9 for some examples of good letterhead
design.

When you do not have a printed letterhead, you
must use a personal heading, which includes your return address (don't forget that ZIP code) and the date
of the letter. (Look at the personal-business letter, Figure 2 – 8.) Start your heading two inches from the top
of the page, and use single spacing. The longest line of
this heading should end at the right margin unless you
are using the full-block style, in which case you will
begin the inside address at the left margin. Below are
some correct return addresses:

Rural route

Route 3
Torrance, California   90507
November 7, 1968

Post-office box

P. O. Box 250
Riverside, California   92502
November 7, 1968

Street address

6648 Dawes Street
Oakland, California   94615
November 7, 1968

Notice that abbreviations are not used. Notice
also that the up-to-date writer omits *st*, *rd*, *nd*, *th* after
the date of the month. However, in the body of the
letter, when the day precedes the month or the month
is not named, these ordinal endings are used, or the
date is spelled out: "the 5th of December," "the 5th,"
"the fifth of December," or "the fifth." Another thing
to notice is that two spaces are left before the ZIP code.

*Note that "P. O. Box"
is an exception to the
"no-abbreviations" rule.*

precedes
ordinal

BERTRICK ASSOCIATE ARTISTS, INC.   2188 Jackson Avenue, Seaford, N.Y. 11783

516 826-4286

TIME
THE WEEKLY NEWSMAGAZINE

TIME & LIFE BUILDING
ROCKEFELLER CENTER
NEW YORK 10020
JUDSON 6-1212

CBS
Columbia Broadcasting System, Inc.
51 West 52 Street
New York, New York 10019
(212) 765-4321

BORIS
FINE JEWELRY ◆ 721 MADISON AVENUE
NEW YORK CITY 10021
telephone: PLaza 2-4186

PROCESS MATERIALS CORPORATION ■ 53RD AVE. AT 11TH ST., LONG ISLAND CITY, N.Y. 11101 ■ 212/729-4444

Georgian Lithographers Inc. • *175 Varick Street, New York, N.Y. 10014*

Telephone WAtkins 4-4820

Figure 2 – 9
Some Business Letterheads

Inside Address

This part of the letter identifies the name and address of the person or company receiving the letter. Single spaced, it begins at the left margin of the letter, from four to ten lines below the date line (depending on the length of the letter).

    Names of individuals should be preceded by a title. If the person has no title, use the ordinary courtesy form: *Mr., Mrs.,* or *Miss.* The National Secretaries Association suggests you use *Ms.* when you are in doubt as to whether a woman is married. The following are common forms:

courtesy

```
Mr. Paul Chivers      Miss Alice Mackey   Messrs. Thomas Jay
Dr. John Nelson       Mrs. Alan Michel      and James Sims
Professor David Dunn  Ms. Eileen Nolan    Misses Alice and Jane Clark
                                          Mr. & Mrs. Edwin Slade
```

Several items should be noted: *Professor,* like *Reverend* and *Honorable,* is generally spelled out. When addressing two married women or an unrelated man and woman, each name is given its proper title, and one name is listed below the other. Also, watch your spelling of the plural of *Mr.* One inaccurate typist wrote "Messes," which caused no little embarrassment. Be sure you use *Messrs.*

embarrassment

    A person's title in an organization may be used after his name. To maintain uniformity of line length, the title may be typed on either the first or the second line:

```
Mr. James L. Whitford, Manager     Mr. James L. Farmingdale, III
Industrial Exhibitors Mart         President, Ace Company
```

If the title is more than one word — as, "General Manager" — place it on a separate line:

```
    Mr. James L. Whitford
    General Manager
    Industrial Exhibitors Mart
```

    Use abbreviations sparingly in the inside address. Except for *Mr., Messrs., Mrs., Ms., Jr., Sr., Esq.,* and

Esq. is the abbreviation for Esquire.

academic degrees, write out all words and titles. Note that the abbreviation *Esq.* may be used following the names of attorneys, judges, congressmen, and other government officials. When it is used, no other title or degree may be used with it:

Don't be redundant.

      `Mr. Philip King`
`or` `Philip King, Esq.`
`not` `Mr. Philip King, Esq.`

The same is true when you use academic degrees:

      `Dr. Martin Jason`
`or` `Martin Jason, M.D.`
`not` `Dr. Martin Jason, M.D.`

Numerical street or avenue names up to and including ten are spelled out. Some offices still use the ordinal endings — *st, nd, rd, th* — after street and avenue names, but many are omitting them:

      `795 Fifth Avenue`

      `55 25th Street`
`or` `55 25 Street`

      `396 East 116th Street`
`or` `396 East 116 Street`

Cooperate with the Post Office: Use those ZIP codes! Remember to allow two spaces after the state name before you type the ZIP.

Salutation

Type the salutation two lines below the last line of the inside address. A colon follows it if you use mixed punctuation (see Figure 2 – 2); the colon is omitted in open punctuation (see Figure 2 – 4).

The salutation agrees with the first line of the inside address. In the singular, the preferred salutation is *Dear Mr.* (Mrs., Miss, Ms.) *Smith. Dear Sir* (or *Dear Madam*) is considered "icy" and poor public relations.

In the plural, use *Gentlemen* for several men or for a group of men and women, and use *Ladies* or *Mesdames* for several women. (*Ladies* is more commonly used today.) Following are some typical names with their accompanying salutations:

Stack Supply Store	Gentlemen
Floridale Women's Club	Ladies
Miss Margaret Murn	Dear Miss Murn
Mrs. Jack Barnes	Dear Mrs. Barnes
Mr. Wilson Hathaway	Dear Mr. Hathaway
Box 564, Fresno Times	Gentlemen
Professor Frank Statler	Dear Professor Statler
Dr. Martin James	Dear Doctor James
Messrs. Swift and Throne	Gentlemen
Ms. Catherine Block	Dear Ms. Block
Misses Marie and Dora Smith	Ladies

Note that *Doctor* is written out in the salutation, where the given name is not used.

When you are writing to a company but know that your letter will be serviced more rapidly by a specific individual or department, you direct the letter to his or the department's attention. In that case, because the first line of the inside address is plural, the salutation must be plural:

Acceptable	**Better**
Glen Service Center	Mr. Arnold Pope
1215 Trane Road	Glen Service Center
Omaha, Nebraska 68112	1215 Trane Road
	Omaha, Nebraska 68112
Attention Mr. Arnold Pope	
	Dear Mr. Pope
Gentlemen	

Body of the Letter

The body — that is, the content — of the letter begins two lines below the salutation. Single space the letter with double spacing between paragraphs.

Some correspondents use a special line to precede the body of the letter. We call this the *subject*

correspondents

line. It identifies the message — it gives it a title. The use of the subject line enables you to begin your letter directly and to avoid dull résumé beginnings.

Modern treatment	**A little old fashioned**
Dear Mr. Harnack	Dear Mr. Harnack
Request for Credit Information	Subject: Request for Credit Information
Body of Letter	Body of Letter

Complimentary Closing

Refer to Figures 2 – 2 and 2 – 3. Notice that the closing line is written two spaces below the body of the letter, either at the left margin or in the center, according to the style you use. Be consistent in punctuation and style. Place the comma after the complimentary close when a colon follows the salutation; omit it when no punctuation follows the salutation.

The usual business letter ends with one of these closing lines:

Only the first word is capitalized.

Yours very truly
Very truly yours
Sincerely yours

Make the closing fit the situation.

Match the closing to the salutation.

Custom, more than anything else, dictates the use of these closing lines. But the tone of the letter or the relationship between the writer and the addressee may call for other forms, such as *Cordially* or *Respectfully yours*. A cold *Dear Sir* salutation takes an equally cold *Yours truly* closing. Many correspondents feel that both the salutation and the complimentary close are trite and outmoded; they simply omit both of them, as illustrated in the simplified style (Figure 2 – 5). But this style has not yet gained wide business acceptance.

Signature

After you have typed the complimentary closing, give your writer four lines in which to sign his name. Type the name, followed on the next line by his title.

The writer should sign his name in full. Naturally, when he is friendly with his reader or when he writes to him frequently, he may sign only his given name. However, the typed signature must include his full name. A married woman should indicate her status (Mrs.) preceding her typed signature. In social usage, she should type her married name in parentheses beneath her written signature.

preceding

By the way, why don't you decide right now exactly how you will sign your name. Will you use your middle initial, write out your middle name, or even use an initial for your first name? Choose an official signature. Then be consistent; don't switch.

Social and business usage	Business usage	Social usage
Sincerely yours	Sincerely yours	Sincerely yours
Michael L. Story	*Mary Murphy*	*Janet Hardy*
Michael L. Story	(Mrs.) Mary Murphy	(Mrs. Frank J. Hardy)
Personnel Manager	Credit Division	

Identification Line

"Who typed this letter?" said the boss to the supervisor of the typing group. "It's beautifully done." Flush with the left-hand margin, a space or two below the last line of the signature section, Mary Jones's initials told the tale. Because the writer's name had already been typed on the signature line, only the typist's initials appeared. This line can be treated in many ways depending on the practice followed by a company, but the typist's initials in lower case suffice.

lower case
(That is, not capital letters.)

Sincerely yours,

Alfred Hossler

Alfred Hossler
Transfer Department

mj

Typist is Mary Jones.

Other Notations

In addition to the items we have just discussed, some letters require one or more further notations.

SECOND-PAGE NOTATION AND CLOSING

What identifies the second page of a letter? If that second page is lost or misplaced, it must find its way back to the first page — of the correct letter. Therefore, nine lines from the top edge of each page after the first one (using plain bond paper, not letterhead), you should type the name of the addressee, the page number, and the date:

Mr. Jerome Hickman   -2-   June 6, 1968

Or you may type these items one beneath the other, with the first line placed nine lines from the top and beginning at the left margin:

Mr. Jerome Hickman
Page 2
June 6, 1968

Allow three lines below the second-page notation before continuing the body of the letter.

The closing changes somewhat on the two-page letter. Since the letterhead is not used, the name of the company is included in all capitals two lines below the complimentary closing.

Very truly yours,

APEX CORPORATION

William Starris

William Starris
Credit Manager

ENCLOSURE NOTATION

The enclosure notation works two ways: It saves time for you when you check to see that you have included

the items mentioned in the letter. And the addressee
quickly ascertains from the notation whether he has
received the correct materials.

    When extra material accompanies the letter, make
the notation immediately below the typist's initials. The
usual method is to type the word *Enclosure* (use a
plural notation for several enclosures); then list the
enclosed item or items.

One enclosure	More than one enclosure
jfb	jfb
Enclosure	Enclosures
Check $10	Check $10
	Signed contract

CARBON-COPY NOTATION

Very often you want to send a copy of the letter that
you are typing to a third party for his information. Make
a carbon-copy notation following the identification line
— or the enclosure line if there is one.

With enclosure

Very truly yours,

Herbert Jones

Herbert Jones
Manager

ji
Enclosure
  Check $10
cc Mr. Patrick Downes

Without enclosure

Very truly yours,

Herbert Jones

Herbert Jones
Manager

ji
cc Mr. Patrick Downes

POSTSCRIPT

As an added note to attract special attention, to add an explanation, to mention an idea unrelated to the letter, or to include information that was omitted from the body of your letter, you use a postscript. Type it following the carbon-copy notation if there is one.

omitted

```
ji
Enclosure
   Check $5
cc Mr. Robert Peters, Accounting

P.S.    Remember to circle that date
        on your calendar--Monday,
        September 5.
```

Double space.

calendar

MAILING NOTATIONS

When a letter is sent by a special mail service, type *Airmail* (unless airmail stationery is used), *Special Delivery*, *Certified Mail*, *Registered Mail*, or *Insured Mail* on the envelope and on the letter itself so that the information is available for possible reference.

```
Certified Mail

Mr. John Starkweather
224 West Ninth Street
New York, New York    10038
```

Inside address.

Envelope Address

addressee

Since your addressee sees the envelope before he sees the letter, you must pay as much attention to it as to the letter itself. The address on the envelope must agree exactly — in wording, spelling, and so on — with the inside address on the letter. However, spacing may differ: On the envelope, double space a three-line address; single space a four- or five-line address.

Note hyphenation of these compound adjectives.

For a letter typed on regular 8½ by 11 paper, the business-size envelope may be used (Figure 2 – 10). If you include an enclosure or if your letter is more than one page, use a legal-size envelope (Figure 2 – 11).

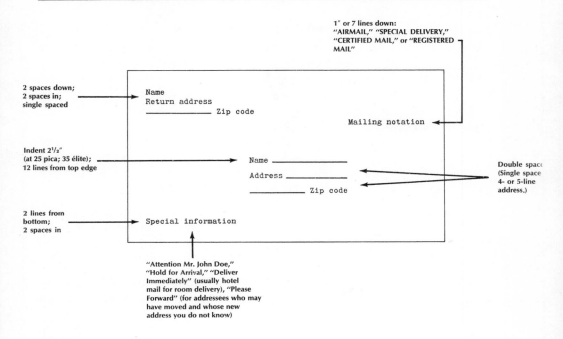

Figure 2 – 10
The Business-Size Envelope

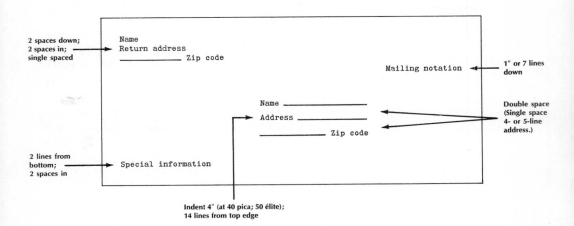

Figure 2 – 11
The Legal-Size Envelope

BE YOUR OWN SEVEREST CRITIC

up to date
(No hyphens are used when compound adjective follows the noun.)

Your letter, no matter how correct and up to date in style and form, must be a model of accuracy and neatness. It must look professional. To judge your letter's appearance, answer these questions:

Make corrections neatly.

1. Where you made a correction, does your correction show? If it is obvious, it is still an error even though you tried to erase and hide it. Did you strike that key so hard when you corrected the error that you spotlighted the correction?

Use your typewriter skillfully.

2. How about your touch? The electric typewriter must be on the correct pressure if you are to have even type. The manual needs your even touch to obtain sharp, clear letters.

Help your typewriter help you.

3. Think of the typewriter itself — are you maintaining a clean machine free from grime and eraser particles? Look at the individual letters. If they are filled in, blurred, crowded, spread, your machine should be serviced. Keep it clean and in optimum working condition. If your type is faded, change your ribbon.

Check the overall appearance of your letter.

4. How is your placement? Check the space from the top of the page to the date line. Now check the space between the last line of the letter (probably the initials) and the end of the page. Is there about half an inch more space at the bottom? Are the left and right margins even, or is one much wider than the other? Have you been able to maintain a fairly even right margin? Are the parts of the letter correctly spaced?

SUMMARY

We have now described the four letter styles business most commonly uses. When you write a business letter in an office, you will probably use either the modified-block or the semiblock style, the most popular styles today. Many firms, however, are now adopting the newer, time-saving full-block style, and others are accepting the simplified style — the latest on the scene. It will be to your advantage to know each of them.

You have also learned how to handle special situations. For the formal letter of invitation, thanks, or congratulation, you will find the official-business style adds dignity to the communication. For the innumerable times that you write to other members of your company, the interoffice memorandum provides an efficient form. And there is the personal-business letter, in which, as we have noted, you usually do not use letterhead paper. You include your return address above the date, and you omit the typist's initials.

congratulation

Your punctuation form must also be correct and consistent. The two most used forms — open and mixed — were described.

The purpose and prescribed usage of each part of the letter should now be familiar to you: letterhead, date line, special mailing notations, inside address, attention line, salutation, subject line, body of the letter, second-page notation, complimentary closing, typed signature and title, and closing notations (initials, enclosure, carbon copy, and postscript).

prescribed

The envelope, too, must receive your careful attention. You learned the correct forms for business-size and the legal-size envelopes. Remember to include all the information required for rapid delivery.

Before you mail your letter or interoffice memorandum, check it carefully for correctness of style and professional appearance.

Double checking always pays.

[1] SPELLING

a. Do you know when to use one e and when to use two? Fill in the blanks below:

prec___de   proc___dure   prec___ding   proc___d

b. Correct the misspelled words in this paragraph:

To our embarassment, it seems we omited your new calenders from our preceeding shipment. We are now sending them along seperately. Thank you for your curtesy in calling our attention to this ommission. May we take this ocasion to send you a complementary copy of our popular "Congradulations to Charlie" cartoon cards?

c. Do you know the correct use of *correspondents* and *correspondence*? Fill in the blanks in this sentence:

The _____ department has requested that all _____ study the principles of business writing before they write their own letters and that all _____ be checked by the supervisor before being mailed.

[2] VOCABULARY

a. How would you define these words?

avant-garde   ascertain   addressee   imperative   prescribe

b. Use each of the following words in a sentence. Your sentences should show that you understand what these words mean.

adopting   watermarked   appraisal   lower case

c. What are *ordinal* numbers? What are *cardinal* numbers?

[3] HYPHENATION

In a number of places in this chapter, two or more words were hyphenated to form a compound adjective. Do you know when to use a hyphen? Here are some general rules:

RULE: *When two or more words having the force of a single modifier precede the noun, they are hyphenated.*

two-page letter   social-business letter
well-polished corridor   up-to-date writer

RULE: *But, when such words are used as a predicate adjective — when they follow the noun — they are usually not hyphenated.*

the corridor that is well polished
the writer who is up to date

RULE: *When the first of two words is an adverb ending in* ly, *the hyphen is omitted.*

a truly good man
his fairly interesting report

Although you should learn these rules and follow them, it is always a good idea to have a dictionary handy. Some prefixes, such as *self* and *quasi* are hyphenated, while others are part of the word that follows and take no hyphen — for example, *anti*, *non*, and *semi*. Always check your dictionary when you aren't sure about hyphenating prefixes.

Correct the hyphenation in the following paragraph. You will have to add hyphens in some places and remove them from others. (Some hyphens in the paragraph may be correct.) Make a list of the correct forms.

A well-known business executive delivered a first rate speech on the impact of the income tax law on the spending habits of individuals. He mentioned that the post war era has brought many changes in tax laws. Middle-income people have seen how their money making plans have benefited the tax-collector. As a result, they have had to forego non-essential items. Many reasonably-intelligent people do not realize that it is after-tax income that really counts. This well-known executive further stressed the importance of keeping up-to-date where taxes are concerned.

[4] SETTING UP THE LETTER

Use sheets of plain paper for these problems. Set up the parts of each letter, including the current date, in their proper positions. Capitalize and punctuate; spell out abbreviations except where abbreviations are approved. You may choose your own style and punctuation.

	Dictated by	Transcribed by	Sent to
a.	john f gersten president	ella gibbons	mrs leonard houghton 9907 engels dr bethesda, md 21811

Special instructions: Salutation? Complimentary close?

	Dictated by	Transcribed by	Sent to
b.	michael f thomas sales dept	gerald turman	gibbs construction co 735 s jackson st denver, colo 80210

Special instructions: Attention of mr alfred charlton; carbon copy to edward cusack. Salutation? Complimentary close?

	Dictated by	Transcribed by	Sent to
c.	howard timms purchasing agent	ann massey	frances lockwood 1347 shady ave pittsburgh, pa 15217

Special instructions: A check for $10 is being sent with the letter. The subject is order 5670. Salutation? Complimentary close?

	Dictated by	Transcribed by	Sent to
d.	peter knight general mgr	florence egan	bruce lineman treasurer national optical co 2000 penn ave ann arbor, mich 48103

Special instructions: Airmail.

	Dictated by	Transcribed by	Sent to
e.	you	you	messrs klein & smith attorneys at law 1545 dickens st sherman oaks, calif 95681

Special instructions: You are writing about a legal case, *Prentis* v. *Hill*. Salutation? Complimentary close?

[5] THE ENVELOPE

For each case in Exercise 4, write envelopes (business size). Be sure to include all the necessary information. Assuming that all companies have printed envelopes, you need use a return address in only one case.

[6] FORM AND PUNCTUATION

Correct any errors in the form and punctuation of the following:

a.

Apr. 21st, 1967.

Chandler & Jones
33 1st Ave. 30303.
Atlanta, Ga. 30303.

Att.--Albert Coughlan.

Dear Mr. Coughlan,

Respectfully yours

James Bliss

James Bliss

JB/f.f.v.

b.

December 9, Dec. 67

Mr. George Wattel, Esq.
219 Empress Dr.
Houston, Tex. 77034.

Dear Mister Wattel.

Very Sincerely Yours,

Carl Riskin

Carl Riskin.

Incl.
UF

c.   May 15th 1967

Box 989
The Tribune
Park Ridge, Ill.

Via Air Mail

Dear Gentlemen--

                                        Yours very Truly,

                                        Jack Nichols
                                        Jack Nichols
                                        Sales Mgr.

P.S.   See you Monday.

JN:w.w.d.

d.   February 30, 1967

Prof. Kenneth Newell
3936 Red Bud Ave.
Cincinati, O.   45229

Dear Prof. Newel

                                        Sincerely Yours

                                        Jayne Wayne

                                        Jayne Wayne
                                        Consultant

cc Philip Hart
jh

e.   March 10, 1867

Fontana Sisters Style Shop,
1231 2nd Ave.
Walla walla, Wash.   99362.

Dear Ladies,

Respectfully

Donna Stevens

Assistant Buyer
Donna Stevens

Inc.
　　Cheque $10.00
you/ds

f.

Jan**uary** 14**th**, 1967

~~Dr.~~ Robert Lodge, M.D.
Chesterfield, Massachusetts 00000

December
~~Re~~ Boston speech 1~~2~~/2, 1966

Dear D~~ick~~ Lodge**:**

Very **t**ruly **y**ours,

Vern Safford

Vern Safford

~~Convention program~~ Enclos~~ure~~
at
convention program

[7] SALUTATION

You are writing letters to the following. Select the correct salutation to cover each case.

Gentlemen a. Box 143, <u>New York</u> <u>Times</u> f.　Mrs. Otto Eckner
Ladies b. Hopedale College Alumnae g.　William Hart, Ph.D.
Gentlemen c. Messrs. Wright and Clark h.　Irma Morton
Professor Frye d. Professor Milton Frye i.　Reverend Arthur Starbuck
　　e. Mr. Robert Brown j.　Kenneth Hammer Associates

[8]   PARTS OF THE LETTER

Name the part of the letter indicated by each letter in the illustration below:

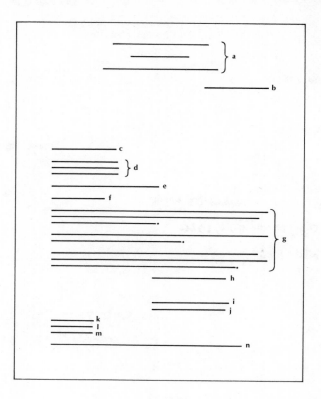

[9]   SPECIAL PROBLEMS

How would you handle these situations?

a.   You are 1¾ inches from the bottom of the page. You must still type
     a three-line paragraph to complete your letter. Which of the following
     would you do?

1. Complete the letter on page 1.
2. Complete the paragraph on page 1; place the closing lines on
   page 2.
3. Type the entire paragraph and closing lines on page 2.

4. Break up the paragraph with two lines on page 1 and one line on page 2, or vice versa.

b. You are 1½ inches from the bottom of the page. You have a four-line paragraph to type to complete the letter. Choose your course of action.

1. Complete the letter on page 1.
2. Break up the paragraph with two lines on each page.
3. Complete the paragraph on page 1 and place the closing lines on page 2.

c. You are at the end of the final line of page 1 of a two-page letter. The bell rings when you type the *re* in "recapitulation." What would you do?

1. Finish typing the word.
2. Type the entire word on page 2.
3. Hyphenate the word and finish it on page 2.

d. Your company uses plain bond paper for the second page of its two-page letters. Would you use the same closing lines as on a one-page letter? If so, why? If not, what changes would you make?

e. You are ready to begin the second page of a two-page letter. What information should you include in the heading of page 2? In what order?

[10] CHOOSING THE RIGHT FORM

Here are some situations you may encounter in your letter-writing. You want to be sure to match your salutation and complimentary closing with the tone of the letter. Would you make any changes in the following? List them.

a. You are writing a fourth letter trying to collect a long-overdue bill from Henry Agar.

Dear Henry: Cordially yours,

b. This letter is to a customer, Harold Lowery, who is also a good friend.

Dear Mr. Lowery: Yours very truly,

c. Here is one to the president of your college, whom you would like to interview for your club newsletter.

Dear Mr. Dewey: Sincerely yours,

d. You are writing to the Cornwall Paper Company to ask about their new paper products.

    Dear Sirs: **Very truly yours,**

e. You are writing to Mrs. Mary Gray to ask her when she plans to visit your college on her annual recruitment drive.

    Dear Miss Gray: **Respectfully yours,**

3 | Organize Your Thinking

NOW THAT we have seen how business letters are put together, let's turn to the body of the letter, the message itself. When you have seen many business letters, you will recognize that effective letters have several things in common. They are well organized, complete but to the point; their language is clear, precise, and grammatical; and their information is accurate. The effective letter is the result of careful planning, the proper use of language, and attention to detail.

OUTLINE YOUR PLAN

List Facts in Order

The preplanning of letters — organization — is one of the most difficult tasks for you as a novice to learn. You must jot down the ideas to be included, carefully consider whether you have omitted any item of information, then put all points in the order in which you should cover them.

novice

Check for Omissions

Businessmen who answer many letters a day too often feel that it is not necessary to plan each letter. Their return mail is filled with requests for follow-up material.

casualty

The red-faced insurance broker.

> I do not understand why my new auto-
> mobile casualty-insurance policy
> AF12403657 does not include towing
> service as my previous policy did.
> Will you please add this to my policy
> and bill me for any additional
> charges.

liability

> I am also interested in increasing my
> liability coverage to $100,000-
> $300,000. Please tell me the differ-
> ence in the premium.

Lack of service from a service organization.

> Thank you very much for the informa-
> tion on job opportunities in the
> field of social work. Have you for-
> gotten to include the list of accred-
> ited schools that offer degrees in
> social work?

The slipping office manager.

> Of course we will route all orders
> through the new agency in Dallas, as
> you request. Can you tell us the name
> of the man who will take charge of
> our account?

Don't let this happen to you.

judgment

Even the expert letter writer will take the time to outline difficult letters. Mr. Espersen, the vice president of a leading bank, did not finish his working day at five o'clock. After dinner, he reviewed a financial problem that required his judgment. He made copious notes to be incorporated in a report he planned to dictate the next morning, showing the step-by-step reasoning behind his decision to refuse a $150,000 loan to an expanding industrial firm in the community. Then he listed the points he would include in his letter to the head of the firm. He planned his reports, his letters, his memos; that was one reason for his success.

Delete the Unnecessary

Clear organization demands that you exclude non-essential information, which not only takes time to write and to read but clouds the essentials. The reader wonders why you put that sentence or phrase in the letter. Is he missing the point? Does this carry an implication he isn't aware of? Be careful to include only relevant information and to delete the extraneous facts that detract from the unity of your communication.

relevant; extraneous

Put Your Outline to Work

Shall we try organizing our responses in several business situations? Remember the procedure: List the ideas, check for completeness, eliminate irrelevant information, arrange in logical sequence.

Follow this procedure.
irrelevant

In the first case, assume you are employed as a clerk in a college during the summer months to fill requests for catalogs and brochures on special programs, adult-education courses, and foreign-student guidance. The requests for the brochures on the Certified Professional Secretarial Examination have been so heavy that you have run out of them. You have 25 requests you cannot fill. What will you do? If you wait until the new supply is received, you will be getting second requests; so you decide to write to the 25 secretaries. What will they want to know?

catalogs; brochures

This is easy for you to answer if you put yourself in the place of the person writing the original letter and answer the question: "What would I want to know if I did not receive this brochure?" You must tell the secretaries:

Put yourself in the reader's position.

The request has been received.
The delay is temporary.
The brochure will be sent by a specific date.
You are sorry for the delay.

As a beginning worker or a part-time summer clerk, of course, you would not send this letter until you had checked with your supervisor. Only after receiving his approval would you prepare the form letter

Hint for good human relations in the office.

to be mailed to all those for whom brochures were not available.

similar

A similar situation arises in this next position. You are a clerk in the office of a local repair shop, and a customer expects her electric broiler to be repaired and ready for pickup the following Saturday. Unfortunately,

distributor

the original distributor has gone out of business, but you are trying to locate the part at one of the other dealers. Rather than wait for the customer to call, you anticipate her irritation and write her this note:

> Please give us one more week to re-
> pair your broiler. The Acme Company,
> who made this broiler, has gone out
> of business, and we are trying to lo-
> cate a new kolar unit at one of their
> dealers' shops.
>
> We will let you know by the end of
> this week whether or not the part is
> available.
>
> We are sorry this is taking so long.

dealers'
(Note how possessive
of a plural is formed.)

To be sure you did not omit anything the customer should know, check your letter against the list of points you made:

The repair has not been made.
Why?
What is being done about it.
A definite follow-up is set.
Apology.

Your next position is a more demanding one, with greater responsibility. You are a full-time employee in the Exchange Import Company, a small company in which you handle the cash sales, the accounts, and the billing as well as the mail. You receive a package from Mr. Frisbee containing a walkie-talkie on which the antenna has been broken. He wishes to have it repaired free under his one-year guarantee. You know that the

guarantee covers any defect of workmanship within a
year of normal use, but it is obvious that the antenna
was snapped off because of carelessness. Repairs will
cost $13, including return postage. You need part pay-
ment of $5 in advance. Organize your thoughts; write
down the ideas you must include in your letter to Mr.
Frisbee; then check your list against these suggestions:

guarantee

> The antenna can be replaced without difficulty.
> The guarantee covers faulty work or materials.
> The antenna was snapped off, probably accidentally.
> Safeguards can be taken to avoid a recurrence.
> Repairs cost $13, and part payment of $5 must be made
> in advance.
> The repair will put the walkie-talkie in operating order.

accidentally
recurrence

Stick to the objective of the letter. Don't digress;
don't tell too much. This letter to a stationery-supply
company has included information that is not necessary
to achieve the objective of the message:

digress
stationery
(spelled with an "e")

> ```
> Mr. Silvers is no longer working for
> us and has accepted a controller's
> job with another company. Therefore,
> remove his name from our letterhead.
> ```

It can be revised efficiently to:

> ```
> Please remove Mr. Seymour Silvers'
> name from our letterhead and include
> the name of Mr. Morris Eisman. Mr.
> Eisman will take Mr. Silvers' place
> as treasurer.
> ```

*When a name ends in
"s," form possessive by
adding " 's" if name is
one syllable or just
apostrophe if name has
two or more syllables.*

It is equally important to include all the necessary
facts. If you were a secretary in the stationery-supply
company, how would you react to this order letter?

> ```
> Gentlemen:
>
> I am starting my own business as a
> consulting engineer. I would like to
> ```

order my stationery from you. Enclosed you will find the letterhead I
have designed.

Will you quote me a price on a thousand letterheads with envelopes to
match?

Sincerely yours,

Sam Enterline

Sam Enterline

quotation

Can you make a quotation on the basis of the information in the letter? Did Mr. Enterline tell you anything about the size, quality, the color of the paper and the envelope, or the color or colors of the printed letterhead? To answer this letter, you must include all the information he omitted. List your ideas. Do they read something like this?

Give quotes on all qualities from the least to the most expensive, and include brochure.
Enclose samples.
Recommend 8½ x 11, but say that any size is available.
Set delivery time for two weeks after the order is placed.
Say that terms are 30 days net.
Thank him for asking.

30 days net
*(The full amount must
be paid within 30 days
of the billing date.)*

Get to the Point Immediately

How will you begin your letter? Don't hesitate; let the opening sentence tell the reader why you are writing. A long or short introduction is not necessary in a business letter; in fact, it detracts from the letter. In one such letter, a personnel manager wrote two pages about his company before he asked for a reference for a former student who was applying for a position there. How annoying to the reader!

personnel
*(He isn't a "personal"
manager.)*

All of us get into habits of doing things, and it is

difficult to change. One habit many businessmen have
acquired is starting a letter with

> `Re your letter of the fifteenth . . .`

> `This is in answer to your letter of`
> `July 15.`

> `We have received your letter of the`
> `fifteenth.`

How unnecessary! Compare these beginnings with this
first sentence:

> `It is a pleasure to send you a copy`
> `of` <u>`Cleaning Your Rugs.`</u>

This gets to the point immediately and avoids the
unnecessary.

Even the "no" letter should include its negative
reply in the opening paragraph. You may want to start
positively; but, if your objective is to say that you cannot do something, say so in the first or second sentence. The answer to your request for a convention
speaker is quickly and efficiently given in this first
paragraph:

> `Thank you very much for inviting me`
> `to be the banquet speaker at your`
> `November convention. I am unable to`
> `accept because I will be speaking at`
> `the University of Hawaii on that date`
> `as part of my fall lecture series.`

Your personal letter in answer to an invitation to
a dinner party could say:

> `I wish I could be with you at your`
> `dinner party on Friday, the fif-`
> `teenth; but I must be at the twenty-`
> `fifth anniversary celebration of my`
> `parents' wedding.`

parents'

Don't waste your reader's time with a long preliminary

discussion. Remember to reply to his request in your
first or second sentence.

Study these opening statements. Note how the
revised sentences get to the point at once.

Original	Revised
We thank you for your letter of the third in which you placed an order for 500 barrels of oil.	The 500 barrels of oil were *Passive "No"* shipped today. Thank you for this order.
Referring to your letter of October 10, we have sent the report you requested on "Health Insurance Under Social Security."	"Health Insurance Under Social Security" was mailed today. *Passive "No"*
In reply to your letter of the first, we regret the error made in your last order in which we inadvertently neglected to include two gross of ball-point pens.	We mailed two gross of ball-point pens by special delivery today. We are very sorry that we made this error.
Mr. William Barnes has applied to us for a charge account. He has given us your name as a reference. Will you be good enough to give us a credit rating on him.	Please complete the enclosed credit report form on William E. Barnes. Mr. Barnes gave your name as a business reference when he applied for a charge account with us.
The Federal Deposit Insurance Corporation has recently increased the amount of insurance to depositors in member banks. Heretofore, individual depositors were insured in a single capacity to a limit of $10,000. Now, the limit has been raised to $15,000.	The Federal Deposit Insurance Corporation now insures your account in our bank to a limit of $15,000. (The previous limit was $10,000.)

USING THE RIGHT WORD

affect √.

effect n.

Your choice of words and the way you use them affect
the clarity of your communication and determine what
effect it will have on your reader.

Avoid Superlatives

So often a salesperson will say, "This is perfect for you." This makes many people's sales resistance zoom — they prefer to make their own decision. And this is important to remember in letter-writing. When a letter states, "This is the best investment on the market for you," the reader will probably comment to himself, "Prove it."

How would you react to these statements? Our opinion is given in the margin.

`This will surely give you a very clear understanding of all the issues.`

This is for the reader to decide.

`We are proud of our exceptionally prompt and most efficient service.`

"Prompt service" is enough.

`Use of our system will produce a tremendous and outstanding improvement in the handling of incoming mail in your office.`

Implication of current inefficiency is offensive.

`We are extremely sorry for the delay.`

Sounds false; omit "extremely."

`Our company is most delighted with your fine and welcome order.`

Writer is a woman who answers many invitations to tea.

`This model is the best television set ever produced.`

At any price?

The business letter and the personal-business letter are written to comparative strangers. Keep them free of superlatives and qualifying adjectives that give a false tone to the writing or tend to draw conclusions for the reader.

comparative

Choose Words for Clarity

How can you write so that your reader knows at first reading what you want to say?

RELATIVE TERMS ARE AMBIGUOUS

Words such as *late, early*; *high, low*; *good, bad*; *productive, nonproductive*; *expensive, inexpensive* are relative terms. They mean one thing to the writer but may mean something else to the reader. To you, "Don't be late" may mean to be home at midnight, but to someone else it may mean to be home at 10 p.m. "My son spent his savings on this expensive car." How much is "expensive"? $10,000? $3,000? $2,000? It varies from person to person and from item to item. A father may consider $3,000 expensive for his son but not for himself. A "productive" grain farmer in India with an average yield of 1,000 pounds of grain annually would be "nonproductive" in the United States, where the average yield is 25,000 pounds.

advertisement

An advertisement for a famous perfume read: "Great savings! Buy now at 20 percent off list price." The customer, not knowing the list price, is unaware of the exact cost or how great the saving actually is. Similarly, when the college newsletter states that a student needs a "high average" for the scholarship grant, a student may wonder whether he needs 85, 90, or 95. What does "high" mean? Does he qualify?

GIVE SPECIFIC INFORMATION

mortgage

A letter from a bank denying a mortgage of $20,000 on a $30,000 house contains the suggestion that the amount of the mortgage be reduced. That letter should have stated:

"Percent" should usually be spelled out.

> If you can see your way clear to a mortgage of $12,000, at 6 percent, for 25 years, we can process it immediately. A $20,000 mortgage in your case, at this time of tight money and high interest rates, may mean a delay of six months.

mortgagor

These precise figures enable the hopeful mortgagor to make his decision.

Which of the following expressions gives you specific information? You are told to come in for an appointment:

early Monday morning, July 18

on Monday, July 18, in the morning

at 9:30 a.m., Monday, July 18   *Type "a.m." and "p.m."*
                                                 as shown here.

The first two sentences leave you wondering when to
arrive. And they make an unfavorable impression, because they convey the idea that you may have to wait   convey
— that no one is expecting you at a special time. The
last sentence sets a definite appointment and gives the
impression that you will get prompt attention at 9:30 a.m.

USE GENERAL TERMS WISELY

It is easy to be specific about dates and prices and
other numerical information. But you can also pinpoint
your meaning by avoiding such general terms as *matter,
situation, area, problem, field, subject, issue, action.*

Vague	Specific
He is an excellent man in his field.	He is an excellent man in electronics.
Help us in this matter.	Discover the error in our account.
We ask your assistance in this situation.	Please extend our credit for 30 days.
This will explain the action of the Board.	The enclosed minutes will explain the Board's opposition to the dividend increase.
Salesmen will visit your area soon.	Salesmen will visit Chicago on August 1.
We shall discuss the issue with you when we meet.	We shall discuss your application when we meet on Saturday.
We will confer about the subject.	We will discuss employment opportunities.

Of course, you don't want to repeat yourself constantly. Sometimes, general words such as those listed above are useful and even necessary. The key to wise use of general terms is *context*. For instance, take the sentences about the Board's action in the list above. Suppose the sentences directly preceding read:

The clarity of words is affected by the company they keep.

> In its March 15 meeting, the Board
> voted not to increase the company's
> dividend. A copy of the minutes of
> that meeting is enclosed.

In this case, using the specific sentence (shown above on the right) would be redundant; the left-hand sentence — "This will explain the action of the Board" — would be more suitable.

redundant

Context, then, can make an otherwise vague sentence precise or a precise sentence redundant. Context is a useful tool — but one that should be used with care. It is better to err on the side of too much clarity than to leave your reader wondering what you are talking about.

The Dictionary Can Help You

.thesaurus

Use a dictionary and a thesaurus to help you choose the right words to express your meaning exactly. By skillful use of these aids, you can develop the ability to select words and to combine them so that they will give you the meaning you desire.

Many words have more than one meaning.

When you look up a word, do you give its meaning only a glance? Take the word *premium*. To the insurance man, it means the money paid for a contract of insurance. But if you do not read beyond the first meaning of the word in your dictionary, you may think that a premium is only a reward or a prize. Are you speaking the same language as your insurance man when you consider your insurance premium a reward or a prize?

And the word has other meanings. The personnel

manager may offer his employees premium pay to work on a late shift. To him it is a bonus offered to spur his workers to work at odd hours. When the broker sells a $10 par value stock at a market value of $25, he sells the stock at a premium of $15. In this case, the premium represents the sum above the nominal or par value of the stock. The jeweler sells only premium merchandise — that which has an exceptionally high value. And so on.

nominal

Most words in our language can be interpreted in different ways. And words may even be used as more than one part of speech. *Well,* for instance, has several meanings as a noun; it is also a verb; and it is also an adverb.

Many words have more uses as any of several parts of speech.

Aside from the meanings of a word, what other information will you find in your dictionary?

1. The correct spelling of a word — such as *phlegm* or *queue.*
2. Preferred spelling when more than one spelling is correct — such as *judgment* or *judgement, advertise* or *advertize, enclose* or *inclose.*
3. Grammatical information:
   a. The part of speech.
   b. Irregular plurals — such as *foot, feet; notary, notaries.*
   c. Principal parts of verbs — such as *give, gave, given.*
   b. Irregular plurals — such as *foot, feet; notary,* tives and adverbs — such as *good, better, best; well, better, best.*
   e. Cases of pronouns — such as *I, my* or *mine, me; we, our* or *ours, us.*
4. Syllabication.
5. Pronunciation.
6. Whether to use a hyphen with a prefix or suffix or to join it to the word — such as *self-interest, selfish, businesslike.*
7. Whether a term is one word, two words, or hyphenated — such as *openhearted, open-air, open house.*
8. Synonyms. (These are not given for all words.)
9. Capitalization of proper nouns and adjectives.
10. The origin (etymology) of the word.
11. Examples of uses of the word.

Each dictionary has its own way of showing this material; to get the most from yours, you should read carefully the explanatory notes at the front.

A dictionary, like any reference book, is no better than your ability to use it correctly. Get yourself a good dictionary, study its method of presenting its information, and then be consistent in using it. Develop the look-it-up habit.

consistent

When you are trying to find exactly the right word, or a synonym for a word you are using too often, or perhaps the opposite of a word, turn to a thesaurus for help. Here you will find many more synonyms than the dictionary provides, and you can discover antonyms as well.

Finding a more precise word.

For example, you want to say that John is a skillful politician, but you have used "skillful" in the preceding sentence. So you make use of your thesaurus, where you find numerous synonyms, among them:

> dexterous, adroit, expert, apt, handy, quick, deft, ready, smart, proficient, good at, master of, a good hand at, masterly, accomplished

Now you can choose among other words to describe John, and you find that "adroit" not only replaces "skillful" but, in this instance, even improves upon it.

Avoiding a colloquialism.

Sometimes you may want to replace a phrase that is too colloquial — for instance, "in a jiffy." If you look in the index under "jiffy," you will be referred to a section that gives you such substitutes as these:

> moment, instant, second, minute, twinkling, flash, breath, crack, burst, flash of lightning, stroke of time

Finding an antonym.

Still another way to use your thesaurus is to find antonyms. Since words are usually grouped in a thesaurus according to ideas (rather than alphabetically), you can find contrasting words in adjacent entries. If you look up "attraction," for instance, you might find that the next entry is "repulsion."

If you will get into the habit of utilizing your dictionary and thesaurus, you'll find your vocabulary expanding and your writing skills improving rapidly.

FORMING SENTENCES

Choosing the right words is only the first step. In order to communicate ideas to the reader, you must combine words into sentences. What constitutes a sentence?

"I cashed my check" is a *simple* declarative sentence. The doer of the action, "I," is the subject. The action, "cashed," is the verb. And the thing acted upon, "my check," is the object.

The simple sentence.

Now let's add a qualifying word, an adjective. "I cashed my *first* check." You immediately picture a new employee happily counting his first salary payment — an important occasion. Or we can add an adverb — "I *quickly* cashed my check." What picture does this call to mind? Qualifying words (modifiers) help make your writing more specific and more interesting.

qualifying

Here are two simple sentences:

```
I cashed my check.
I paid the bill.
```

There can be no question that the two thoughts are closely related. So we can make an improvement here if we add the coordinating conjunction "and" and delete the period. See how much more smoothly the sentences read when they are combined:

The compound sentence

delete

```
I cashed my check, and I paid the
bill.
```

Note use of comma between clauses.

Whenever two clauses are closely allied, you can use a *compound* sentence to add variety to your style and to help your reader understand relationships between thoughts.

The other coordinating conjunctions — *but, or, nor, for* — can also be used to connect two thoughts. Which would you choose to connect these sentences?

coordinating conjunctions

```
The president of the company wishes
to appoint Mr. James head of the Ad-
vertising Department. The Board of
Directors has not yet acted on his
proposal.
```

Use "but."

Use "for."

These data will provide the basis for
his report. They show future trends
in sales.

Use "or."

Will you join the group in Hawaii?
Will you catch up with them in the
Philippines?

Now look at this sentence:

Because I needed money, I cashed my
check.

Here we have combined two related thoughts in a
different way. Instead of a compound sentence (two
simple sentences joined by a coordinating conjunction
The complex sentence. such as "and"), we now have a *complex* sentence. It is
independent composed of an independent clause — "I cashed my
check" — and a dependent clause — "because I needed
money."

A dependent clause is simply one that cannot
stand alone — it leaves the reader waiting for the rest
of the sentence to follow. Read the following dependent clauses. Do you notice that you are waiting for
something else to follow each of them, that you have
a feeling of incompleteness?

After reading this,	You remark:
If you cannot pay your bill by the end of the month	What will happen?
As I have already said	Something is coming that I should know.
Because the capital-investment tax refund has been temporarily suspended	What will result?
When you apply for a position	What should I do?

These clauses need the support of an independent
clause because they do not contain a complete thought
when they stand alone.

In the examples above, *if, as, because,* and *when*

are subordinating conjunctions (as are *since*, *until*, *while*, and *after*). You can see that a subordinating conjunction is what makes a clause "dependent"; you use it when you want to write a complex sentence.

subordinating conjunctions

You have now seen how conjunctions can be used to connect whole clauses to make your writing smoother. But you may also see the conjunctions *and*, *or*, and *nor* used to connect parts of a clause — verbs, adjectives, phrases, nouns.

> You should <u>take</u> the initiative and <u>see</u> the job through to completion.

Verbs.

> The student is <u>industrious</u>, <u>efficient</u>, and <u>alert</u>.

Adjectives.

> This subject is not taught <u>in the high schools</u>, <u>in the colleges</u>, or <u>in the universities</u>.

Phrases.

> Neither <u>Professor Cooper</u> nor his <u>assistant</u> can speak to the group.

Nouns.

For and *but* are also used as prepositions:

> Do this for him.

> All but the last figure have been checked.

Placement Affects Emphasis

USE THE INDEPENDENT CLAUSE FOR EMPHASIS

While you are organizing your thoughts, consider the point of emphasis. In the following sentences, we determine the topic of the conversation by placing it in the main clause:

> I did my assignment while watching television.

> I watched television while doing my assignment.

The topic in the first sentence is "my assignment." In the second "watched television" is the topic.

Another way to spotlight a word or idea is to make it the first or last word in the sentence. Conversely, burying it in the middle of the sentence will often keep it from attracting attention.

PARALLEL CONSTRUCTION AIDS EQUAL EMPHASIS

There are times when each unit of a sentence or paragraph is of equal importance. Using language that is

parallel

parallel in construction will show this equality. For example, when you receive the following information in a letter from the admissions office of the college to which you are applying, you realize the importance of each of the three requirements:

> To be considered for matriculation at Wooley College next February, you must complete the following requirements before November 15:
>
> 1. Complete an Admission Form.
> 2. Have a transcript of your record sent from your high school.
> 3. Take the College Entrance Examination.

What do we mean by parallel construction? If you look at the example, you will see that equal units are presented identically. Each unit starts with the same part of speech — in this case a verb — and is followed by a similar construction — in this case a direct

requisites

object. To neglect any one of the three requisites would deny you the chance to be considered for entrance to the college. The three are parallel in importance, and parallel construction is used to make this clear to you.

But parallel construction is more than a matter of equal emphasis; it is part of adherence to correct grammar. When coordinate conjunctions connect statements that are parallel in form, they should connect noun

with noun, verb with verb, phrase with phrase, clause
with clause, and so on.

> If you select a gift and if you pay   *Clause with clause.*
> for it now, ~~It will be shipped~~ today.
>
> We are concerned about taxes, about   *Phrase with phrase.*
> crime, and about inflation.
>
> Select your material, take it to the   *Verb with verb.*
> desk, and pay your bill.
>
> The treasurer prepared the statement,   *Noun with noun.*
> and the president signed it.

Note how the revised sentences correct the errors
in parallel construction in the original sentences:

Unparallel	Revised
Landing on a carrier for the first time and to cope with a defective engine upset the young pilot.	Landing on a carrier for the first time and coping with a defective engine upset the young pilot.
We plan to build fine homes, to pave highways, and develop educational systems.	We plan to build fine homes, to pave highways, and to develop educational systems.
His notes read: Attend the meeting of the board on the tenth, contact AMS for convention information, plan sales analysis report, and presentation of high merit award at the sales conference.	His notes read: Attend the meeting of the board on the tenth, contact AMS for convention information, plan sales analysis report, and present high merit award at the sales conference.
It is important to enlist the seniors, juniors, sophomores, and the freshmen in student government.	It is important to enlist seniors, juniors, sophomores, and freshmen in student government.
Keep the motor in tiptop condition, good tires, and a tankful of high test.	Keep the motor in tiptop condition, equip the car with good tires, and fill the tank with high test.

This paragraph shows how the President made effective use of parallel construction:

> In a land of wealth, families must not live in hopeless poverty. In a land rich in harvest, children must not go hungry. In a land of healing miracles, neighbors must not suffer and die untended. In a land of learning, young people must be taught to read and write.
>
> Lyndon B. Johnson
> Inaugural speech, January 20, 1965

Avoid Fractured English

Correct use of antecedents, participles, and tenses and proper agreement of subject and verb are some of the essentials of good, clear writing.

ANTECEDENTS

```
The teacher told the student that he
could go home at three.
```

Who could go home at three — the teacher or the student?

```
Mr. Johnson explained to the salesman
that he would attend the sales con-
ference in October.
```

Would Mr. Johnson attend the conference, or did "he" refer to the salesman?

antecedent

By placing the pronoun near the antecedent to which it refers and by planning carefully that the pronoun cannot refer to anything else in the sentence, you will keep your message clear.

Check the revised sentences to see how they clarify the meaning:

Unclear	Clear
`The teacher told the student that he could go home at three.`	`The student was told that the teacher could go home at three.` `The teacher said the student could go home at three.`

When Mr. Smith spoke to the
treasurer, he told him that the
figures were incorrect.

Mr. Smith spoke to the treasurer and told him that the
figures were incorrect.

Equally disturbing to the careful reader is the
"this" in the second sentence of each of these type-
written reports:

Unclear

The president and the board of
directors felt that the dispute
between labor and management
could be resolved quickly. This
kept them in a relatively good
frame of mind. No cutbacks in
production were foreseen.
(Does "this" refer to the feeling or to the
possibility of resolving the dispute?)

During the dissolution proceedings, the partners agreed to
equal distribution of assets.
This surprised their business
associates.
(What surprised the associates? Was it
the fact that the partners could agree on
anything? Was it that the assets were to
be distributed equally?)

Clear

Because the president and the
board of directors felt that
the dispute between labor and
management could be resolved
quickly, they were in a relatively good frame of mind. No
cutbacks in production were
foreseen.

Their business associates were
surprised because, during the
dissolution proceedings, the
partners agreed to an equal
distribution of assets.

Watch your antecedents; they can make your
writing ambiguous.   **ambiguous**

PARTICIPLES

What about this sentence?

While walking down the street, the
car hit the man.

"The car hit the man" is grammatically correct, but
what about the initial participial phrase, "while walking
down the street"? Which noun does it modify? Obviously, the phrase is intended to refer to "man," but
because of the construction of the sentence it actually

modifies the subject — "car." As it stands, the sentence says, "While the car was walking down the street, it hit the man." This construction is clearly an error, and it is a common one in writing as well as in speaking.

You can solve the problem in several ways. Notice how each of the following avoids the ambiguity of the original sentence:

```
While walking down the street, the
man was hit by the car.

As the man was walking down the
street, the car hit him.
```

Here is another example. Note the different meaning that is conveyed in the corrected sentence.

```
When applying for a position,       When applying for a position,
the personnel director requires     an applicant is required to
the completion of an applica-       fill out an application blank
tion blank.                         for the personnel director.
```
(Is the personnel director applying for the position?)

AGREEMENT

You know that the verb must agree with its subject. You say: *I do, you do, they do,* but *he does, I am, you are, he is, they are.* But finding the subject sometimes requires special care. You may encounter a few difficulties that you can easily resolve if you are aware of them. For example, in the sentence "I will buy one of the suits that are on sale," *that* refers to *suits* and takes the plural verb. However, in the next sentence, "In this scene Joe is the only one of the students who escapes," *who* refers to *one* and takes the singular verb (only one escapes). Which verb is correct in each of these sentences?

```
You are one of the many who (has,
have) applied for federal jobs.
```

```
You are the only one of the many ap-
plicants who (has, have) been ap-
pointed.
```

In the first sentence, since the antecedent of *who* is *many*, the verb must be *have*. You are correct if you picked *has* in the second sentence, because *who* refers to *only one*.

Another problem you may have is distinguishing the subject from intervening additions. Check the sentences below:

```
The president, as well as the board
members, agrees to this statement.
```
The subject is "president."

```
The students, in cooperation with the
teacher, plan the field trips for the
class.
```
The subject is "students."

```
The society, in association with the
business firms in the community,
sponsors the yearly conference in re-
tailing.
```
The subject is "society."

```
Mr. Richard Peters, together with his
wife and family, was invited to join
the club.
```
The subject is "Mr. Peters."

TENSE

You know that verb tenses denote the *time* of an action, and you can choose easily among the past, present, and future tenses. But what do you do when you want to show whether one past action has preceded, occurred at the same time as, or followed another? Look at the following example:

denote

```
At the end of the month, I paid my
bill for everything I had bought dur-
ing that month.
```

In this sentence, the writer has indicated that the action of buying preceded the action of paying the bill.

He has done this by using the past tense — *paid* — and the past perfect — *had bought.*

Compare these sentences:

The student corrected all the errors that the instructor <u>marked</u> on his theme.	**The student corrected all the errors that the instructor <u>had</u> <u>marked</u> on his theme.**

Did the instructor mark the errors *before* the student corrected them? Yes. Then you must use the past perfect for the teacher's action.

The present perfect is useful for a different purpose. It enables you to show an action started in the past and completed at any unspecified time up to the present. Here are two sentences:

Since January, when we sent you our estimate, prices <u>have</u> <u>risen</u>.	**Prices <u>rose</u> on the stock exchange today.**

Both sentences speak about an action that was started and completed in the past — that is, before the moment at which the sentence was written. However, the sentences are different. The one on the right (which uses the straight past tense) indicates a *specific* time or period during which the action took place. By contrast, the sentence on the left (which uses the present perfect) indicates only that the action happened *sometime between January and now.*

But what if you want to go further and say that prices are still going up? They went up this morning, they have gone up since this morning, and they are continuing to go up as you write the sentence. To show this sort of *continuing* action, you must use one of the *progressive* forms of the verb *rise.*

Prices are rising on the stock exchange today.

If you suspect that prices will stop going up shortly — or if you aren't sure — you might say:

```
Prices have been rising on the stock
exchange today.
```

There are also other progressive forms: *will be rising* shows continuing action in the future; *had been rising* shows sustained action in the past.

You can see from these examples that the progressive forms are made by using some form of the verb *be* plus the present participle (the *ing* form) of the main verb.

Forming the progressive.

Be sure that you understand these verb forms. If you use them properly, they will contribute to the precision of your writing and facilitate your reader's comprehension of it.

PARAGRAPHING FACILITATES READING

You have learned the importance of choosing the right words and of forming them correctly into sentences. But there is another step you must take to write a good letter: paragraphing. Paragraphing facilitates the reader's comprehension of your message; it says to him, "Here are the organized parts of the whole." The unparagraphed letter appears as a mass of information that he will have to take apart to understand.

facilitates

No formula determines how many paragraphs you should have or how long a paragraph should be, but the most important criterion is meaning. Each paragraph should have its own central idea or topic; a new topic usually calls for a new paragraph. Compare the unparagraphed and paragraphed forms of the letter shown in Figures 3 – 1 and 3 – 2.

Many business letters, however, are short and concern only one main topic, so a single paragraph should suffice. However, appearance is a second criterion of paragraphing, and even a short letter looks better if it contains more than one paragraph. In addition, you should try to keep your paragraphs short, since the eye is attracted to shorter units. This is espe-

criterion

simms, inc.

896 Brattleboro Avenue
Boston, Massachusetts 02111
(617) TR 6-6700
showrooms: Middlebury, Vt. / Pittsfield, Mass.

May 15, 1968

Mr. James S. Johnson
70 Lincoln Street
Martins, Vermont 05201

Dear Mr. Johnson:

You and your friends are cordially invited to visit the new Simms
Showroom in Middlebury, Vermont, which was built in 1956 to
celebrate our 100th anniversary. It is a red building of modern
architecture with a casting pool and is located directly on U. S.
Route 7. Many visitors have commented, "It's the finest in the
East." The interior of the building is attractively paneled with
striated plywood, and it is uniquely lighted from overhead as
well as from wall showcases, the design of which came from
England. A large fireplace and comfortable chairs make you
feel at home. Needless to say, we have a wide variety of the
finest in fishing tackle, including all the rods Simms makes,
for your inspection and actual trial in our pool outside; but, in
addition to this, the showcases are filled with a great assortment of imported items. Country clothes and specialties--
collectors' items such as Gibbs' miniature birds and rare crystal
jewelry--will keep your interest high as you look around. Right
off this main showroom is a new women's shop in which the
ladies in your party can browse while you are attending to your
hobby. They will see beautiful imported sweaters, skirts, and
many other things dear to a woman's heart. Our showroom has
something to interest and please the whole family. We are open
Monday through Saturday all year 'round. Come to see us.

Cordially yours,

Frank Stampler

Frank Stampler
Showroom Manager

hf

Figure 3 – 1
A Mass of Information
Is Uninviting

simms, inc.

896 Brattleboro Avenue
Boston, Massachusetts 02111
(617) TR 6-6700
showrooms: **Middlebury, Vt.** / **Pittsfield, Mass.**

May 15, 1968

Mr. James S. Johnson
70 Lincoln Street
Martins, Vermont 05201

Dear Mr. Johnson:

You and your friends are cordially invited to visit the new Simms
Showroom in Middlebury, Vermont, which was built in 1956 to
celebrate our 100th anniversary. It is a red building of modern
architecture with a casting pool and is located directly on U. S.
Route 7. Many visitors have commented, "It's the finest in the
East."

The interior of the building is attractively paneled with striated
plywood, and it is uniquely lighted from overhead as well as from
wall showcases, the design of which came from England. A large
fireplace and comfortable chairs make you feel at home.

Needless to say, we have a wide variety of the finest in fishing
tackle, including all the rods Simms makes, for your inspection
and actual trial in our pool outside; but, in addition to this, the
showcases are filled with a great assortment of imported items.
Country clothes and specialties--collectors' items such as Gibbs'
miniature birds and rare crystal jewelry--will keep your interest
high as you look around.

Right off this main showroom is a new women's shop in which the
ladies in your party can browse while you are attending to your
hobby. They will see beautiful imported sweaters, skirts, and
many other things dear to a woman's heart.

Our showroom has something to interest and please the whole
family. We are open Monday through Saturday all year 'round.
Come to see us.

Cordially yours,

Frank Stampler
Frank Stampler
Showroom Manager

hf

Figure 3 – 2
The Value of Paragraphing

cially true of that first paragraph; a long first paragraph is an obstacle the reader hesitates to encounter. When you paragraph correctly, you will like the break that white space gives, and so will your reader.

CHECK THE ACCURACY OF FACTS, FIGURES, AND DETAILS

Business demands accuracy. Writing letters entails the responsibility of checking every fact, every figure, every word. Develop the habits of careful proofreading, of looking up information, of confirming figures and dates. For you to *think* it's correct indicates that you are a **marginal** employee, the first to go when your employer can find someone better. The worker who *knows* his work is right has reached a level of competence that leads to positions of higher responsibility.

Errors may be expensive — a misplaced **decimal** point or comma can cost your employer many hundreds of dollars. The secretary who wrote "1,000 barrels of oil" instead of "100 barrels" could hardly believe that one little zero could so disrupt the plant's operations. There was no place to store the extra 900 barrels. The company's fire-insurance policy would not cover an accidental fire under these conditions. The delivery was made on Friday, and a regular pickup could not be made until the following Monday morning. What happened? The extra 900 barrels were returned at the expense of a special trucking service at overtime pay.

With modern data-processing, errors are even more costly; that same misplaced decimal point can cause millions of other complications at the flick of a switch. How can you avoid errors? Simply make it a habit to check your facts and figures carefully. When you enclose a check for $65.56, compare that figure with the original bill. You can easily reverse figures without knowing that you did it.

Always double check figures.

Another common error is the day-date mixup. The invitation to the office party read, "Be sure to come on Friday, December 12." The phone rang all morning, and important tasks had to be put off. The frantic secretary should have made a tape recording of the answer she had to give to all callers: "Sorry, the date is *Thursday,* December 12, same time, same place." Add to the cost of the office party the time, the phone calls, the irritation, and the work interruption caused by that simple error.

An incorrect letter of the alphabet can change the meaning of a phrase. Take the embarrassment caused by the letter sent to a group of experienced reporters who were honoring a colleague at a dinner. **colleague** The man to be feted was described as: "A reformed actor, bon vivant, and raconteur, and a degenerate city editor." Several hundred letters were mailed before someone caught the mistake. The typist should have typed "regenerate city editor." But this was a word she did not know. What should she have done? Be- *Always check your* cause she was in doubt, she should have looked it up; *spelling.* and, if she was still unsure, she should have asked her supervisor. Why don't you check the meaning of those two words. Would you have been embarrassed?

A cursory reading will not always catch the mis- **cursory** use of a word. Catch this one if you can:

```
The members were invited to attend an
an open meeting of the board.
```

If you were alert, you saw the two *an*'s, one at the end of the line and the other at the beginning of the next line.

A professor affixed his signature to a letter in which his secretary failed to correct this sentence:

```
The event has past, and we must move
forward to better things.
```

The verb *passed* should have been used. *Past* is either a noun ("His *past* came before him") or an adjective ("*Past* events proved this to be true").

You must check grammar, spelling, punctuation,

and usage as you write. You must double check all facts and figures. And you must always proofread carefully. Be sure that your written communications are correct in every way.

SUMMARY

You will be on your way to successful letter-writing if you will spend some time in thought before you sit down at the typewriter. Your preliminary work must include a careful outlining of the points you wish to discuss so that you will be certain to include all necessary information and to exclude extraneous material.

Then, when you write that first sentence, make it get to the purpose of the letter immediately.

Next, choose words and phrases that have precise meanings, and avoid generalities that keep your reader guessing. If you rely on the dictionary or thesaurus, you can use your words correctly and add variety to your language. And remember, you can make context work with you to achieve clarity and brevity.

When typing, organize your sentences into one-idea paragraphs to aid your reader's understanding.

Before you mail anything you have written, check the accuracy of facts, figures, and details. So important is accuracy in the business world that you must make checking and proofreading one of the integral parts of writing. No letter should be signed and mailed unless you are certain that it is correct.

3 | Exercises

[1] SPELLING

a. The endings *ence, ance, ent,* and *ant* often give us trouble. Can you
    fill in the correct letter in the following words?

    independ__nt   irrelev__nt   recurr__nce   consist__nt

b. The *er, ar, or* endings are another source of frequent spelling mistakes.
    Which is the correct ending for each of these words?

    mortgag__r   distribut__r   simil__r

c. In the following list, some of the words are misspelled, and others are
    spelled correctly. Write the correct spelling of the words that contain
    errors.

comparitive	priviledged	garantee
judgment	decimal	advertisment
delete	parellel	brosures
accidently	qualifying	redundent
colleague	qualified	catologs

[2] VOCABULARY

a. As you know from the discussion of *premium* in the chapter, many
    words have more than one meaning. Look back at the chapter to see
    how the words *liability* and *quotation* were used (the words in the
    margin will help you find them). Is this the way you would usually
    use these words? See if you can give another definition for each word.

b. Sometimes a word can be used as any of several parts of speech.
    Drink, for example, can be a noun ("Have a *drink*") or a verb ("I *drink*
    tea"). The words *requisite* and *antecedent* can each be used as a noun
    or as an adjective. Write two sentences for each word, using it first
    as a noun, then as an adjective. (If you aren't sure of the different
    meanings of these words, check your dictionary before you begin.)

77

c.   Give a synonym for each of the following words. (If you cannot think of a one-word synonym, you may use two or three words.) Be sure your synonym is the same part of speech as the original word.

   casualty   ambiguous   marginal
   cursory   facilitate   denote
   digress   convey   criterion

d.   What is the meaning of *extraneous*? of *nominal*?

e.   Businessmen often use the expression *30 days net*. Explain briefly what it means.

f.   What is a *novice*?

[3]   **SOUND-ALIKES**

Words that sound alike often trouble us. As we go along, we will be checking on a number of these bothersome terms. The ones we've come across in this chapter are: princi**ple**, princi**pal**; station**e**ry, station**a**ry; **a**ffect, **e**ffect; person**nel**, person**al**. If you are not sure when to use any of these words, study their meanings in the dictionary before you do the exercise below. Then choose the correct word in each of these sentences:

a.   Interest of 4 percent is earned on the (*principal, principle*).

b.   The (*principal, principle*) spoke to the senior class.

c.   Do you think we can (*affect, effect*) some changes in procedures during the next month?

d.   A (*personal, personnel*) letter to your congressman may (*affect, effect*) his vote on the amendment.

e.   This is the (*principal, principle*) reason for our writing.

f.   The appearance of your (*stationary, stationery*) (*affects, effects*) the reader.

g.   The new revenue law may (*affect, effect*) the outcome of the election.

h.   The (*personal, personnel*) manager explained the (*principals, principles*) of management to the audience.

i.   Their position remained (*stationary, stationery*) for three years.

j.   The (*stationary, stationery*) department in their Pittsburgh store has been their (*principal, principle*) source of revenue.

k.   Our class president is a young man of high (*principal, principle*).

l.   An agent has the power to make contracts for his (*principal, principle*).

[4] AGREEMENT OF SUBJECT AND VERB

The "heart" of a sentence is the agreement of the subject and the predicate. Your first step is to identify the subject. Is it singular (one) or plural (more than one)? A singular subject takes a singular form of the verb; a plural subject takes a plural form of the verb.

Let's begin to clear up some of the common difficulties concerning agreement.

> RULE: *Words that come between the subject and the predicate do not affect the number of the verb.*

> The men who play on the team are our employees.

The subject is *men*; therefore, the verb must be plural — *are*.

> The manager, together with his assistants and advisers, has written the report.

The subject is *manager*; therefore, *has*, the singular verb, is needed.

> RULE: *When two or more subjects are joined by and, whether the subjects are singular or plural, they form a compound subject which is always plural.*

> Mary and Jack have formed the new club.

More than one has formed the club; therefore use the plural verb.

Let's apply these rules. How well can you achieve agreement between your subject and verb in these sentences?

a. The proposal to offer stock options to all officers of the company (*was, were*) opposed by minority shareholders.

b. The file on James and Smith (*doesn't, don't*) seem to be in the proper place.

c. The retention of a major portion of our earnings (*has, have*) helped build the new factory.

d. The engineer, as well as the superintendent, (*was, were*) present at the meeting.

e. One of the senior accountants employed at the company headquarters (*has, have*) prepared these reports.

f. Mr. Jones, accompanied by his secretary, (*has, have*) arrived at the office.

g. The report and the statements of the people involved in the accident (*has, have*) been studied.

h. Linda, with her fellow officers, (*is, are*) responsible for the club's success.

i. Changes in design, in performance, and in safety (*results, result*) in greater customer acceptance.

j. Filing tax returns on schedule and making quarterly payments (*keeps, keep*) you on the safe side.

[5] PUNCTUATION: THE APOSTROPHE

Can you form possessives correctly? Remember these simple rules:

> RULE: *Add 's to the singular noun if it ends with any letter but s, or if it is a one-syllable noun ending in s. To nouns of more than one syllable that end in s, you need add only an apostrophe.*
>
>> woman's heart; dealer's stock; boss's desk, James's office; Jonas' kitten

> RULE: *Add only an apostrophe to plural nouns ending in s. Add 's to plural nouns not ending in s.*
>
>> collectors' coins; parents' attitudes; women's shop; the Jamesons' house

Revise the following sentences so that they use the possessive case, as in the following example:

> The books of the girls are in the library.
> The girls' books are in the library.

a. The library of the children is open during the afternoon.

b. The fur of the fox has a glossy sheen.

c. They had a special sale on hats for women.

d. The son of Mr. Jones spent several days in Canada.

e. Inventories of the dealers must be reduced.

f. The boss of Miss Simmons offered her a promotion.

g. The statement of the accountant had an error in addition.

[6] PROOFREADING

The following letter has been typed for the president to send out to his employees. You are to check it for accuracy before it is duplicated and distributed. List any errors you find, and tell how you would correct them. Use your dictionary if you need it.

February 30, 1968

To the Members of the Staff:

Once more it is my privilige and obligation to report to you the results of our operations during the passed year as they effect our Profit-Sharing Plan.

The too categories of principle interest to you involve the following figures:

1. a payment to you Fund for the year of 15% of 1967 compensation;
2. a dollar value per unite as of November 30, 1967 of $18.08.

While the $18.80 figure is lower than the $18.64 unit value of a year ago, I think you will share my pleasant surprise that the decrease is not greater in view of the decline in security values generaly.

Those employes who have qualified for participation in the Defered Plan will soon recieve certificates indicating the number of profit-shareing units placed to his credit this year, and the total number credited to day.

[7] PROBLEMS

a. List the points you would include if you were to write a letter under the following circumstances: You hold a position in the admissions office of Valley Military Academy, a boarding secondary school for boys. You receive this inquiry from a Ralph Trainor — the father of a prospective student:

My son, Colin, will be eligible to attend secondary school in September of 1968. I have heard about the excellent reputation of Valley Academy, and I would like him to attend school there.

Please send me a brochure showing the course of study at the Academy.

Is it possible to pay the annual tuition in installments? Must my son take the SAT examination in order to

qualify for entrance, or will his school grades be accepted? Is there an opportunity to have an interview
before he applies to Valley Academy?

Thank you for your help.

b.   Outline the points your letter would cover in this situation: On March
     30, you receive a second invoice for $1,250 from Prebilt Corporation
     for five filing cabinets. You have already paid for the cabinets, and you
     have your canceled check to prove payment.

c.   You are secretary of your high-school alumni organization. Outline the
     points you would include in your letter to the group asking them to
     contribute to a fund for construction of a new swimming pool at the
     school.

d.   In each of the following, choose the sentence which you think would
     be the better opening sentence for a letter:

     1.   This is in answer to your inquiry of June 10.
     2.   The answer to your inquiry of June 10 is "yes."

     1.   Our most recent price list has been mailed to you today.
     2.   We have noted your request for our most recent price list.

     1.   Could you please give me the credit rating of Donald Brown, who
          has an account with you?
     2.   Donald Brown has applied for a charge account at our store. He
          has given your name as a reference.

     1.   We hope that you have enjoyed reading the books you purchased
          two months ago. However, do you realize that you have not yet
          sent us your check in payment of your account?
     2.   May we remind you that we have not yet received your check for
          $8.69, which was due us last month?

     1.   Your account at the Fulton Bank now earns 5 percent interest.
     2.   If you have been following the financial news, you realize that the
          State Banking Department has given permission for mutual savings
          banks to pay a maximum of 5 percent interest on all savings
          deposits, an increase from the 4½ percent interest formerly paid.

     1.   We're planning to build a new office building in Akron, so we
          would like to have your bid for the job.

2. This letter is being sent to all local contractors who may be interested in placing their bids for our new office building, which is to be built in Akron.

1. We have received your letter of September 15, in which you inquire about the basketball schedule for the coming season.
2. Here is the complete schedule of basketball games for the coming season, which you asked about in your letter of September 15.

1. We are very sorry to read in your letter of February 1 that your orders have not been delivered on time because we have been addressing the packages incorrectly.
2. You have every reason to complain about your orders arriving late because of our incorrect method of addressing the packages.

1. In this rapidly changing world, it is essential that a young man have adequate training before he applies for an accounting job. I am that young man.
2. Will you consider my qualifications for a position in your accounting department? I have a B.S. in Accounting and have completed 16 credits toward my M.A.

1. In recent months, there have been many changes in the various health plans offered to the public. You may be interested to know that a major change is the increase in the allowable number of days of hospitalization from 14 to 21 days completely paid up.
2. Health plans now offer 21 days of completely paid-up hospitalization — an increase of 7 days over previous plans.

e. Where necessary, rewrite the following sentences so that their meaning is clear and accurate. (Watch for generalities, vague terms, and superlatives.)

1. The meeting of shareholders takes place on Monday morning at the Grange Hall in Springfield.

2. The holiday shopping season began early this year.

3. How can you resist such an inexpensive mink?

4. We have the finest display of radios in the entire world.

5. Do not worry about the bill. The cost of repairing your watch will be nominal.

6. Our area has tallied up the highest dollar volume of Christmas sales in history.

7. This is an issue that will come up at the next meeting of the committee.

8. Your savings account at the Dollar Bank earns money at the rate of 4 percent.

9. Your welcome order arrived at our office today, and we were very delighted to receive it.

f. Use coordinate conjunctions (*and, but, or, for*) to produce smoother sentences:

1. Fifty applicants took the test. Only ten passed.

2. The planes were grounded. The entire area was fogbound.

3. The accountants are working. The tax report will be ready soon.

4. Will you enter by the rear? Will you enter by the front?

g. Correct the unparallel construction in these sentences:

1. I want to take this opportunity to remind you of the annual campaign of the City College Fund, which is now under way, and urge you to renew your generous support.

2. Your thoughtful response in the past has enabled The Fund to open new avenues of opportunity for our students and provided direct financial aid for young men and women in need who would not otherwise have been able to continue their education.

3. Won't you take a moment to read it and send your check today to the City College Fund?

4. We offer attractive rates, steady employment, and our working conditions are pleasant.

5. We find that Wick Investing Corp. incorporated under the laws of this State, June 21, 1962, filed a Certificate of Amendment with change of name, September 2, 1965, name changed to Mountain Equities Inc., and is in existence and good standing at the present time.

h. Rewrite these sentences for clarity:

1. When Mr. Saxon handed Mr. James the award, he smiled.

2. Because John's father is a lawyer, he chose this as a profession.

3. The managers told the foremen that they would make the decisions.

4.   Flying high in the sky, I saw the plane.

5.   The auditor told the accountant that he could prepare the statements.

i.   Paragraph this business letter:

> It is with great pleasure that we announce to our clients that as of January 2, 1967, our firm will join the well-known New York Stock Exchange Member Firm, Halsey and Moore. Our headquarters will be at a new branch office of the combined firm of Halsey and Moore at 535 Madison Avenue; our telephone number will be 753-4300. We plan to occupy this space on January 3, 1967, or as soon thereafter as practicable. Your representatives and the present senior partners, who will become limited partners of Halsey and Moore, will handle your accounts and will continue to provide all the services we have in the past. Our research and floor partners will be general partners at the main office of Halsey and Moore at 30 Broad Street. We trust that the confidence you have shown in us for 30 years will continue, and we wish to extend to you at this time the season's greetings and our best wishes for a healthy prosperous and happy New Year.

4 | Your Reader's Response

A GOOD business letter does not merely transmit information; it begins or continues a relationship between you and your reader. Of course, you want your reader to understand your message; but you want to accomplish more than that; you intend your letter to arouse the reader's interest and to elicit a positive response **elicit** from him — you want him to act on your proposal, buy your merchandise, accept your apology. Whether or not you are successful depends on the impression your words make on the reader. Ideas cannot always speak for themselves; the way you present your message, the point of view from which you write, and the impression of you that your words evoke — all these play a part in **evoke** the success of your communication.

SPOTLIGHT THE READER

First, and most important, write with the reader in mind. We all see other people and things only through our own eyes and from our own point of view. We may be

altruistic

influenced by others, pressured by circumstances, tamed by culture; we may be sympathetic and altruistic, but we are each the center of our own world. So, too, the reader is the core of his world. To get him to read your message and act upon it, put him in the center of the stage — tell him what your message can do for him, answer his questions, use language that is meaningful to him.

Address Yourself to Your Reader's Interests

Use *you* and *your*, not *I, we, my, our*. This puts you and the reader in the right frame of mind. Notice how the sentences at the right improve the originals:

We are delighted to have customers write us to ask about our personal bank loans.	You may take out a personal bank loan up to $1,000 by visiting us tomorrow.
We appreciate the order for one dozen blue plaid shirts and will be pleased to send them immediately.	Your order for one dozen blue plaid shirts is on its way to you today. Thank you.

Remember, your letter will get a better response if it impresses the reader with his importance and with your concern for him.

Also, show the reader how you are serving him. **benefit** You write to benefit yourself and your business; but you **benefited** will be benefited most if you can convince your reader that what you propose is to his advantage. For example, compare the following approaches to the dunning notice. Which message would get your vote?

We wish to have a check to meet your overdue account so that we can bring our books into balance for our annual audit.	Your check in the mail before June 30 will maintain the sound credit rating of your business. Of course, your credit reputation is a valuable asset that you want to preserve; but your account is now three months past due. Please don't delay another day.

The businessman in financial difficulty would not care whether or not his creditor's annual audit was taking place. But he could not afford to lose his own credit standing — it could mean loss of his business. Credit allows him to stock what he needs and to pay for it later, out of the income from his future sales. The second approach would get our vote. Did it get yours?

    Now consider this paragraph from a sales letter:

> The new Scout is the best car we have
> ever made. We know that it is better
> than any other car on the market to-
> day. We are offering a special trade-
> in on your old Scout and a low price
> on the new model.

Your boast certainly doesn't interest the reader. How about this instead?

> Give yourself the pleasure of driving
> the new Scout. As the owner of a 1968
> Scout, you will realize the greater
> efficiency, finer performance, and
> improved safety of the new model. By
> trading your old Scout this month,
> you will get the highest price toward
> purchasing the new safer Scout.

Greater safety, more effective performance, special trade-in bonus are *his* as a new Scout owner.

    What would you do with this opening to redirect the major interest to the reader?

> The enclosed brochure, <u>Priceless</u> <u>Hol-</u>
> <u>idays</u>, contains 42 pages describing
> exciting travel adventures, including
> trips to many world capitals, priced
> as low as $399 for 15 days.

One answer might be:

> See the capitals of the world. You've
> begun your trip when you read <u>Price-</u>
> <u>less</u> <u>Holidays</u>. From 42 pages of travel

audit

Underline titles of pamphlets and brochures (or type in all capital letters).

capitals

adventures, you will be able to select a tour that excites the imagination. Just think--you may choose a
vacation trip of 15 days for as
little as $399.

Enter the Reader's World

How do you know what the reader wants to know, how
he feels about price, what is the best way to serve him?

Look through former correspondence with him if
there is any. Is he an old customer or a new one? Is
your customer a man or a woman? In what business or
engaged   profession is he engaged? Does his style of writing give
you any clues to his personality? Is it usual for him to
tarry in paying his bills?

Take the case of a clerk who was hired for the
summer months and therefore did not know the business or its customers. Trying to impress her employer
with her efficiency, she mailed out second notices at
the end of a ten-day waiting period with a typed remark: "Did you forget? Your bill is overdue!" One
customer of 20 years' standing, piqued by this, sent in
her check, the second notice, and a little note, addressed
to the owner, that read: "No, I did not forget, but you
can forget to include me in your list of customers for
immediately   the fall season." The owner immediately called to
apologize to this good customer, who had been one of
his first. He knew that she was away during the summer
months, but the new clerk had not checked with him.

Anticipate your reader's reaction to your statements. How do you do this? Write to him as if you were
looking at him. Will you get a smile or a frown? Will
rebuff   you get cooperation or a rebuff? Will you get action or
delay?

Reach into your own experience to develop an
understanding of your reader's reaction. If you remember how you felt when you did not receive one of your
textbooks on time, you will know how to answer the
angry complaint you receive as a part-time assistant in
the college bookstore. You would not irritate the student with a postcard saying:

> The textbook you ordered has not come
> in. The expected delivery date is
> February 15.

February

You would assuage him with the message:

> You can pick up your textbook on
> February 15. Your instructor knows
> that the book will not be available
> until that date.

Another part of writing from the reader's point of view is awareness that his background and interests may be different from yours. Your business, like every other field of endeavor, has its own specialized vocabulary. Will your reader understand that vocabulary? As a stockbroker, for instance, would you write this letter to a college freshman?

> We recommend the purchase of Ajax
> common stock for long-term capital
> gains. The stock has a 16:3 ratio by
> 1968 projections, a low evaluation by
> historical standards. A capital ex-
> penditure of $900 million to develop
> new products suggests a base adequate
> to support a doubling of the price of
> Ajax within the next two years.

Note that "million" is usually written out to avoid many ciphers.

If you did, it might not make much sense to him. To the sophisticated investor, this language is clear; but the college freshman would better understand the language of the following letter:

> Begin your investment program with
> the purchase of shares of Ajax, a
> stock that should make your money
> grow. The current price of the stock
> is low in comparison to the firm's
> probable earnings this year. In addi-
> tion, Ajax is introducing many new
> products that will have broad appeal
> to customers. Sales and profits
> should increase enough to cause the
> price of Ajax to double within the
> next two years.

knowledge

Thus, the stockbroker must write different letters to the international banker and the teacher, to the new investor and his active customers. So you, too, must use your own experience and your knowledge of people's reactions to meet them at their level of interest.

To Your Reader Be True

When you write that an order will be shipped next week, is this just a delaying action to keep your customer from going to your competitor? Are you planning to write him next week to tell him that there has been an unfortunate delay for another week? How would you feel if someone played this game with you? Such

integrity

a lack of integrity causes loss of respect for your company. It also takes away your customer's right to make a decision that may be important for his business;

subterfuge

through subterfuge, you have forced him to wait two weeks for his order.

When the new clerk received this order letter, he was concerned because the delivery could not be made:

```
Please send the electric clock radio
No. 6680 for $22.95 which is adver-
tised in your Christmas brochure on
page 16. Here is my check for $22.95.
```

What should the clerk tell the customer? This was his answer:

```
Dear Madam:

Your order for the electric clock
radio and your check were received
today.

The order will be filled as soon as
possible.

                    Very truly yours,
```

The clerk submitted the letter to his supervisor, who suggested the following:

Dear Mrs. Jones:

Thank you for your order for the electric clock radio.

Unfortunately, there has been a delay in our shipment. We will notify you as soon as the order goes out, which should be within a week or two.

Notify customer of delay.

We are sorry for this delay.

Apologize.

                    Very truly yours,

Before the letter was mailed, the sales manager made a special request to the office manager. Noting that the shipment had been "hijacked" and that the order was to be duplicated, he requested all clerks to refer orders for the electric clock radio to him. This was his answer to Mrs. Jones:

Dear Mrs. Jones:

Your electric clock radio No. 6680 will be shipped on December 20.

The hijacking of our truck on December 10 prevented your receiving the radio on time, but the manufacturer is duplicating the shipment immediately. We are sorry for this delay.

Give explanation whenever possible.

We shall not cash your check for $22.95 until the order is shipped.

                    Sincerely,

The third letter gives the reader a clear understanding of the situation and the reason for it. She can accept the order subject to the delay or cancel it.

You must believe that what you are writing is true — that the car will give safety and top performance at a low price, that you will pay on August 31, that the order will be shipped on December 20. If it is not true, the deception will soon be discovered; and the relationship between you and your reader will be destroyed.

Use semicolon before a conjunction when a comma is used in either independent clause of a compound sentence.

For example, when a businessman purchases something on credit, he has established a relationship between him and his creditor that is important to his business. If he cannot pay his bill on time, how can the businessman preserve that good relationship: What about this letter?

> Please give us an extension of 60 days on our account. We have run into a serious problem. As you know, tight mortgage money has slowed down con-struction of new homes in Allentown, and our heating units have remained unsold.
>
> We expect to be able to pay our ac-count in full by August 31.

incurred

Think of the angry collection letters that need not be written, the expense of writing them that will not be in-curred, and the reassurance the creditor now has that his customer is honest and is not merely trying to avoid payment.

Truthfulness goes hand in hand with sincerity. The following sentence from a form letter is an insult to the reader's intelligence:

capitol

> I am writing this letter to you per-sonally to give you an opportunity to subscribe to our magazine, <u>News from the Capitol</u>, at a reduced rate.

He knows that thousands of copies of this letter are

being mailed. Therefore, he will ascribe to everything   **ascribe**
that follows the same lack of sincerity found in this
first sentence. Interest in the reader must be genuine,
or it will backfire.

Remember the Amenities

How do you react to these commands?

> Pick up the papers on the floor.
> Answer the phone.
> Close the file drawer.

Do you feel that the person issuing such orders is
imposing on you? These peremptory statements can be   **peremptory**
softened by the addition of "please" or "will you."

In your business communications, too, you must
preface your request with the magic word "please." No
matter how interested you are in brevity, this word may
not be omitted.

Courtesy also requires an apology for an over-
sight, a late response, a negative reaction, or an error.
The customer's anger is dissipated with "I am sorry" or
"I apologize."

Finally, include a "thank you" for your reader's
assistance, for the action he has taken, for the time and
attention he has given to a proposal. Otherwise, you
will be guilty of being discourteous.

All your business communications win friends by
using courteous terms. Make it a point to include
"please," "thank-you," or "I am sorry" when they are
needed in your business communications.

A PICTURE OF YOU

You have learned the importance of writing from the
reader's point of view. Even when you do that, however, your letter will give the reader a picture of you.
What kind of impression will that be?

Recently the director of a large summer resort

catering to varying age groups received this letter and assigned the three vacationers to Cottage 148 on the far side of the lake.

> 386 East Avenue
> Aro, Wisconsin   53289
> July 30, 1968
>
> Winnebago Resort
> Fond du Lac
> Wisconsin 53276
>
> Dear Sir:
>
>   Re your advertisement on Vacation Lakes in the travel section of the <u>Times</u>, I would like to reserve a cottage on the lake for the two weeks, August 15th to August 31st. The cottage must have at least three bedrooms, inasmuch as there will be three of us renting it.
>
>   Pursuant to the stated requirements, I am enclosing herewith my check in the amount of $50.00 as down payment and will pay the remainder upon our arrival on August 15th.
>
>   Looking forward to a delightful vacation, I remain,
>
>   Very truly yours,
>
>   *Ilka Krauss*
>
>   Ilka Krauss

Would you use these terms?

re

15th; 31st

inasmuch

pursuant; stated requirements; herewith

remainder

I remain

The three occupants of Cottage 148 were surprised to find that they had been placed with the more mature vacationers — those 60 years old and older. But the director of the resort was even more startled to see

three shapely young 20-year-olds crossing the bridge as
they made their way into his office to complain about
their assignment to the quiet side of the lake. But the
letter had been written in language of the nineteenth
century — surely no modern young woman would have
used such outdated expressions, such old-fashioned
form. Red-faced, Ilka realized that she had followed the
pattern used by her own employer.

The business world is populated by many Ilkas
who imitate the past and by many employers who make
frequent use of outdated, trite expressions. These ex-   trite
pressions tell the reader that he is communicating with
an old, staid stick-in-the-mud. What do you think of
these expressions taken from typical business letters?
Would they be used in face-to-face conversation? What
improvement in language can you suggest?

Worn-out expressions	Suggested revisions
Re your letter of the tenth, I would like to order the textbook.	Please send the textbook.
inasmuch as	because _or_ since
in accordance with the requirements	as required
I am enclosing herewith	here is
thanking you in advance, I remain	thank you
In reply to your letter, I believe that we can make an adjustment forthwith.	Your account was adjusted today. (We adjusted your account today.)
We acknowledge receipt of your check for $10.	Thank you for your check for $10.
We are in receipt of your order.	You will receive your calculator in ten days.
you will please find enclosed	here is
due to the fact that	because

in accordance with the	according to
We would like to express our appreciation.	Thank you.
prompt consideration of the matter	Please verify the data promptly.
pursuant to	according to
We value your patronage.	Thank you for your business.

You can easily avoid these clichés by "talking" your letter. Would you say what you have written in a telephone conversation? No, then rewrite it. Replace those expressions that have worn thin with the easier, shorter, more pointed language of today.

But avoiding the outdated expressions of the past does not mean selecting the jargon of the present. Our everyday talk is peppered with such expressions as: "Oh, yeah!" "I don't get it." "Come again?" "He's a right guy." A student can be heard suggesting that another student "con" the teacher into giving him a better grade. Slang is appropriate in conversations with friends, but it is out of place in business correspondence. It characterizes you not as modern but as non-professional and flippant.

Consider the suggestions at the right to replace the slang expressions at the left:

He's a right guy.	Mr. Jones gets along very well with his co-workers as well as with his supervisors.
We're hitting on all cylinders.	Every worker is reaching his production level.
We've made it now.	We have achieved success.
The Democrats are in.	The Democrats have been elected.

The successful letter writer does not lean on the clichés of the past or the jargon of the present; he chooses his own expressions.

LANGUAGE TO CREATE INTEREST

If you can approach the reader on his own level and can leave him with a good impression of yourself as a business person, you're off to an excellent start. But your message itself must also leave a favorable impression. Let's look at some ways to accomplish this.

Elastic Sentence Length

The length and complexity of your sentences should be tailored to the type of message you are writing. If your objective is rapid understanding, keep your sentences short enough to be absorbed at a glance. In a sales letter, for instance, you may have to catch the reader's attention and get your message across before that attention wanes.

tailored

In a different situation, you might use a series of short, declarative sentences to show a cold analysis of facts:

> You charged $520 worth of goods in
> October. However, you have not yet
> paid your bill or contacted us. Why
> have you delayed payment for three
> months?

The technical writer — the scientist or mathematician — might also use this staccato effect. You can see each arrow hitting the mark in this series:

staccato

> The fourteen patients were given the
> drug. Seven patients showed marked
> improvement. These seven patients had
> a common form of the disease. The
> drug is likely to be effective against
> one form of this disease.

Complex and compound sentences, on the other hand, enable you to qualify your statements, to add nuances that broaden and deepen your meaning, to bring clearer understanding. (Review Chapter 3 on compound and complex sentences.) For example, the an-

nuances

swer "I will" may be qualified by the clause "if it doesn't rain." Or, the cold statement "you have delayed paying your account for three months" can be softened by the addition of "although you have been one of our best charge customers over the past five years." The student who reads "your application for matriculation in January 1967 has not been accepted" knows he has been rejected — but he does not know why. The clause "since it was not filed before the November 1 deadline" clarifies his understanding of his situation.

complemented
*(with an "e"; not
"complimented" with
an "i")*

Flowing thoughts and lively writing usually call for a variety of sentence lengths. In most situations, a mixture of short, simple sentences complemented by longer, smoother ones will best hold your reader's attention. You should remember, however, that too long a sentence is burdensome. It usually requires rereading, and that is a waste of the reader's time. Just try this for sentence size:

> Although there has been a tremendous drive by our employees to improve production quotas, and although production has been increased by 10 percent, it is imperative that, in an attempt to meet the new request by management for production to be increased another 25 percent, an extra shift of 50 men be added between the hours of 8 p.m. and 2 a.m. for the months of October, November, and December.

Did you grasp the meaning of the sentence the first time you read it? Break it down to shorter units of thought for quick, easy reading:

Use numerals for percents.

> The cooperation of our employees in improving quotas increased production by 10 percent. To meet the new 25 percent increase set by management, we should add another shift of 50 men. We can schedule the shift from 8 p.m. to 2 a.m. for the months of October, November, and December.

The average sentence has between 16 and 22 words. If you find that your sentences consistently go beyond this average, you will certainly want to cut them.

Varied Approaches

In addition to varying the length of your sentences, you can add interest to your letter by varying sentence structure.

Personnel directors are accustomed to getting letters of application that begin:

```
I would like to apply for the posi-
tion of
```

and continue in the second paragraph with:

```
I was graduated from Long Beach High
School in June, 1968. I had a B aver-
age. I was also active in school
affairs.
```

and repeat the ubiquitous "I" even in the final paragraph with:

```
I will be glad to come in for an in-
terview. I have listed my phone num-
ber on my data sheet.
```

The repeated subject-verb sentence beginning dulls any message. You get the feeling that you are back in elementary school reading that first primer. To add that vital touch to your written communications, vary the beginnings of your sentences.

Don't begin each sentence with a noun or pronoun	Try these ideas
The company wishes to order a transistor for its specially designed machine.	<u>verb</u>: Please send transistor No. 17 for our automated drill press.

Transistor No. 17 is no longer being produced.

conditional clause: Because we have replaced it with another type, No. 17 is no longer being produced.

The increase in voltage output will increase the efficiency of the machine.

phrase: In fact, with the increase in voltage output, the drill press should operate more efficiently.

Reactions that are quick and alert can save your life.

adjective: Quick, alert reactions can save your life.

The key to high production is selecting personnel carefully.

adverb: Carefully selecting personnel is the key to high production.

Election Day is just another holiday to some people.

preposition: To some people, Election Day is just another holiday.

The ability to write clear effective messages requires organized thinking.

gerund: Writing clear, effective messages requires organized thinking.

We can only hope that a man live his life to its fullest degree.

noun clause: That a man live his life to its fullest capacity is all that we can ask.

It is a trying problem for the youth of today to choose the right vocation.

infinitive: To choose the right vocation poses a trying problem for the youth of today.

The secretary opened the mail as she was waiting for her employer.

adverbial clause: While the secretary was waiting for her employer, she opened the mail.

Nothing about your writing should happen accidentally. You must work at it. Planning for variety in your sentence beginnings will give your communication vitality.

Continuity

In the credits for motion pictures, you often see the listing "Continuity." If one scene does not lead smoothly into the next, confusion results. The same is true in business communication. Without continuity, your writing lacks punch. It jerks along, forcing the reader to expend extra effort in jumping the hurdles between ideas, as you will notice in the following paragraph:

expend

> The modern version of <u>Carmen</u> is receiving rave reviews. It opened in New York in November. Tickets are to be ordered for any Friday in December. The tickets cost $6 each. The Business Club is going. The cost of the tickets is high for college students. Twenty-five tickets will be ordered. Student Council is asked to make a loan of $150 for the purchase of tickets. This has been the procedure in the past.

For amounts of money, use figures. Omit decimal and zeros.

Use words, not figures, at beginning of sentence.

With a little organization and with the use of transitional phrases, the same report reads:

> The Business Club selected the modern version of <u>Carmen</u> for its theater party in December. Since the critics acclaimed this production for its excellence of musical interpretation and staging, the members are willing to purchase tickets for $6.

Underline titles of plays, operas, ballets.

> Following the procedure of last year, the Business Club asks Student Council to extend a loan of $150 for 25 tickets at $6 each so that the Club can pick up the tickets immediately. Repayment of this loan will be made within two weeks.

Use figures for numbers over ten.

Organization, as we said in Chapter 3, has much to do with continuity; but the simple technique of using transitional words keeps the reader with you. Bridge the gap for him with such expressions as:

> in the second place, finally, of course

```
however, nevertheless, therefore
as you see in the attached memoran-
dum, in Section II
when I telephoned you
after that
in reviewing the first case
to summarize
```

Without such transitions, the reader loses time in reading and comprehending your ideas; with them, he reads easily and smoothly.

Choosing Words for Added Effect

Verbs and nouns can increase the vitality and punch of your writing or make it dull; they can keep a moderate tone or introduce a note of harshness. As always, choosing the right word for the right purpose enhances your communication.

enhances

VERBS OF BEING VERSUS ACTION VERBS

Verbs such as *am, seem, feel, was, were, are,* and *is* assume a condition or state of being:

```
I am tired.
They feel that it is not true.
We are right.
```

These "being" words are useful when you want to speak generally, to avoid being specific, or to de-emphasize something you must say. For these purposes, they are important. Usually, however, you want to *add* action and life to your writing, and overuse of verbs of being slows your business writing to a crawl. Compare the pairs of sentences below:

"Being" verb	**Action verb**
There is a balance of $87 due on your account.	You owe $87 on your account.

We are the largest manufacturers of ski equipment in this country.	Our company manufactures more ski equipment than any other company in the United States.
This is your opportunity to buy at low prices.	Now you can buy at low prices.
It is my opinion that I can help you increase your profits.	I believe that I can help you increase your profits.
There is evidence that Mr. Jones is a reliable credit risk.	We rate Mr. Jones a reliable charge customer.

Notice how changing the verb converts a quiet, lifeless sentence into an active, emphatic one. Action verbs bring your sentence right to the point and tell the reader just where responsibility for the action lies. When you have completed a letter, count the number of times you used *it is*, *there is*, or *there are*. Did you mean to write this kind of letter? Or can you add power to your letter by eliminating these drowsy words and phrases?

PASSIVE VOICE VERSUS ACTIVE VOICE

Do you like the straightforward person who always gives you a direct answer and who does not hedge? If your answer is "yes," you will want to exhibit this same straightforward approach in your own writing. To do this, use the active voice. When you make the subject of your sentence the doer of the action, you employ the active voice. When you make the subject the receiver of the action, you use the passive voice.

hedge

Passive voice	Active voice
I was made a better letter writer by taking this course.	I write better letters because I took this course.

In the first sentence, you passively accept what is being done to you; in the second, you actively participate in achieving writing skill.

Now look at the sentences below. Notice the vagueness and lack of directness of those at the left. Do you see how the active voice in the sentences at the right emphasizes the doer and adds forcefulness to the sentence?

Passive voice	Active voice
The figures have been checked by the auditor.	The auditor has checked the figures.
It is noted that your business is improving.	The Board noted the improvement in your business.
Your assistance is appreciated by us.	We appreciate your assistance.
The procedures manual has been prepared by the personnel department to help new employees.	The personnel department has prepared the procedures manual to help new employees.

onus

Under certain circumstances, however, the passive voice can be useful. If, for instance, you don't want to place blame on the subject (or if you don't know who is to blame), the passive voice will shift the onus of responsibility from him — as in the following sentences:

The company was forced to close its doors.

permitted
(When the accent is on the last syllable, form the past tense by doubling the final consonant and adding "ed.")

John was not permitted to attend the conference.

(Do you get the implication that it was not the company's fault? Do you understand that John was not absent by his own choice?)

Or perhaps you must tell your reader that he is at fault, but you want to keep his goodwill. By using the passive voice, you can avoid the clear-cut, definite statement that gives offense. Compare the following answers to the housewife who complained about her malfunctioning washing machine:

Active voice	Passive voice
Because you have made unauthorized adjustments on your Speedex, we cannot service your machine under the guarantee.	Because unauthorized adjustments have been made on your Speedex, your guarantee has been invalidated.

Remember, the active voice is direct, specific, and positive; and it keeps your writing moving. In most cases, these are the values for which you strive. The passive voice, on the other hand, is indirect and general, and it removes the emphasis from the doer of the action. Limit its use to the times when these are your goals.

THE LONG-WINDED ABSTRACTION

Many writers try to impress their readers with abstract words and long-winded phrases. In most writing, however — and especially in business letters — the best way to say something is usually the simplest way, and the most suitable word is frequently the shortest one. Compare the following sentences:

Analysis of the situation indicated the ineffectiveness of his plans in ameliorating the food shortage for a thousand people.	His plans had not included transportation for the hundred tons of rice; without it, a thousand people starved.
Try to effectuate some changes in your plans so that we can utilize these tickets.	Try changing your plans so that we can use these tickets.
The exigencies of the situation demand that the government decrease its monetary expenditures.	The financial crisis makes it necessary to cut government spending.
We anticipate that the optimum remuneration we can offer you is $8,000 per annum.	We think that the best salary we can offer you is $8,000 a year.
We are in a position to assist you without further delay.	We can help you now.

Notice how difficult it is to understand the sentences on the left. Formless, abstract words and convoluted phrases detract from the clarity and force of your writing. They obscure your meaning; in some cases (as in the first and third sentences above), they may lose it entirely.

*Build your vocabulary
— then use it well.*

It is important to build an extensive vocabulary — the more words you know, the more precisely you will be able to express yourself. However, you must remember that the major purpose of your business writing is to communicate with your reader; and that means choosing the clearest words, not necessarily the longest ones. Save the "big" words for those cases where a simpler word will not do.

SUMMARY

A powerful dimension of your business-letter writing is the relationship created between you and your reader Focus on him as an individual by appealing to his interests, by showing him that you want to serve him, by placing yourself in his position so that you write his language, by being honest with him.

Your reader should get a picture of you as an up-to-date writer. Don't let him find you trapped in the dead language of the past. "Talk" your letters to give them a natural tone. Vary the length and construction of your sentences to retain interest, and make your thoughts flow smoothly with transition words. Pack power into your writing by using action verbs; the active voice; concrete words; and short, specific words and phrases.

Develop a positive attitude toward your reader, and you will get his positive reaction.

$$4 \quad | \quad \text{Exercises}$$

[1] SPELLING

a. Misspellings often result from the omission of a letter rather than from the use of an incorrect letter. Correct the spelling of these words by adding the missing letters:

Febuary   immediatly   knowlege   curteous

b. Correct any misspellings you find in this sentence:

He incurred the dislike of his associates by his constant subtrefuges and his lack of integrety.

c. Do you know when to double the final consonant in forming the past tense? What is the past tense of each of the following?

benefit   incur   permit   audit   elicit

[2] VOCABULARY

a. Look back to see how the words *tailored, engaged, audit,* and *hedge* were used in this chapter. (The marginal notations will help you locate them.) What does each word mean as we used it? Do you know another meaning for each word?

b. What is the difference between *evoke* and *elicit*?

c. Use each of the following words in a sentence, being sure that the sentence shows you know the word's meaning:

altruistic	staccato	trite
subterfuge	nuances	ascribe
peremptory	enhance	expend

109

[3] SOUND-ALIKES

Be sure you know the difference between *accede* and *exceed*, *complement* and *compliment*, *capital* and *capitol*. Now get a perfect score on the sentences below.

a.   Please accept our (*complements, compliments*) on your excellent display.

b.   If he (*accedes, exceeds*) to our request, we'll have our full (*complement, compliment*) of engineers.

c.   There is not sufficient (*capital, capitol*) to finance the proposal.

d.   The (*complement, compliment*) of 88 is 12.

e.   If your debts (*accede, exceed*) your assets, we cannot (*accede, exceed*) to your request for credit.

f.   The (*capital, capitol*) in most state (*capitals, capitols*) is an impressive building.

[4] MORE ON AGREEMENT

In Chapter 3, you learned not to be confused by a group of words that intervenes between subject and verb. Here are some hints for solving other agreement problems.

> RULE: *When your subject is one of the following words (or is modified by them), the verb must be singular:* every, each, everybody, everyone, every one, anybody, anyone, any one, nobody, everything, anything, somebody, something, someone, some one, many a, more than one, nobody, no one, nothing.
>
> > Everyone misses a class from time to time, but no one skips an exam.
> > Many an idea is lost in the discussion.
> > No one is above suspicion.

Even when *each* or *every* is part of a compound subject, the subject is considered singular:

> Each student and teacher keeps his own records.

Collective nouns (that is, nouns, such as *committee* or *group* or *audience*, that refer to several individuals together) also confuse many writers.

> RULE: *Treat the collective noun as singular if it refers to a group acting as a unit; treat it as plural if it is a group whose members are acting as individuals.*

The committee has announced its decision.
The committee have left for their homes.

Be sure you understand these rules; then try your hand at these sentences:

a.   Every one of the employees (*wishes, wish*) to order (*his, their*) own stationery.

b.   Each of us (*is, are*) obliged to sign (*his, their*) name.

c.   The audience (*has, have*) given (*its, their*) approval of the performance.

d.   Every regional director and supervisor (*has, have*) sent in (*his, their*) work reports.

e.   Many of the workers (*has, have*) gone home.

f.   Our team (*is, are*) going to vote on it tomorrow.

g.   None of the boys (*is, are*) leaving.

h.   Many a miracle (*has, have*) been wrought.

i.   Somebody among us (*knows, know*) the answer.

j.   (*Does, Do*) some of the children get tickets?

k.   The Scholarship Board (*has, have*) ordered (*its, their*) lunches.

[5] PUNCTUATION: COMMA

The comma is the punctuation mark that gives most people the most trouble. Let's look at two rules for using it.

RULE: *Use a comma between the independent clauses of a compound sentence.* (An independent clause is one that can stand alone as a sentence; a compound sentence is one in which two or more independent clauses are joined by one of the coordinate conjunctions — *and, but, or, nor, for.*)

Interest in our new product is high, and sales have doubled.

Remember, a clause has both a subject and a verb. Don't be fooled by sentences like the one below. It has only one clause, since there is only one subject; therefore, it has no comma.

Roger went fishing with his father last week and brought home seven bluefish.

RULE: *Use a comma following introductory clauses or phrases.*

When John finished eating, he went out to find Dave.

Of all the possibilities, you had to choose this.
If I didn't know better, I'd say you did that one.

With these rules in mind, punctuate the following sentences.

a.   Since you are learning to write correctly you will be a successful correspondent.

b.   The secretary called the meeting to order at noon and read the minutes immediately.

c.   Attend the stockholders' meeting and write me a complete report of the day's activities.

d.   When Sally and Jo finished riding Sam applauded them.

e.   The case has closed but our lawyer has not yet received his fee.

f.   The editor read the copy quickly and made the necessary changes.

g.   If I were to go he would surely recognize me.

h.   Either James went to the conference or he got news of the decision from Henry.

 [6] PARALLEL STRUCTURE

Remember our discussion of parallel structure in Chapter 3? Review it if you don't; then rewrite the following sentences to make them conform to the rules of parallelism.

a.   Our new dacron shirts wash easily, drip dry quickly, and you can wear them right away.

b.   Come join our company, where the pay is high, working conditions are pleasant, and to succeed is possible.

c.   The mechanics are trained in repairing all makes of domestic cars and in foreign-car repairs.

d.   The personnel manager said that this employee is intelligent, alert, and has been a capable worker.

e.   Trying to get ahead in business is not necessarily to succeed in it.

[7] PROBLEMS

a.   Do the sentences below emphasize the reader's point of view? Make any changes in them that you feel are needed.

1.   We are happy to send our new price list to all our customers.

2.   This new model is our latest in a long series of "firsts" in the industry. We were first in producing a low-cost radio. We made the first portable television. Now we are first in portable color television.

3.   *Good Times* has been read by thousands of people who have benefited from its excellent suggestions. They have always found dozens of ideas for making their money stretch by reading our fine publication.

4.   I am applying for the position of junior accountant in your office. I feel that my grades prove that I am intelligent and capable, and I know I can do a good job for you.

b.   Do these statements ring true? Can you improve them?

1.   Although delays in shipment are normal at this time of the year, we will see to it that your orders are the first to leave our shipping room.

2.   Yours is the first complaint our store has ever received.

3.   Place your account with Withers and Company, and watch your money grow. We don't make mistakes.

c.   If you remember the amenities, you can make these sentences sound a little friendlier:

1.   Send me the travel folder you advertised in *This Week.*

2.   We have received your order of February 20.

3.   Will you consider my application for employment?

4.   Your account is now up to date.

5.   Return the questionnaire to us soon so that we can publish our findings early next year.

d.   Below is a letter to an eighth-grade pupil who wrote to a broker to ask about buying ten shares of Goode Motor Company. Does it enter the reader's world? What changes, if any, would you make in it?

Dear Harold:

Thank you for your letter asking our opinion about your purchasing ten shares of Goode Motor Company.

The performance of the stock has been rather erratic of
late. Undoubtedly it has been subjected to selling pressure by those taking tax losses.

However, its P/E ratio is now only 15 to 1, which we
consider to be quite favorable under the circumstances.
We do not foresee that the stock should decline much
more. As a matter of fact, our projections indicate that
the company has an excellent future.

Congratulations on wanting to buy stock for your future.
But, since you are a minor, you cannot purchase the
shares yourself. An adult will have to open a custodian
account for your benefit. We will be glad to help you in
any way.

e.   Too much writing is marred by old-fashioned expressions. Below are
sentences taken from an 1880 publication; notice that they are still
in use today. How would you bring them up to date?

1.   Enclosed please find a check for $10.

2.   Please be advised that your order will be shipped within a short
period of time.

3.   I enclose herewith an order to which you will please give your
earliest attention and forward, with as little delay as possible, as
per shipping instructions attached.

4.   Your letter dated July 25th has been duly received and noted.

5.   Referring to your letter of the 5th, we beg to state that there has
been no error in your statement.

f.   Avoid the too-casual language in the following sentences:

1.   We goofed! We charge you $15.75 for the radio when it should
have been $50.75.

2.   Why don't you get with it? Join the crowd. Buy this new outdoor
pool.

3.   You'll have a ball when you shop at Tracey's.

g.   Rewrite each of the paragraphs below so that it is clear and reads
smoothly.

1. Your insurance man can give you automobile insurance. He can give you life insurance. He can sell you health insurance. He can insure your boat and your personal property.

2. We would like to know whether, during the several weeks in which you have been considering our estimate to paint and refurnish your office, you have made any decision to go ahead with the work.

3. Since I am delighted to accept your kind invitation to speak at your club meeting on Monday, January 5, 1968, at 8 p.m., on any topic I deem advisable, I have decided to say a few brief words on that ever increasing hazard to our national physical health — air pollution.

4. We do not have a large enough work force. We cannot bid on this job. Please ask us again when you have another job. We may be able to bid at a later date.

✳ h. Rewrite these sentences using the active voice.

1. Your letter of the fifth has been read, and the order will be shipped immediately.

2. These fabrics have been produced by Glenn Company for the past 75 years.

3. Your itinerary will be carefully drawn up by one of our experts, and all details will be handled by him.

4. Our report was considered by the board, but no definite recommendations were made.

SOCIAL-
AND
PERSONAL-
BUSINESS
WRITING

5 | Simple Statements

YOU HAVE reviewed and mastered discrete principles of business writing. Now let's practice what we preach — let's integrate these principles into the complete business communication.

discrete
(not "discreet")

THE SIMPLE REQUEST

Suppose we start with a simple written communication typical of our normal personal-business life. While reading the *Times* last Sunday, you clipped this item:

> McDONNELL & COMPANY
> REPORTS ON
> TRANS-AMERICA CORPORATION
>
> To receive your copy,
> just send a postcard to us at
> 228 Vista View Road
> San Francisco, California   22203

pertinent

This report may contain some data pertinent to your economics project, so you have decided to send for it.

This is a simple problem, but you must organize your thoughts to be sure that you receive the report quickly. Remember that a postcard is requested; don't burden the mail room with a letter that must be opened and then routed.

When a firm uses an ampersand (&) in its name, type the symbol, not the word "and."

Now let's read a few of the requests received by McDonnell & Company the next morning. The first was this postcard:

```
Dear Sir:

Send me your report advertised in
Sunday's paper.

                    Yours truly,

                    Bert Jones
```

Sad to say, Bert never received the report. Of course, you know why — he did not include his return address. Is that unusual in personal communications? Not at all. Ask any radio or newspaper advertiser how often he receives requests he cannot answer because of lack of a return address — and sometimes even of a name.

Include all the facts.

Although Bert's one-sentence request was short and to the point, it certainly did not include all the facts. First, there was no date. In personal-business communications, as well as in regular business correspondence, the first thing you must remember is to include the date. Second, the phrase "your report" is not specific enough; "the report on Trans-America Corporation" would have indicated clearly which report Bert wanted. This is especially important if McDonnell & Company is distributing other companies' reports. Third, do you know what paper Bert was referring to? Would it not

Be specific.

companies'
(Remember how to form the possessive of a plural?)

have been just as easy for him to have said "Sunday's *Times*"?

Yes, Bert omitted many facts in this simple communication. Have you noticed other errors? What about the salutation? Do you address a company as "Dear Sir"? Of course, the salutation should be "Gentlemen." Finally, what is the word that must precede the command "send me"? You're right — that word is "please."

Use correct mechanics.

Remember the amenities.

Can you rewrite Bert's one-sentence postcard to make it a more effective personal-business communication?

Here is another card received by McDonnell & Company:

```
                585 Benefit Street
                San Jose, California   95103
                October 5, 1967

Gentlemen:

I have seen your ad in Sunday's Times
of October 2 re Trans-America Corp. I
would appreciate it if you would send
me a copy of this report. I must
write a paper for my course in eco-
nomics, and having this report should
be a great help to me.

Thanking you in advance, I am

                Yours truly,

                Sheila Kissel

                Sheila Kissel
```

Sheila Kissel did get the report because she included all the information that McDonnell & Company needed. But her communication, too, could be improved. She took too long to write something simple, which wasted

*Include only the neces-
sary facts.*

her own time and that of the person receiving the
message. Her organization was poor because she included unnecessary information concerning the use of
this report in writing her economics paper.

In addition, anyone receiving this communication
would believe that the writer was an older person. Can
you see why? Who else would use such outmoded expressions as "re" and "thanking you in advance, I am"?

*Use the language of
the 70's.*

Sheila has another common problem: "I" trouble.
Just count the number of sentences beginning with
that pronoun.

But all in all, her communication was more effective than Bert's. Why? She received the report.

The third request received by McDonnell & Company on Monday morning was superior to the first two:

```
                717 Depot Street
                Santa Clara, California    95052
                October 5, 1967

Gentlemen:

Please send me a copy of the report
on Trans-America Corporation that you
advertised in the Times on October 2.

Thank you.

                Yours truly,

                Patrick Muskie

                Patrick Muskie
```

*Get to the point in the
first sentence.*

Notice that Patrick got to the point immediately; he
included the facts necessary to obtain his request, but
no others; and he built good human relations by remembering to say "please."

choose
(not "chose")

Would you choose Patrick's postcard as the one

you would send? Can you make any improvement? If you are eliminating unnecessary elements, you can also omit the salutation and the closing. And, by moving the return address under your name, you make it easier for the typist at McDonnell & Company to address that report to you.

```
                              October 5, 1967


     Please send me a copy of the report
     on the Trans-America Corporation, as
     advertised in the Times of October 2.

     Many thanks.

               Robert Newriter
               225 North Avenue
               Los Angeles, California    90021
```

ADDING SOME COMPLICATIONS

Now we are ready to go on to a more difficult problem — one that involves more data. The newly elected secretary of the Cap-It Bowling Club, John Foresight, must prepare the notices for the first fall meeting of the club to be held at the Arbor Avenue Alleys on Friday, September 15, at 8 p.m. All members and their guests are invited to be present. Refreshments will be served.

Let's work through this problem with the secretary. Not only must he contact each of the 25 members, but he must reactivate their interest in the club after the summer respite. The success of the year's activities   respite
really depends on the turnout for the opening meeting, and getting a good turnout is his responsibility.

In outlining his plan, he realizes that he does not have all the information. First, he must look up the exact address of the Arbor Avenue Alleys. Second, since refreshments must be ordered and alleys must be re-

ascertain
(Remember this word?)

served, he must ascertain from the Arbor Avenue Alleys' manager the deadline for reservations. One more item remains — the fee. The officers tell him that the cost of refreshments will come out of club dues, but each person who attends will be asked to pay $2 in advance or at the door for use of the bowling facilities.

insistent

And now an insistent voice should be saying, "Mr. Secretary, don't slip up on checking the date. Be sure that Friday is September 15 and that the date and time have been reserved at the alleys for your club." Checking must be an integral part of a writer's preplanning.

Check accuracy of dates.

integral

The secretary has collected and checked all the pertinent facts. What form of communication will he use? Will a postcard do? How will he get the RSVP's? He decides that a mimeographed card would be most economical. Therefore, he presents this card to the vice president for his suggestions before duplicating it for the membership:

Omit th, st, rd, nd *when date follows month.*

Use figures before a.m. *and* p.m.

Use figures for amounts of money. Omit decimals and zeros for amounts in dollars.

```
                                    September 1, 1967

Dear Member:

The Cap-It Bowling Club is holding
its first fall meeting on Friday,
September 15th, at 8 p.m., at the Ar-
bor Avenue Alleys, 251 Arbor Avenue,
Beverly Hills.

Since this is the first meeting, we
are planning to serve refreshments.
Wives and guests are invited. The
price is $2.00 per person, payable in
advance or at the door.

Please let me know by September 12th
if you are coming.

                    Yours truly,

                    John Foresight

                    John Foresight
                    Secretary
```

Mr. Foresight has included almost all the necessary information, but almost is not enough. He may not get many responses, for he has made it difficult to answer by omitting his address and telephone number. The vice president advises that he add his address and asks him to highlight the date and time. The card is rewritten to read:

advises

                                September 1, 1967

The Cap-It Bowling Club is holding
its first fall meeting on FRIDAY,
SEPTEMBER 10, at 8 p.m., at the Arbor
Avenue Alleys, 251 Arbor Avenue, Beverly Hills.

Refreshments will be served. Guests
may be invited by members. The price
is $2 per person.

Please let me know by September 7 the
number of reservations you wish to
make. You may send me a check or pay
at the door.

            John Foresight, Secretary
            228 Fourth Street
            Beverly Hills, California   90211

Avoid passive voice; use "You may invite guests."

At this time, the president joins the other two officers and comments, "For this first meeting of the fall season, why don't we send a letter?" (How wise he is to consider the reaction of the membership. A card would detract from the importance of this first meeting.) "Wouldn't a tear-off form at the end of the letter and a self-addressed, stamped envelope make it a cinch for our members to answer?" (He is not concerned with economy in this case — it amounts to only a couple of dollars. He wants to make it easy for his members to say "yes.")

detract

The secretary is quick to accept these suggestions, for he knows of the president's past success as secretary

intramural

mimeographed

already

received
(Remember this word?)

all ready

misconception
preoccupation

advice

of the college's intramural sports program. Together they rewrite the announcement (Figure 5 – 1), which is then mimeographed and mailed to the members on September 1.

Three days later, an amazed John Foresight reports to the president and vice president that 20 of the 28 members have already answered and that 15 of them plan to bring one or two guests. The members must have mailed back their forms the day they received them or the following day. The president had been right in making the responses easy. Only two or three minutes were needed to complete the form, and it was all ready to be inserted in the envelope and mailed back to the secretary. In arranging this, the president had also made it easier on John, who was now thinking of a follow-up. On the twelfth, he would telephone every member who had not responded. There would be very few, if any.

Thus, John Foresight had learned from his first experience as secretary. He had made every effort to gather all the information he would need for the first postcard he wrote; but, like Bert Jones in his request for the Trans-America report, John made a glaring omission — he did not include his return address.

Did you notice, however, that John did exclude the unnecessary information that the cost of refreshments was to come out of club dues?

Of course, John's major misconception was his preoccupation with economy. The objective was not to inform the members of the meeting in the most economical way; it was to get the total membership out to the first meeting. He had forgotten to put himself in the reader's place. Besides, the difference in cost between 25 postcards and 25 first-class letters (including stamped return envelopes) was minimal.

John quickly accepted the president's advice, however, and was very glad he had done so when he realized how good the response was and how much easier the follow-up would be.

THE CAP-IT BOWLING CLUB

                                    BEVERLY HILLS, CALIFORNIA
                                    September 1, 1967

TO ALL MEMBERS:

Our first fall meeting has been scheduled:

            Date: Friday, September 15
            Time: 8 p.m.
           Place: Arbor Avenue Alleys
                   251 Arbor Avenue
                   Beverly Hills
       Admission: $2 per person

Don't miss this opportunity to get together after our two-
month summer vacation. If you wish, you may invite guests
to this first meeting. Refreshments will be served at
10:30 p.m.

Your Executive Committee has been busy setting up the team
schedule and the final tournament for the year. You may pick
up copies of their proposals at the meeting. They will be
discussed at the October meeting. This promises to be a
great year!

Please make your reservations by September 12. Just complete the form below, and send it to me in the enclosed
envelope. We're hoping that every member will come.

                        Sincerely,

                        John Foresight

                        John Foresight
                        Secretary

- -

Please detach and mail by September 12 to: Mr. John Foresight
                                            228 Fourth Street
                                            Beverly Hills
                                            California 90211

I ___ will (___ will not) attend the September 15 meeting and
will bring ___ guests.

___ My check for $___ is enclosed. (Please make check payable
    to the Cap-It Bowling Club.)
___ I will pay at the door.

                        _____
                        Name

Figure 5 – 1
A Good Letter Suits Its Purpose

SUMMARY

When writing your business communication, choose the form that suits the situation. Use a postcard for that short notice or request, a form letter for large mailings, and an individually typed letter for more personal communications. In deciding which form to use, consider the purpose of your letter and the reaction you want from your reader. Individually typed letters are not a suitable way to send sale notices to hundreds of charge-account customers, but they are the only correct way to request an extension of credit from two or three of your suppliers.

Whatever the form, follow the correct writing procedures. Include all the necessary facts, be specific and to the point, use correct mechanics, keep your language natural, and by all means remember the amenities. Before you sign and mail that card or letter, read it through carefully to verify its accuracy. No matter how short or simple the communication is, following these procedures saves time and trouble.

[1] SPELLING

Correct the spelling in these sentences:

a. If I could acertain its meaning, I could chose the right answer.

b. Please send the members mimiographed copies of the letter.

c. He was very insistant, so I chose one of the magazines.

d. Have you recieved a parcel recently?

[2] VOCABULARY

a. A *misconception* and a *mistake* are both errors of a sort. What is the difference between them?

b. Give an antonym for the word *pertinent*.

c. Write a sentence using *intramural* and showing that you know what it means. Do the same for *integral*.

d. In your own words, define the following: *respite, preoccupation, detract.*

[3] SOUND-ALIKES

In reading this chapter, you should have learned the difference between *all ready* and *already*, *discreet* and *discrete*, *advice* and *advise*. Use this knowledge to select the correct word in each of these sentences:

a. When the meeting began, the directors were (*already, all ready*) to answer questions.

b. A (*discreet, discrete*) person would never make an insulting remark about someone's intelligence.

c.   We have (*already, all ready*) sent the check to pay the premium.

d.   The teacher's (*advise, advice*) was to use several (*discreet, discrete*) steps in solving the problem.

e.   We knew the plans were (*already, all ready*), but we had to be (*discreet, discrete*) in speaking about them.

f.   The Constitution requires that the President get the (*advise, advice*) and consent of the Senate.

[4] MORE ON AGREEMENT

Occasionally the structure of a sentence may mislead us into treating the wrong word as the subject. As we saw previously, this can occur when words intervene between subject and verb. It also happens when the verb precedes the subject.

> Are the file cabinet and the duplication equipment in the same room?

The compound subject — "cabinet and equipment" — takes a plural verb — "are."

> Clearly visible on the desk were the statements for the past five years.

The subject is "statements," so the verb is "were."

> RULE: *When the sentence begins with* there is, there are, here is, here are, *locate the true subject and make the verb agree with it.*
>
> > Here is an idea that should be accepted.
> > Here are several ideas that should be considered.
> > There is, in Salt Lake City, a beautiful capitol.
> > There are, in Salt Lake City, many private gardens.

> RULE: *The expletive* it *requires a singular verb, even when the real subject is plural.*
>
> > It is the blue and green copies that belong there.
> > It is the figures we are questioning.

In the sentences below, make the correct choices:

a.   There (*is, are*) some meetings to be held in the president's office.

b.   Included in his baggage (*was, were*) a tape recorder, a sheet of instructions, and a reel of tape.

c. To all the scientists and engineers who worked on the project (*go, goes*) our appreciation.

d. It (*is, are*) our systems and procedures that we must overhaul.

e. During the early hours (*is, are*) the best time to get work done.

f. Here (*is, are*) the opportunity you have been seeking.

g. There (*is, are*) the letters you requested.

h. There (*is, are*) many a mile to go.

i. Here (*is, are*) each of the reports you were promised.

[5] PUNCTUATION: COMMA

RULE: *Use commas to set off items in a series.*

Red, white, and blue are the colors of our flag.
He was working too hard, getting too little sleep, and eating poorly.

You will notice that some writers do not include the comma before the *and* or the *or* at the end of a series. However, it is good practice to make a habit of including it, since your meaning will not always be clear without it. That final comma leaves no doubt in the reader's mind that the last two members of the series are to be considered separately. For instance, look at this sentence:

Orders arrived from Abraham and Straus, Lord and Taylor, Saks and Macy's.

Abraham and Straus is one store; so is Lord and Taylor; but Saks and Macy's are separate stores. If you place a comma after "Saks," the reader knows how many stores there are.

Now use the comma rules you have learned in Chapters 3, 4, and 5 to punctuate the following sentences:

a. When the final figures are released quotations in the New York San Francisco Chicago and St. Louis markets will be affected.

b. This stationery is available in pink blue yellow and white.

c. Professor Allen his wife and their two children came to the class play.

d. By next year our company will be selling its products in Japan Australia and the Common Market countries.

e.   John Pat and Mary represented us at the science exhibit but Bill Jack and Irene represented us at the business show.

f.   When you were a student you should have read works of Dickens Emerson and Poe and seen paintings of Monet Turner and Matisse.

[6] PARALLEL STRUCTURE

Correlatives are *either . . . or; neither . .   nor; not only . . . but also; whether . . . or; both . . . and.*

RULE: *The elements following correlatives must be parallel.*

Not   Our temporary employees are not only proficient, but they are loyal.

But   Our temporary employees are not only proficient but loyal.

Not   Either Mr. Stack wants our financial statement or a letter of recommendation.

But   Mr. Stack wants either our financial statement or a letter of recommendation.

Not   The treasurer's plans both worked out in theory and in practice.

But   The treasurer's plans worked out both in theory and in practice.

Correct these sentences:

a.   The ruling of the traffic department both affects drivers and those who enforce the laws.

b.   Either pay your bills now, or you will have to deal with our attorney.

c.   The company not only found an excellent site for its new factory but also a good market for its products.

d.   Mr. Hanson will either arrive on the early plane tomorrow or in the afternoon by train.

e.   Moore's Department Store expects not only to add a furniture department but also an appliance section.

f.   Under current economic conditions, we can obtain funds neither from the security markets nor the banks.

[7] PROBLEMS

a. Send a postcard to Poor and Rich, 826 Averill Street, New York, New York   10003, asking for a copy of the brochure, *Timely Investments*, which was advertised in the Wall Street *Journal*, January 9, 1968.

b. Your instructor asks you to type a postcard requesting a copy of the new text, *The Keynesian Outlook in 1968*, by Robert Ross, published by the Oakhurst Press, New Haven, Connecticut   06512.

c. As the elected secretary of the safety squad in your plant, you are asked to send an announcement to all members of the squad of a meeting for Friday, January 15, at 1 p.m., in the dining room. The group will discuss the need for protective devices. Ten accidents occurred last week.

d. Tramp Trips offers a free Caribbean folder if you will write a postcard to Air and Sea Travel Service, Hudson Avenue Hotel, 228 West 56 Street, New York, New York   10019.

e. Station WROY offers a free sample of Lazy Day Soap Powder to anyone who sends a postcard to Lazy Day Soap Powder, 250 Barome Street, New Orleans, Louisiana   70160. Write for your sample.

6 | The Social-Business Letter

IN YOUR social-business life, you will have to write many types of letters. Your social commitments usually require you to write a thank-you note from time to time. If you participate in any group activity, you may find yourself writing invitations to speakers or guests to attend your meetings, forums, receptions, dinners, conferences, sports events. Since we all manage to get at least one vacation each year, it is often necessary to write a letter reserving a hotel or motel room or a cottage by the sea. Then there are the "no" letters, particularly troublesome when they must be written to your employer or to someone in authority; the congratulatory messages; the notes of sympathy or condolence; the cancellations. Let's take four types of social-business letters — the thank-you letter, the social-business invitation, the reservation letter, the "no" letter — and work through some problems you may encounter.

commitments

condolence
cancellations

THE THANK-YOU LETTER

One of the most abused forms of communication is the thank-you letter. Many people write because they have

hypocritical

to, not because they want to. They hide behind hypocritical phrases and weary expressions. The real gem of a thank-you letter is the one that is truthful.

Here is a situation in which you have to write a thank-you note to your host and hostess. The faculty adviser of the Business-Management Club, Professor Ross, invited you, as president, and the other members of the club's executive council to his home for dinner, to be followed by a council meeting. Professor and Mrs. Ross were very gracious, and the group were made to feel very much at home. After dinner, the council planned the term's activities, which would be presented to the membership for consideration at the first club meeting. As president of the club, you face the double responsibility of expressing both your own appreciation and that of the council.

However, each member of the council will also write his own note. Bill Fischer wrote his that very night. It was late, and he was tired; but he had enjoyed the dinner and wanted to say so. In his usual flamboyant way, he dashed off this note:

council

Note use of collective noun as plural — "group were."

flamboyant

Spell out numbers up to and including ten.

Spell out "Professor."

Avoid slang: "loads," "swell," "invite."

"Would have" is correct.

> October 9, 1968
>
> Professor Richard Ross, Adviser
> The Business-Management Club
> 5 Campus Road
> Collegetown, California   92012
>
> Dear Prof. Ross:
>
> Here I am, home after a full day.
> This was completely different from my
> usual--I had dinner at your home.
>
> Thanks loads for the swell dinner. It
> was a real treat not to have to eat
> in the cafeteria, where I would of
> eaten otherwise.

I hope that I and the other club members will get another invite from you again some time.

                    Truly yours,

                    Bill

                    Bill Fischer

"Sometime" is one word when it means "at another time."

Use a more up-to-date closing.

Professor Ross appreciated this letter from Bill — so few students remember to say thank you. But Bill seemed much more interested in the food than in the company, saying in effect that anything was better than eating in the cafeteria. And he was certainly brash in asking to be invited again. Can you see the amusement on Professor Ross's face as he read the last sentence?

brash

If Bill had given a little more thought to his host and hostess and had corrected his language and form, the thank-you note would have looked something like this:

Dear Professor Ross:

Thank you very much for inviting me to your home tonight. It was a real treat for all of us to have dinner with you and Mrs. Ross.

I am glad that I was elected to office in the Business-Management Club and that I am helping to plan the year's activities. What a first meeting!

                    Sincerely yours,

Angie Jewkes was a timorous writer. She tried to write her letter three times, but she just couldn't get

overwhelmed

started. Finally, she asked an older friend to help her. When she finished, Angie was so overwhelmed by the strangeness of the language that she couldn't believe she had written it. (Neither could Professor Ross.)

Avoid wordy or out-moded expressions and ones that sound insin-cere.

Dear Professor Ross:

<u>May I take this opportunity</u> to ex-press my sincere appreciation for the very enjoyable <u>repast</u> I and the other members of the executive council had at your home yesterday. I was <u>indeed</u> pleased to have been invited to your home.

This occasion <u>afforded</u> the members of the council the opportunity <u>to become better acquainted with</u> one another and to give <u>further consideration</u> to the development of a worthwhile pro-gram for our club for the <u>forthcoming</u> term.

<u>Let me express again</u> my <u>deep grati-tude</u> for a very fine evening.

                    Respectfully yours,

Again, watch that out-dated closing.

Angie wrote her thank-you note without delay — an important point to remember. Her letter was polite; she got to the point at once; she closed with an extra thank you. But she forgot to be natural. Her language depicted not the vital, sharp gal of the twentieth cen-tury but the old-fashioned stereotype of the 1890's. Let's ask Angie a question: What would you say to Professor Ross if you met him on campus? Her answer:

depicted

stereotype

"Professor Ross, thank you so much for that won-derful evening we had at your home. Will you tell Mrs. Ross how much we enjoyed it.
"It was great of you to have the executive council. We did so much and had such a good time doing it that we feel we can't miss this year."

If Angie wrote her letter in these terms, it not only would sound like her but would leave the impression that she really did enjoy herself. Note how she would adapt her verbal expression to the written form: **adapt**

> Dear Professor Ross:
>
> Thank you very much for the wonderful evening we had at your home last Tuesday. Please tell Mrs. Ross how much we enjoyed it.
>
> It was very thoughtful of you to have the first meeting of our executive council at your home. We accomplished so much and had such a good time doing it that we feel this will be a very successful year.
>
> Thanks again, Professor Ross.
>
>   Sincerely yours,

Now it's your turn. How will you start that letter? How can you tell Professor Ross how much you appreciate what he has done? How can you thank his wife? You start four times:

> Thank you very much . . .
>
> We want to thank you sincerely . . .
>
> Many thanks . . .
>
> Our sincere thanks . . .

Since you are writing for the whole committee as well as for yourself, you decide to use the last idea — and also to mention Mrs. Ross in that first sentence:

> Our sincere thanks to you and Mrs. Ross for the dinner meeting you planned for our executive council on Tuesday. We certainly enjoyed our-

selves. You made us feel very much a
part of this college.

In the second paragraph, you want to mention
the council meeting. This is easy, because the members
of the group were glowing as they left Professor Ross's
home, saying such things as: "What a program!" "The
kids will love it!" "To think that we could really get
him as a speaker!" So you write easily:

*You found "stature" in
the thesaurus under
"importance."*

*Use active voice:
"helped greatly."*

The council is proud of the proposal
for the year's activities and is especially impressed with the stature
of the speakers you suggested. Your
guidance and advice were of tremen-
dous help. We cannot wait to present
the proposal to the members next
week. This looks like a great year!

The last paragraph is yours personally:

I want to add my own personal thank
you, Professor Ross, for inviting me
to your home and for doing so much to
make our club successful.

stationery
*(Remember, not "sta-
tionary.")*

You type your letter on stationery bearing the
college seal, using the formal style of official-business
correspondence. Of course, you make an extra carbon
for the club's files, and you always make one for your
personal file. You are happy to sign your name to this
letter, which you send through the intracollege mail.

intracollege

October 11, 1968

Dear Professor Ross:

Our sincere thanks to you and Mrs.
Ross for the dinner meeting you
planned for the executive council on
Tuesday. We certainly enjoyed our-

selves. You made us feel very much a
part of this college.

The board is proud of the proposal
for the year's activities and is especially impressed with the stature
of the speakers you suggested. Your
guidance and advice helped greatly.
We cannot wait to present the proposal to the members next week. This
looks like a great year!

I want to add my own personal thank
you, Professor Ross, for inviting me
to your home and for doing so much to
make our club successful.

> Respectfully yours,

> Philip Martinson

*In official-business let-
ters, a formal closing is
proper.*

Professor Richard Ross, Adviser
The Business-Management Club
Five Campus Road
Collegetown, California   92012

*Remember change in
placement of inside ad-
dress in official-business
style.*

There are numerous occasions that call for a letter
of appreciation — a gift, the return of a lost article, a
speech, the attendance of a famous guest at a reception, the participation of a panelist, a letter of recommendation. Remember to get to the point immediately,
to be natural, to say no more than is necessary, and to be
sure that your thank you sounds genuine.

numerous

THE SOCIAL-BUSINESS INVITATION

As you become more and more involved in group
activity, you will be inviting speakers to meetings, guests

dignitaries

data

counsel

alumnus

to receptions, dignitaries to conventions. Just as the special party invitations include basic points of information for your guests — purpose, date, time, place, host and hostess — so your written social-business invitations must include these data.

As secretary of the fraternity, you are asked to write to the president of the college and his wife to invite them to attend the annual Christmas banquet on December 21 as guests of honor of the fraternity. It's to be a gala affair — the national officers will attend, and this year your fraternity is to be presented with the National Service Award for service to the college, the community, and the national office of the fraternity. It is important that the president of the college be present at the ceremonies.

You compose the letter shown in Figure 6 – 1 with the help and counsel of your fraternity's adviser. Then, after getting Walter's signature and addressing a legal-size envelope in double-spaced form, you deliver the invitation personally to the president's secretary.

The executive board and the national officers give you another job. They want you to invite the state senator, who is an alumnus of Kensington and a Phi Nu member, to be the guest speaker. How do you address a state senator? Your reference manual shows the following:

Address	Possible salutations
The Honorable James Jones	Sir:
The State Senate	Dear Senator Jones:
Albany, New York 12209	My dear Mr. Jones;

You know that you want to get to the point immediately, but you must be formal with a state senator. Four openings suggest themselves:

Please be our guest speaker.

Will you please be our banquet speaker.

Kensington City College

BETA CHAPTER

FRATERNITY
128 Martindale Road
Kensington City, California 95402

November 22, 1968

Dear Senator Winner:

You would be honoring us in Phi Nu in a special way
by addressing the twenty-fifth annual Holiday Banquet
on December 21. The banquet will be held in the
Starlight Room of the Hotel Madison, Santa Barbara,
at seven o'clock. We will be happy to have you choose
the topic of your address.

It would be a special privilege to present our fore-
most alumnus on this occasion. Our chapter has been
named to receive the National Service Award this year.
It represents outstanding service to the college, to
the community, and to the nation. The national officers plan to make the presentation following your
address, and they would like you to participate in
the ceremonies.

We hope that you will be our banquet speaker on the
21st. It would make our evening a certain success.

                    Respectfully yours,

                    Michael Scriber

                    Michael Scriber
                    Secretary

Senator David G. Winner
The State Senate
Sacramento, California 95825

Figure 6 – 1
A Social-Business Invitation

It would be a special honor for us in
Phi Nu . . . .

You would be honoring us in Phi Nu in
a special way by addressing the
twenty-fifth annual Holiday Banquet
on December 21, in the Starlight Room
of the Hotel Madison, Santa Barbara.

adopt

You adopt the last choice; but the sentence is too long,
and you must shorten it. By placing a period after "21,"
you can include the rest of the information in the next
sentence:

The banquet will be held in the
Starlight Room of the Hotel Madison,
Santa Barbara, at seven o'clock.

In order to give the senator freedom to speak on any
topic, you write:

We will be happy to have you choose
the topic of your address.

prestige

If the senator would consent to be the banquet speaker,
it would ensure the success of the banquet and would
add to the prestige of your fraternity. You really mean
it when you say:

It would be a special privilege to
present our outstanding Phi Nu alumnus on this occasion. Our chapter has
been named to receive the National
Service Award. This represents outstanding service to the college, to
the community, and to the nation. The
national officers will make the presentation following the address, and
they wish you to participate in the
ceremonies.

*You have used "out-
standing" twice in this
paragraph. Check a the-
saurus or dictionary for
a synonym.*

reiterate

The final paragraph should reiterate your request:

*Mention the date again
for emphasis.*

We hope that you will be our banquet
speaker on this occasion, for that

```
would make our evening a certain
success.
```

You use your fraternity stationery and type very carefully the letter shown in Figure 6 – 2. When you are ready to mail it, you hesitate — should you include a self-addressed, stamped envelope to ensure an answer? The president's secretary responds: "That would be an affront to the senator. He will use his own stationery and matching envelope to reply."

affront

In writing the social-business invitation, be sure to include all the facts, spotlight the reader, and state clearly the special purpose of the affair. It's hard for the reader to say no to such an invitation unless he has another commitment.

THE RESERVATION LETTER

Making a Reservation

The bus was delayed by the storm — not just an hour or two, but four hours. When the four girls trudged into the ski lodge, they were fatigued and cold; but they expected warm, comfortable rooms that had been reserved by telephone two weeks before. The night clerk looked nonplussed. There were no rooms reserved for them — in fact, there were no rooms available in the lodge. What had happened? The telephone reservation had not been recorded.

trudged

While it is occasionally necessary to make a last-minute reservation by telephone or telegraph, it is safer to write; and you should know how to compose your own communication for this purpose. The reservation letter is an official record, and a confirmation assures you that your reservation will be waiting when you arrive.

Remember, a letter is an official record.

Once again, follow the simple rule: Be brief and right to the point, but be precise. You cannot assume that your reader knows what you want. If you write simply "Please reserve a room for me on April 22,"

Kensington City College

BETA CHAPTER

Φ N FRATERNITY

128 Martindale Road
Kensington City, California 95402

November 21, 1968

President and Mrs. James A. Wells
Kensington City College

Dear President and Mrs. Wells:

Beta Chapter of the Phi Nu Fraternity cordially invites you to be our guests of honor at the annual Holiday Banquet on Saturday, the twenty-first of December, in the Starlight Room of the Hotel Madison, at seven o'clock in the evening. It would mean a great deal to us in Phi Nu to have you with us on this evening.

This year, our chapter has been named to receive the National Service Award. The presentation will be made at the banquet by the national officers of Phi Nu. Representatives of other chapters are expected to attend, and many of our alumni are returning.

We are proud to bring this honor to Kensington, and we hope that you will be able to be with us on the twenty-first to share our success.

Sincerely yours,

Walter R. Furst
President, Beta Chapter

Figure 6 – 2
A Formal Request

don't be surprised to find yourself in a luxury room that you do not need and cannot afford. *You* know what you want, and you must state it clearly.

Where will you stay when you are in another city? There are a number of excellent directories in which you may find complete hotel information. When you are employed in an office, you will probably have access to the *Hotel Red Book*, which is published annually by the American Hotel Association. Regional directories published by the American Automobile Association also supply listings and ratings of hotels and motels. Several excellent guides, such as the *Guide Michelin*, list hotel accommodations in foreign countries. These directories indicate the number of rooms, the rates, and whether (in the case of a hotel) it is operated on the European or American plan. (Under the European plan, the rate represents the cost of the room only; under the American plan, the rate includes the cost of your meals as well as the cost of the room.)

When you make a reservation by mail, these points should guide you:

1. *Kind of room.* If you want a room with air conditioning, cross ventilation, or television, you must say so. If the location of the room makes a difference to you (overlooking the lake, on a certain floor, near an exit), be sure to put that in the letter, too.
2. *Type of accommodations.* You should state whether you want twin beds or a double bed and, especially in foreign countries, the lavatory facilities you want.
3. *Approximate rate.* Tell how much you wish to pay for your room. Naturally, you should use common sense in quoting a rate that would be commensurate with the type of accommodations and location you have requested. Requesting a room for two on the sixteenth floor, with shower and a view of the ocean, but insisting that this room cost no more than $6.50 is ludicrous.

access

to

too
accommodations

commensurate

two

ludicrous

advisable

4. *Number of persons in your party.* If there are children in the group, it is advisable to mention this fact also and to tell their ages.

5. *Date and probable time of your arrival.* You might also indicate your method of travel because of possible delays in transportation at certain times. If there is any likelihood of delay, be sure to ask that the reservation be held for you until you arrive.

6. *Length of stay.* Tell the reservations clerk how long you expect to stay so that he will know when he can accept the next reservation for the room.

7. *Request for confirmation.* A confirmation of your reservation may be especially helpful to you in a city where hotel rooms are at a premium, such as Washington, D.C., during the Easter holidays.

The message below is short but complete enough to enable the room clerk at the Hotel Elizabeth to make a reservation for this student from California:

```
                          65 Carolyn Oval
                          Ana, California    94104
                          December 15, 1968

        Airmail

        Hotel Elizabeth
        Ste Adele
        Montreal, Quebec

        Attention Room Clerk

        Gentlemen:

        Please reserve a single room with
        shower, at a rate not to exceed $15,
        for the night of Thursday, January 2.

        I am scheduled to arrive in Montreal
        on Canada Airways Flight 128, at
```

exceed

4 p.m. on that day. Please hold my
room until I arrive.

Please confirm this reservation.

Sincerely yours,

John Walker

John Q. Walker

John was careful enough to send the reservation airmail
so that he could be sure of receiving the confirmation
before his trip.

Now let's plan a vacation with Carol and Anne.
They wish to spend a one-week vacation at a winter
resort. After reading the following ad, they have decided
to make a reservation at Red Maples:

resort

Red Maples Is the Place for You!
SPECIAL WINTER VACATIONS!

$48 per week for each person, including meals. Fun
and rest await you! Olympic-size heated pool. Skiing,
skating, tobogganing, dancing nightly, indoor tennis
courts. Excellent food. Write: Red Maples, Box T,
Mapletown, New York   10550.

---

skiing

Carol wrote this letter and asked Anne to check
it before she typed it in final form:

567 Locust Street
Neva, Pa.
Dec. 28, 1968

Red Maples
Box T
Mapletown, N.Y.

Dear Sir:

I have read your ad in the Sunday paper. Please reserve a room for me and

*Would you make any
changes in this letter?*

Note use of possessive.

> my friend Anne Martini for a week's
> stay beginning the second week in
> January, the 22nd.
>
> Our school closes on Jan. 22 and we
> are looking forward to enjoying the
> many activities you listed in your
> ad.
>
> Let me know if you wish a deposit.
>
>   Cordially,
>
>   *Carol Giles*
>
>   (Miss) Carol Giles

Having just completed a course in writing business letters, Anne was able to make the following suggestions for improving the letter:

Write out abbreviations.
Include the zip code in the return address and the inside address.
Use the correct salutation: "Gentlemen."
Get to the point in the first sentence: "Please reserve a room with twin beds and bath for Anne Martini and me."

explicit

Be explicit as to dates: "for a week's stay, from January 22 to 29."
Omit the second paragraph; it isn't necessary.
Refer to the ad and the name of the newspaper in which you read it when you state the cost of the room and meals for each person.
Ask for a confirmation — just to be sure.
Use correct closing: "Sincerely yours."

Following these suggestions, Carol rewrote the letter:

567 Locust Street
Neva, Pennsylvania   19133
December 28, 1968

Red Maples
Box T
Mapletown, New York   10550

Gentlemen:

Please reserve a room with twin beds
and bath for Anne Martini and me for
a week's stay, from January 22 to
January 29.

According to the advertisement in today's Inquirer, the room rate, including meals, is $48 per week for
each individual. Is it necessary to
send a deposit before we arrive?

Please confirm this reservation.

Sincerely yours,

Carol Giles

(Miss) Carol Giles

*Underline names of
newspapers and maga-
zines — or type in caps.*

Another type of reservation you can make by mail
is one for renting a car. Russell planned to fly from San
Francisco to Chicago. He wished to rent a car for a
week, and the following advertisement caught his attention:

BUDGET RENTAL SYSTEM

A Corsair costs only $5 a day and 5 cents a mile.
You buy only the gas you use. Our cars are equipped
with automatic transmission, radio, seat belts, and
heater; and they are covered by proper insurance.
Airport pickup service is available at no extra charge.

Use figures with cents.

Why did Russell's message cause the Budget Rental agent so much trouble?

Include date.

Spell out "East."

Use "Gentlemen."

Omit "st" when date follows the month.

license

```
                      672 Hollywood Boulevard
                      Los Angeles, California    90028

            Budget Rental System
            35 E. Wacker Drive
            Chicago, Illinois    60601

            Sirs:

            I want to rent a Corsair as adver-
            tised in a recent issue of The Far
            Horizons.

            I shall arrive at O'Hare Airport at
            3 p.m. on Omega Airlines Flight 628.
            I should like the car to be delivered
            to the airport. The car will be
            driven for a week and will be re-
            turned to the airport on March 1st at
            2 p.m.

            My Hatton Bank credit-card number is
            A560-331. I have a California driv-
            er's license, No. 061-2347.

                            Very truly yours,

                            Russell Warren

                            Russell Warren
```

You were right if you noted that Russell omitted the date of his arrival at the airport. What date should the car be delivered to the airport? Did Russell remember that this is leap year and that there are 29 days in February? Will he arrive on February 23 or 24? By making slight changes in the second paragraph, Russell will find his car waiting for him when he arrives in Chicago.

Always double check dates.

I shall arrive at O'Hare Airport on
February 24, at 3 p.m., on Omega Air-
lines Flight 628. Please deliver the
car to the airport. I will drive it
for seven days, February 24--March 1,
and will return it to the airport on
March 1 at 2 p.m.

Canceling a Reservation

Sometimes you find it necessary to cancel a reservation
you made for a room or for a trip. Courtesy dictates
that you write a letter as soon as you learn you cannot
keep that reservation. A simple note of apology should
be written, explaining that you are sorry for the inconvenience caused by your cancellation.

Let's take the preceding reservation made by
Carol Giles at Red Maples. Carol sent the reservation on
December 28. On January 2, she learned that she and
Anne were required to attend a special school confer-
ence on January 23, 24, and 25. She wrote to Red
Maples immediately:

*preceding
(Remember how to
spell this word?)*

                    567 Locust Street
                    Neva, Pennsylvania   19133
                    January 2, 1969

Red Maples
Box T
Mapletown, New York   10550

Gentlemen:

Please cancel my reservation of December 28 for a room with twin beds
and bath for Anne Martini and myself
for the week of January 22 to January
29.

I am sorry that we cannot come to Red
Maples as we had planned. It is now
necessary for us to attend a special

*If possible, give a rea-
son for your cancella-
tion.*

college conference from January 23 to
25.

I hope that this cancellation does
not cause you any inconvenience.

                            Sincerely yours,

                            Carol Giles

                            (Miss) Carol Giles

In writing letters either making or canceling a reservation, use clear, precise language. Keep your letters short and to the point. If you are making the reservation, request a confirmation. Then your vacation can be a pleasure, not a fiasco.

fiasco

THE "NO" LETTER

Difficult as the letter of refusal may be to compose, it must be written. Your knowledge of human nature and your ability to use language will help you. Remember to think in terms of your reader. A refusal is always difficult to accept. The first reaction of the recipient is "why?" If the reader of a "no" letter does not get an acceptable answer to this question, you may never get another invitation or request from him.

enmeshed

Here is one "sticky" situation in which Mary Jo Elting is enmeshed. As a part-time clerk in a law office, she received an invitation to be the senior attorney's guest at an important political meeting at which the 25 people in the office were expected to be present. She was first excited to have been included and then totally dismayed when she realized that it coincided with her sister's engagement party. She discussed it with the attorney's secretary and was even more distressed when the secretary said, "Mr. Styles doesn't like it when people refuse." She needed this job for the next semester, but she had to say no. Keeping her job depended on how tactfully she wrote that letter.

This is one time she did not want to get to the point in the first sentence. The second sentence, however, had to state the facts. Mary Jo typed the following letter:

```
                                December 1, 1968

        Edmond J. Styles, Esq.
        Styles, Bridges, and Brown
        18 Board Street
        San Franciso, California    94129

        Dear Mr. Styles:

        Thank you very much for inviting me
        to attend the Mayor's Conference on
        Urban Affairs on December 19. Unfor-
        tunately, my sister's engagement din-
        ner is taking place that same eve-
        ning, and I must be there.

        I know the importance of this confer-
        ence and am very sorry that I cannot
        attend. Please accept my apologies.

                        Sincerely yours,

                        Mary Jo Elting

                        Mary Jo Elting
```

"Esq." — a courtesy title often used for lawyers — is always abbreviated (see Chapter 2).

Her letter was simple, but she hoped Mr. Styles would understand that she really was sorry she had to miss the meeting. He did; she kept her job.

Whatever you do, don't get involved in fabrications designed to impress an employer or supervisor with the gravity of the situation that caused your refusal. One supervisor remarked, "That's the second

fabrications

appendectomy

appendectomy his mother had in six months — she's making medical history." Six months before, the worker had written a note to a representative in another city using this excuse, and it had been reported to his present supervisor. So it backfired the second time.

procrastination

Another temptation to avoid is procrastination. Since "no" letters are unpleasant, you put them off until tomorrow. This makes the letter more difficult to write and puts the reader in an antagonistic frame of mind. Think of the hostess who receives a refusal on the day of her dinner party — or the chairman of a panel discussion who receives a note just before the meeting saying: "Sorry I am no longer able to speak at the panel discussion on 'Automation and the Job Market' this afternoon."

When you write a letter of refusal, you show your concern for the reader by answering immediately, giving a clear and valid excuse, expressing regret, and apologizing.

SUMMARY

adept

As we develop business letters, you will become adept in applying the general principles of letter-writing. In the case of each of the social-business letters we have studied in this chapter, certain specific ideas come to the forefront.

When you write your thank-you letter, overcome your inertia — do it at once. Get to the point in the first sentence, and follow through with language that develops your thoughts naturally. Make the tone of your letter sound genuine. There is no need to write a lengthy letter; the fact that you write to say "thank you" is important.

In your social-business invitation, exercise caution when you mention places, dates, and times. Too many embarrassing situations have arisen as a result of errors in matching days with dates or as a result of neglecting to include specific times and places. Take that little extra time to verify your information. Write so your reader gets the impression that he is really important and really wanted. If you remember to tell him the purpose of the affair and why *he* is being invited, you increase your chances of getting an acceptance.

In your reservation letter as well, you must have precise data. These data include dates of arrival and departure, number in your party, type of accommodation, rates you will pay. For your own protection, request a confirmation of your reservation. You wouldn't be happy if you arrived at a hotel, after a long day of travel, only to find you had no room because your letter had not arrived. Carry that letter of confirmation with you.

If you find it necessary to cancel a reservation, have the courtesy to write a letter giving the precise details necessary for the reservations clerk to locate the record and make the cancellation. Be sure to apologize and, if possible, to give a reason for your cancellation.

When you encounter the unpleasant task of writing a letter of refusal, do not delay your answer. Keep your letter straightforward and factual. Instead of beating around the bush, come out with your refusal honestly and clearly. Again, remember the amenities; say you are sorry.

Notice that the basic principles of letter-writing apply regardless of the type of letter you write. Type all your letters neatly and with correct letter style. Organize your thinking before you write. Use up-to-date language, "talk" your letter, be grammatically correct. Let your letters answer completely the problems they are meant to solve.

[1] SPELLING

a. A frequent source of errors in spelling is "double letters." Do you know when to use them? Correct any mistakes you find in these words:

committments	proceed	excede
cancellations	preceed	access
acommodations	apendectomy	

b. "Double letters" are particularly troublesome when you want to change the form of a word. In Chapter 5, you learned when to double the final consonant of a verb in forming its past tense: *When the accent is on the final syllable, double the final consonant.* Follow this rule to form the past tense of *commit* and of *cancel*.

c. Correct the spelling in these sentences:

Your condolance letter should not sound hypocrytical.
It is adviseable that licence applications be submited on letterhead stationary.
He was overwelmed by the numberous choices available to him.

d. The English language contains many foreign words or words of foreign origin. Sometimes, especially in the case of Latin words, these terms have irregular endings — for the masculine, feminine, plural. *Data*, for instance, is a plural noun (although it is becoming acceptable to use it as a singular one). What is the singular form of *data*? *Alumnus* is even more complicated. It is the masculine singular, and it has a feminine-singular form, a masculine-plural form, and a feminine-plural form. Can you spell these three other forms of *alumnus*?

[2] VOCABULARY

a. What is the opposite of *explicit*? What do the two terms mean?

b. You know what *resort* means when it is used as a noun (e.g., "a beach resort" or "his last resort"). Write a sentence using *resort* as a verb.

c. Using language well requires that you train yourself to notice subtle differences between similar words. There is usually some difference — in meaning or tone — between a word and any of its possible synonyms. In some contexts, synonyms are interchangeable; while in others, choosing just the right word provides the nuance that expresses your meaning exactly. Let's illustrate: First, give a synonym for each of the words listed below. (You may check your dictionary for the definition of any word not familiar to you.) Then, pick three of these words, and explain how each is different from your synonym for it.

trudged	flamboyant	fabrications
prestige	commensurate	procrastination
ludicrous		

d. What does *intracollege* mean? How does it differ from *intercollege*?

e. Write a short paragraph (or several single sentences) in which you use each of the following words at least once. Show by the context that you know the words' meanings. (You may change the tense, number, or part of speech of any word, but be sure to spell the new form correctly.)

depicted	brash	stereotype
reiterate	enmeshed	dignitaries
affront		

[3] SOUND-ALIKES

The following sound-alikes were introduced in this chapter:

council	adapt	to
counsel	adopt	too
	adept	two

Be sure you understand the differences among them before you tackle the sentences below.

a. We have already (*adapted, adopted*) the plant to meet our particular situation.

b. The members of the (*council, counsel*) believed that the building project was far (*to, too, two*) expensive.

c. (*To, Too, Two*) many people are willing to offer (*council, counsel*), which may not always be good.

d. The firm of Johnson and Jackson acted as (*council, counsel*) for the defendant.

e.   If management should (*adapt, adopt, adept*) this proposal, there should not be (*to, too, two*) many problems encountered.

f.   The company treasurer is (*adapt, adopt, adept*) in handling his funds so that he is never short of cash.

g.   The effects of the measure that was passed by the (*council, counsel*) will be felt by the taxpayers for years to come.

h.   Be sure to follow the advice of (*council, counsel*) in legal matters.

[4]   MORE ON AGREEMENT

When singular subjects are joined by *or* or *nor*, the verb should be singular. When plural subjects are so joined, the verb is plural. But what happens when one subject is singular and the other is plural?

> RULE: *When a singular subject and a plural subject are joined by* or *or* nor, *the subject closer to the verb determines the number of the verb.*
>
> Neither the employees nor the supervisor was able to attend the meeting.
> Neither the supervisor nor the employees were able to attend the meeting.

Another agreement problem arises when a noun or pronoun follows a linking verb (*be, feel, taste,* etc.). Such a noun or pronoun is a *predicate nominative*; it is a complement that explains or identifies the subject.

> RULE: *The verb must agree with the subject, not with the predicate nominative.*
>
> Our main problem is writing complete reports and getting them into the mail on time.
> Numerous field tests were the cause of the delay.

Let's try these sentences, using the rules above and the one you learned before on collective nouns (see Chapter 4).

a.   Neither heat nor cold (*affect, affects*) these superior duplicating materials.

b.   The jury (*was, were*) out ten minutes before it returned a verdict.

c.   I believe that the central files or this office (*have, has*) the material you requested.

d.   Either he or his partners (*has, have*) the right to sign checks.

e. The council (*has, have*) prepared standards of conduct for its members.

f. Neither the analysts nor the treasurer (*was, were*) able to report on the company's progress.

g. Either the president or the treasurer (*has, have*) an option to purchase shares of stock.

h. His concern (*is, are*) the many people who have come to rely upon his accurate forecasts.

i. The crowd (*has, have*) cheered their hero.

j. The correspondent said that an increasing problem (*is, are*) the many reports and statistical compilations called for today.

[5] PUNCTUATION: COMMA

RULE: *Use commas to set off appositives and parenthetical phrases.*

An appositive is a noun or a group of words substituting for a noun that appears next to another noun or noun substitute and explains or identifies it.

Professor Jones, our accounting teacher, has extensive business experience.

"Our accounting teacher" is the appositive.

A parenthetical expression is a word or group of words that is not directly related to the rest of the sentence.

Our class, I believe, is the best in the college.

Apply this rule — and other comma rules you have learned — to punctuate these sentences:

a. Joe Nelson our star pitcher led the team to victories in 1965 1966 and 1967.

b. The college however claims no responsibility for this student's behavior.

c. You can I believe get these books at your local library.

d. Have you seen the letter from John Burns president of the Acme Company?

e. If David Atkins our club leader has planned a good program for the semester club membership will increase.

f. You, no doubt, have become acquainted with our new model, now that you have had a chance to use it.

g. The class of 1967, we have heard, has donated a fine record collection to the school.

h. William Harvey the agent assigned to the case, has prepared a lengthy report on his findings.

i. The club roster, composed of Bill, Nally, Jack Smith, Gene Ramos, and ten other boys, has been submitted to the adviser.

j. We shall, consequently, ask you to come to the office to discuss the statement.

[6] CAPITALIZATION

Pay careful attention to rules for capitalization. Many writers tend to capitalize too often. Unless you can apply a definite principle that calls for capitalization, do not capitalize. Here is one principle:

RULE: *Capitalize ali proper nouns* (that is, names of particular persons, places, or things — days of the week, months, political parties, governmental bodies and departments, historical events and periods, geographical names, buildings, and so on).

> Empire State Building; Middle Ages; U.S. Department of Commerce; Middle East; Battle of Bunker Hill

Do not confuse proper nouns with the general (generic) uses of the same words.

> U.S. Post Office Department; neighborhood post office
> Austin High School; the district high school
> President Keeler; when Mr. Keeler was president
> Congress intervened; to appoint a congress

Capitalize when necessary in these sentences:

a. The democrats are a majority in the house of representatives.

b. The department of state has an office in Chicago, Illinois.

c. The boys in high school will draw up a constitution for their student government.

d. The St. Louis Chamber of Commerce has its office in the Tower Building.

e. The Supreme Court will make its decision known on Monday, June 10.

[7] THE THANK-YOU LETTER

a. You have applied for a summer job as a lifeguard at the town beach. You have learned that a neighbor has written a complimentary letter of reference about your character and your reliability. Write a letter to your neighbor to thank him for his help.

b. On a recent Sunday afternoon, your car broke down on a busy highway. Hundreds of people passed you before a stranger stopped to help. He would accept no money for his help. You noticed his name and address on an envelope in his car. Write him a letter to tell how much you appreciated his help, especially when so many paid no heed to your troubles.

c. One of your former classmates has seen your name on the Dean's List. He sends you a letter of congratulations on your achievement. Write him a letter to thank him for his thoughtfulness.

d. You have written to the ABX Company to ask if they would allow you to visit their offices to study their administrative procedures. They permitted you to visit, and you learned many things that were especially helpful in preparing a report for your management class. How would you write to thank ABX for their cooperation?

e. You have borrowed someone's tape recorder for your party, and your brother is returning it to its owner. Write a letter for him to take along to thank the owner for the use of the machine.

f. You bought a set of records that were broken in transit. When you wrote to the company to report the loss, they immediately sent you a duplicate set plus an extra record because of your original disappointment. Don't you think it would be nice to write a brief "thank-you" note to the company? What would you write?

[8] MAKING A RESERVATION

a. You and your parents are planning a trip to Glacier National Park for one week, beginning August 10. Write a letter to the Glacier Lodge asking them to reserve two adjoining rooms with bath for six nights. You prefer the European plan. You will pay up to $20 a night for the three of you.

b. On your next visit to New York during the Christmas holidays, you want to dine at the Top of the Sixes Restaurant, overlooking midtown at 666 Fifth Avenue. Write a letter making a dinner reservation for six on December 28 at 7 p.m. Your group would like to sit by a window for a good view of the city.

c.   You are a member of an organization that is holding its annual convention at the Drake Hotel at 357 Longhorn Street, Missoula, Montana 05201 on November 26 and 27. Write to reserve a room at the Drake for the nights of November 25 and 26. Identify your organization and ask for the convention rates.

d.   Assume that you are a secretary of the Accounting Club at your school. At the beginning of the term, it is necessary to reserve a room to use for your club meetings throughout the term. Write a message to the dean's office to reserve Room 432 for weekly meetings every Monday between the hours of 1 and 2 p.m.

e.   Correct the following letter. You will find many mistakes.

> 587 1ˢᵗ Ave.
> Seattle, Washington 12345
> Nov. 1st, 1967

Hotel Astor,
587 Broadway,
New York, New York 12345

Gentlemen:
~~Dear Mr. Astor:~~

I received my
~~Your confirmation of a~~ room reservation ~~was received by~~
~~me~~ last week. Since then I have found it desirable to
change the dates of my stay in New York from Nov. 16-18
to Nov. 25-27. The same kind of accomodations can be reserved for Nov. 25-27 as you had all ready reserved for
the 16-18.

> Sincerely
> ~~Respectively~~ yours,

[9] THE SOCIAL-BUSINESS INVITATION

a.   Invite the president of the Irving Trust Company to speak on "Tight Mortgage Money," at the Business and Economics Club meeting on Thursday, February 10, from 12 to 1 p.m., in Room 239. Ask him to join you and the faculty adviser, Professor Cutts, for luncheon from 1 to 2 p.m., after his speech.

b.   Invite Mr. Peter Bergen of Bergen & Hamilton Associates to address the Economics Club and their parents on "Building Your Investment Portfolio." The Stock Exchange listed him as one of their speakers. Give him a choice of two dates: March 5 or March 12. The time is from

7 to 9 p.m. Ask him to remain for the reception from 8 to 10 p.m., following his address.

c. Ask the Dean of Students to attend the symposium on "The Common Market" at which Dr. Rudolph Maylor, a noted economist from another university, will speak before leading a discussion. Request the dean to say a few words of welcome in behalf of the administration of the college. The meeting is scheduled for March 27, from 12 to 2 p.m., in Room 945. *add information needed*

d. As secretary of the senior class, invite the members of the faculty who have been designated by the Senior Council as guests of the class to the Senior Prom on Saturday, June 11, in the Grand Ballroom of the Winchester Arms, Beverly Hills, at nine o'clock.

e. Invite the members of the student council of another university to cooperate with your college in a leadership conference to be held at Camp Holmes on March 28, 29, and 30. The student council should invite up to 25 of its members to participate. The cost of the conference is $20 a person, which includes dormitory facilities, meals, and transportation by bus. Top-level speakers and counselors have accepted invitations to work with the students at this conference. The deadline for reservations is March 1, but if the college wishes to participate, the secretary of student council must answer by February 15.

[10] THE "NO" LETTER

a. As secretary, send regrets that the Cap-It Bowling Club cannot participate in the Capital City Tournament because you are already completely scheduled in the County Tournament this year.

b. Write saying that the Business Club of Clearcrest College cannot join the Business Management Leadership Conference to be held at the City University campus because no funds were voted for this by the college's student council.

c. Refuse the invitation to speak on the TV panel "What's Your Responsibility as a College Student?" on Sunday, December 16, at 4 p.m. You will be attending a leadership conference. Ask if the vice president of your club, Mr. Fred Bates, can take your place.

d. The student council asks your organization, the Pan-Hellenic Association, to sponsor the toy drive for the local hospital. Your executive committee's reaction is that this toy drive should be sponsored by the executive councils of all houseplans and clubs as well as by the Pan-

Hellenic Association. Write to the council explaining that Pan-Hellenic will not sponsor it alone.

e. You receive a written invitation to join the office bowling team, which meets on Tuesdays from 6:30 to 9:30 p.m. Write a note explaining that you attend classes on Tuesday and Thursday evenings from 6:10 to 9:45 p.m. and so cannot join the team.

7 | The Personal-Business Letter

BUSINESS activity is becoming more and more a part of our personal lives. We are concerned daily with such personal-business matters as insurance, sales taxes, Medicare, charge accounts, checking and savings accounts, bank statements, orders, cancellations, merchandise returns and credits, buy and sell orders of stocks and bonds, brokers' fees. To handle these matters, you must develop proficiency in writing the order letter, the letter of inquiry, the letter of transmittal, and the claims letter. Written communication will enable you to keep your personal-business life functioning smoothly.

merchandise

proficiency

THE ORDER LETTER

Have you looked through a mail-order catalog lately or a department-store sales brochure? Check any mail-order form (see Figure 7 – 1). You must supply detailed information for each item ordered, such as, catalog number, quantity, article and color, unit price, and total

WALLACHS

Ordered by _____

Address _____

City _____ State _____ Zip Code _____ Apt. No. _____

☐ Check here if you have a Charge Account   ☐ Check or Money Order Enclosed

Please list second color choice

ITEM NO.	DESCRIPTION	QUAN.	SIZE	COLOR	PRICE	TOTAL·

Add 5% tax for N. Y. C. delivery. Other N. Y. State deliveries add sales tax rate in effect at place of delivery.
For Phone Orders: Call **EM 1-7500**

No mail orders accepted for less than 4.00
Add 50c postage beyond United Parcel service area.
SORRY, NO C.O.D.'S

TOTAL

Figure 7 – 1
An Order Form

In typing "f.o.b.," use lower-case letters. Notice that you don't space between the letters.

price. A chart gives you the shipping charges you are expected to enclose with your order. Sales taxes must also be added to the cost.

When you write an order letter, it, too, must contain all this information. Nothing can be left to the imagination. State your method of payment, such as check, money order, stamps. Be sure to mention the exact price, and show your calculations, including sales taxes and shipping charges. Watch the price quotations. Such terms as "f.o.b." after a price may mean a big difference in cost. The automobile listed at "$2,400, f.o.b. Detroit," costs much more on the West Coast. "F.o.b."

means "free on board"; therefore, "f.o.b. Detroit"
means that the buyer must pay freight charges from
Detroit to the point of destination.

Here is an order that was processed immediately.   **processed**
It was exact and easily filled:

```
                        884 Fort Williams Road
                        Salem, Oregon    97303
                        January 14, 1968


Chestnut Hill Sports Shop
Six Chestnut Hill Lane
San Francisco, California    94107


Gentlemen:

Please send me the following equipment and
charge my account:

Catalog                         Unit
Number   Quantity  Description  Cost    Total
 3189       1      No. 100
                   reel for
                   right-
                   handers      $28.95  $28.95

 3191       2      Spools for
                   No. 100
                   reel         2.50      5.00
                        Total           $33.95


Since I am leaving on vacation on January
19, please rush this order. Thank you.

                   Sincerely yours,

                   M. Murphy

                   Mark Murphy
```

*When several sets of
numbers, items, and
prices are given, tabular
form is clearer than
writing the information
in sentences.*

Mark had already established his credit with the
Chestnut Hill Sports Shop. There wasn't a tax in his   **there**
area, and there were no shipping charges for goods

delivered within 20 miles of the shop. Notice that he included just enough information to get that rush delivery, and he did not forget to say thank you.

The order below received much slower service because it was not clear and was therefore difficult to fill — and because the credit standing of the buyer had not been established.

Return address missing.

January 19, 1968

Masters Brothers
15 High Water Street
Sacramento, California   95823

Gentlemen:

Lack of definite information.

I am interested in the stove you advertised in the paper last Sunday. I would like it in white with the oven attached. The price was about $240.

Business hint: Personal checks in amounts over $100 may not be accepted.

Can you deliver this stove next Friday? I am enclosing my check in the amount of $240.

Sincerely yours,

Joanna Burns

Joanna Burns

Fortunately, an alert mail clerk did not discard Mrs. Burns's envelope before he had written her return address on the letter. The order department, however, was not happy with the letter. What stove? Three stoves had been advertised in the Sunday papers, ranging in price from $225 to $265. Not one was listed at $240. All the stoves had ovens — one overhead, one below the burners, one to the right of the burners.

unnecessary

every one
(Two words when referring to each individual thing.)

The credit department also had to do extra and unnecessary checking. The advertisements in every Sunday paper were checked. Every one included the statement, "Shipping charges of $10 are not included in the quoted price." Installation charges of $24 were also listed; yet Mrs. Burns made no mention of this either. In addition, since Masters Brothers did not know Mrs. Burns, they hesitated to accept her personal check. Before sending the stove, they would have to wait until the bank cleared the check.

Correspondence had to go back and forth before this order could be filled. Mrs. Burns did not cook on her new stove that Friday!

Let's make Mrs. Burns happy. We'll rewrite that order letter, following correct business procedures, and get the stove installed on Friday — just in time for her to burn Friday's dinner. The way to begin is to get out the advertisement and keep it before you to be sure your order is exact.

```
                228 Clove Lakes Drive
                Sacramento, California   95838
                January 19, 1968

Masters Brothers
15 High Water Street
Sacramento, California   95823

Gentlemen:

Please send me the Kelsey Range, No.
2264, advertised in the Sunday Times,
page 32. I would like it in white
porcelain. This is the stove with
four burners, two storage drawers be-
low the burners, and an oven and
broiler to the right of the burners.

Here is my certified check for $259
to cover the following:

Cost of Kelsey Range, No.
   2264, in white porcelain    $225
Shipping charges                 10
Installation charges             24

    Total                      $259
```

porcelain

Have your bank "certify" your personal check. This means the bank has set aside the amount on the face of the check for payment.

Your shipping department told me this
morning that this stove can be delivered this Friday and installed by
your licensed electrician at that
time. I will be expecting the delivery on Friday, January 23.

Thank you.

                              Sincerely yours,

                              Joanna Burns

                              Joanna Burns

Enclosure
    Certified check, $259

itemize

In writing the order letter, you must clearly identify the objects ordered, specifically itemize costs and
show calculations (double checking all figures), follow
correct business procedures in method of payment, and
thank the company for processing the order.

LETTERS OF INQUIRY

The Solicited Letter

You have already seen (in Chapter 5) how to handle the
simplest form of written inquiry — sending a postcard
to request a report or pamphlet offered in an advertisement. But what if your request is not so simple and a
postcard will not suffice? Take the following newspaper
advertisement:

For more information concerning this homeowners'
insurance, write to Mr. Ralph Moskovis, Stokely
Equity Corporation, Box 701, Topeka, Kansas
66615.

Or perhaps a radio commentator insists that you "find
out more about our investment program by writing to
Investments, Radio Station WRRZ, New York, New York
10026." In both cases, you must write to get more information, and you will have several questions to ask. A
letter is needed.

Whenever you write such a letter in response to
a newspaper or magazine advertisement, a radio announcement, or a television commercial, you are writing
a solicited letter of inquiry. How do you go about it? To   solicited
answer this typical magazine advertisement, you would
write a short letter.

NEW! COMPREHENSIVE!

56-Lesson
Master Correspondence Course
in Advertising

Covers every phase from copy and art to market
research and merchandising.

Diploma awarded.

Free Booklet: "Opportunities in Advertising"

The Raleigh Correspondence School
Box 228
Hollywood, California   91605

Your letter might read:

```
            666 Mylan Road
            Fresno, California    93728
            May 22, 1968


Raleigh Correspondence School
Box 228
Hollywood, California    91605


Gentlemen:

Please send me details on the cost,
number of weeks, educational activi-
ties, and testing program of the Mas-
ter Correspondence Course on Adver-
```

tising that you advertised in the
Retail Sales Management Journal of
May 15.

What type of diploma is awarded?

When you want certain information, ask for it specifically.

I would also like to receive the free
booklet Opportunities in Advertising.

Thank you.

Sincerely yours,

Charles Richards

Charles Richards

As you can see, the writer merely requests information offered by the advertisement, but he makes certain to find out everything he wants to know by asking specific questions and requesting particular information.

The Unsolicited Letter

The unsolicited letter of inquiry demands additional thought. It requires careful organization and the use of **concise** clear, concise language so that the reader can easily understand and answer the questions. When you write your letter of inquiry, list the questions so that they stand out, supply the background information necessary to give the reader an understanding of your problems, give exact dates where records are concerned.

Mary Lou Alpen asks your help in writing a letter to Brockton College requesting readmission as a matriculated student. She has decided to complete her college **absence** career after an absence of two years, during which she has worked as a receptionist at the Dependable Plastics Company.

    You ask her to gather her data: dates of attendance, number of credits, index. Then you discuss questions concerning her status. Should she mention that her index dropped below the readmission level? Should she ask what she can do about it? You answer, "Why not? The registrar has your records in front of him. You may get some help you could not get otherwise." This is the rough draft of Mary Lou's letter:

registrar

Mary Lou should review rules for comma and semicolon:

ago; Compound sentence with commas takes a semicolon.

and, . . . time, Introductory phrase is set off by commas.

I left Brockton two years ago and
since that time I have worked as a
receptionist at Dependable Plastics
Corporation. Now I know what I want
to do. I want to enter the field of
elementary school teaching. Therefore, I must return to college, and
have decided to do this. I would like
to return as a full-time student in
September 1969.

college No comma belongs between two verbs in a single clause.

When I left college I had 56 credits.
In my last term, I did very poorly
because I had lost interest; my index
dropped to 1.97. Will this prevent me
from being readmitted? Can I do anything about the situation?

college, Use comma after introductory phrase.

Please let me know if I may be readmitted to Brockton in September.

You make the following comments:

    Get to the point in the first sentence.
    Give exact dates and precise information.
    List questions.
    Correct the punctuation.

You and Mary Lou revise the letter in this way:

865 Roselawn Street
Palo Alto, California   94306
March 4, 1969

Mr. John Andrews, Registrar
Brockton College
Palo Alto, California   94301

Dear Mr. Andrews:

I am applying for readmission to
Brockton in September as a matriculated student for the 1969 fall term.
Please send me the readmission form I
must complete.

I entered Brockton as a freshman student in September 1963 and completed
my sophomore year in June 1965. At
this time I accepted a position as
receptionist at the Dependable Plastics Company. It is now my intention
to become an elementary-school
teacher. To do this, I must complete
my college education.

sophomore

In June 1965, I had a total of 56
credits. During my last term, my index fell to 1.97. According to the
catalog, an index of 2.0 is required
for readmission.

　　　May I be admitted as a ma-
　　　triculated student on a
　　　limited program?

　　　Is there an appeal I can
　　　file asking for this consid-
　　　eration?

　　　If not, is it possible to
　　　take summer courses to raise
　　　my index to the required 2.0
　　　by September 1969? Or should
　　　I take evening courses dur-
　　　ing the spring term in order

> ```
>           to be considered for fall
>           matriculation?
>
>    I hope you can suggest some way for
>    me to be admitted in September as a
>    matriculated student. Thank you for
>    your help.
>
>               Sincerely yours,
>
>               Mary Lou Alpen
>
>               Mary Lou Alpen
> ```

The registrar answered quickly and without difficulty:

> ```
>    Here is the Readmission Application
>    you must complete. Attach an appeal
>    letter, addressed to the Committee on
>    Academic Standing, requesting a
>    waiver of the 2.0 index in your case.
>    Be sure to give all details.
> ```

waiver

And he closed the letter, "Good luck."

The letter of inquiry must be explicit in its questions (listing them), must supply the background information necessary to give a complete picture, and must include those important words *please* and *thank you*.

LETTERS OF TRANSMITTAL

When you mail checks, applications, reports, or other items, write a short covering letter or letter of transmittal — and be sure to keep a copy. The letter tells the reader what you sent and why; the copy is your record of what you sent, to whom you sent it, when you sent it, and the address to which you mailed it.

transmittal

endowment

Recently a housewife had to mail her endowment policy to the main office of the insurance company. She had been in contact with her broker and had decided to request the cash value of the policy, which, including the interest, came to $10,350. The company was willing to mail her a check upon receipt of the policy. Would you simply put the policy in an envelope and mail it? This housewife did not; she enclosed a short letter.

```
                          485 Eighth Avenue
                          Denver, Colorado    80239
                          February 2, 1968

Registered Mail

The Acme Insurance Company
500 Wall Street
New York, New York   10002

Attention Mr. John Winston, Manager

Gentlemen:

As you requested, I am sending you my
endowment policy, AF145376, which was
paid up on January 31, 1968.

Please send me a check for the amount
of the endowment, plus interest. This
should come to $10,350.

Thank you.

                          Sincerely yours,

                          Joanna Petersen

                          (Mrs.) Joanna E. Petersen

Enclosure
  Policy AF145376
```

Mrs. Petersen wasn't taking any chances with the regular mail service; she sent the policy and letter of transmittal by registered mail and asked for a return receipt. Not only did she have proof that she had mailed the policy, but she would be indemnified if it were lost. And her return receipt would show that the insurance company had gotten the envelope. When mailing valuables, contracts, deeds, policies, or cash, send them by first-class, registered mail. (Only first-class mail can be registered.)

indemnified

When you are sending an ordinary package, however, you should use parcel post and attach your letter of transmittal to the outside of the package. This method enables you to pay the fourth-class rate for the package, and to insure it if you wish, and to pay the first-class rate for the letter only. In addition, the receiver of the package can locate the letter easily.

Jim Johnson knew he had to write a covering letter for his club's biannual report. Here is his letter:

biannual
(Is this the same as "biennial"?)

> July 10, 1968
>
> Mr. John Finley, Adviser
> Committee on Student Activities
>
> Dear Mr. Finley:
>
> I am enclosing herewith the biannual report of the Accounting Club. This report shows very clearly that our club has so far had a successful year socially and financially. We shall continue to try to do well in the months ahead.
>
> Sincerely yours,
>
> *James Johnson*
>
> James Johnson
> Secretary
>
> Enclosure

Would your judgment of this letter include these points? Jim, you're old fashioned! Change that first sentence to: "Here is the biannual report of the Accounting Club." Do you want to attract Mr. Finley's attention to the major accomplishments of the club? Do you want him to notice the financial status of the club? Then refer to these in the letter of transmittal.

> On page 5, you will see a description of the five major social and educational activities the club is sponsoring this year. Every one of them has been successful.

solvent

> You will note on page 8 that our financial statement shows we are solvent. We have a current balance of $50 in the treasury.

As adviser for all student activities, Mr. Finley and his staff were particularly helpful to the club. Shouldn't Jim thank him in the last paragraph?

> Thank you, Mr. Finley, for the help you have given us in making this year a successful one so far. We expect the rest of 1968 to be even better!

Here is another letter of transmittal you may have to write. The local department store reminded Roseann that she had not paid her last bill for $17. She had completely forgotten the bill and, in fact, had misplaced it. She wanted to pay immediately. Could she put the check in an envelope and mail it? Some people do, and

decipher

the department store must decipher the signature, look up the account, check the address, and hope that they are crediting the correct account.

Roseann decided to write and with great effort composed the following letter:

```
                    482 11 Street
                    Waco, Texas    76701
                    March 15, 1968

Huxley's Department Store
585 Fairview Avenue
Waco, Texas    76708

Gentlemen:

Here is my check for $17.00 in pay-
ment of my invoice of Feb. 3rd.

Apparently I inadvertently misplaced
or overlooked the original statement,
so I did not send my check sooner.

I beg to apologize for the delay in
sending my check. Assuring you that
this will not happen in the future,
I remain

                    Sincerely yours,

                    Roseann Blaine

                    Roseann Blaine
```

Add attention line.

Omit decimal and cyphers: $17.
"Statement," not "invoice."
"February 3."

Second paragraph is unnecessary.

Underlined words and phrases are hackneyed.

Enclosure line is missing.

Although Roseann's language was formerly "in" with correspondents, it is now very much out of date. If Roseann made the necessary corrections, updated the language, eliminated the extraneous information, this is the short, efficient letter she would send with her check:

formerly

```
                    482 11 Street
                    Waco, Texas    76701
                    March 15, 1968

Huxley's Department Store
585 Fairview Avenue
Waco, Texas    76708
```

Attention Accounting Department

Gentlemen:

Here is my check for $17 in payment
of my statement of February 3.

I am sorry for this delay.

                              Sincerely yours,

                              Roseann Blaine

                              Roseann Blaine

Enclosure
     Check, $17

The letter of transmittal marks you as a courteous and well-organized person. It identifies the enclosure and calls the reader's attention to specifics. Keep the letter short and to the point, and be sure to use the correct postal or delivery service to safeguard the item you are sending. Also, keep your own copy; it becomes your record.

CLAIM LETTERS

irate

"Wow!" The adjustment clerk exclaimed, "This lady must be furious!" He had just read a letter from an irate customer who was still waiting on January 5 for the Christmas gift she had ordered for her husband on December 5.

He did not criticize her for being angry. But, unless this letter helped her to get the anger out of her system, it served little purpose. It did not get the package to her on time. A telephone call on December 24 might have done more, for the store might then have sent it out by special messenger.

Why do we write the claim letter? We want to correct an error, to get a satisfactory explanation of a change, to obtain better service. Emotion helps little in these circumstances. What is needed?

Clear thinking in identifying the problem or problems.
Simple language in describing the claim or claims.
Constructive suggestions.
Courtesy.

Think positively. When you ask for an adjustment of a claim, you are giving the businessman a chance to correct an error. For example, you may find that a record you ordered has arrived in damaged condition. The reputable seller of that record has no objection to **reputable** your writing to tell him about it; it may help him improve his method of shipping his goods. He would rather have you complain to him directly so that he can make an adjustment for you than to have you become a dissatisfied customer. A seller wants to improve the **dissatisfied** image he presents to his customers.

Here is a case in which a claim letter should be written. Sandy's father had purchased 100 shares of common stock in the Safeguard Company. The company **common stock** had been paying quarterly dividends of 20 cents a share **dividends** on its stock. On April 15, Sandy's father noticed that he hadn't received his dividends since the previous September. Because Sandy was taking a course in correspondence, he asked her to write a letter to find out what was wrong; he even promised to share the dividends with her when the check arrived. Sandy asked Gary and Diane to help compose the letter. Diane wrote:

Sirs:

My father bought some stock in your
company. He has not received money
from you since last September. Because he knows that your business is

Outmoded salutation.

Vague terms: "some stock," "money," "busness is good," "some money."

*"Dividends," not "in-
terest."*

Outdated closing.

> good, he should have received some
> money.
>
> Please send his interest at once.
>
>   Truly yours,

Diane did not clearly identify the problem. Sandy was
surprised to see the incorrect use of the word "interest,"
and she substituted "dividend." Although she used

imperious

"please," Diane's tone was too imperious.
    Gary's suggestion was better:

> Gentlemen:

*Note commas for ap-
positive.*

*Eliminate decimal and
cyphers: $20.*

> My father, Samuel Stone, is the owner
> of 100 shares of common stock in
> Safeguard Company. He received divi-
> dends amounting to $20.00 in Septem-
> ber but has not received any checks
> since then. Apparently there has been
> some error, because I have checked
> the stock page of the newspaper and
> know that dividends have been paid by
> your company.
>
> Please look into this matter as soon
> as possible.
>
>   Sincerely yours,

Gary identified Sandy's father by name, making it easier
for the company's treasurer to locate the shares. He also
listed the number of shares Samuel Stone owned, the
amount of the last dividend check, and the date that
check was received. Sandy would type $20, omitting
the decimal and cyphers, and would delete the worn-
out word "apparently" and the tired phrase "look into
this matter as soon as possible." In fact, Sandy's letter

was clear, concise, courteous, and constructive:

> Gentlemen:
>
> My father, Samuel Stone, owns 100
> shares of Safeguard Company stock,
> certificate number 0413007. He has
> not received dividends since last
> September. (The September check was
> for $20.)
>
> I understand Safeguard paid dividends
> in December and in February.
>
> Will you please check to see why my
> father has not received his regular
> dividends.
>
>   Sincerely yours,

Explicit information.

Polite and constructive.

    Let's take the case of the unhappy customers Jack Leonard and his friend Ralph Sherry. They ordered a set of two walkie-talkies at $37.95 from the Mitsi Electric Corporation. The company advertised that they would receive audible transmission up to five miles. Both Jack and Ralph were disappointed when they tried to use their set. Jack wrote this letter and showed it to Ralph before mailing it:

audible

their

> What kind of a company are you? The
> walkie-talkie set you sent me and my
> friend doesn't have a reception of
> one mile, and you advertised it as
> having a reception of five miles.
>
> My friend and I paid $37.95 for this
> stupid set, and we want you to tell
> us what you do to get a reception of
> five miles--use a megaphone?
>
> I plan to report you to the Better
> Business Bureau for misrepresenta-
> tion.

Ralph didn't like the tone of Jack's letter and said that he would write the letter using a positive approach. After all, the walkie-talkie might not have been working correctly. He thought that a suggestion for settling the claim might be a good idea. Jack agreed with his friend that this letter was more constructive:

Gentlemen:

Will you please tell me how I can get my 56X walkie-talkie set to transmit at a range of five miles? My friend and I have not been able to get any reception beyond a one-mile limit. Does this mean that the set is defective? Is it possible that the buildings in this area are interfering with the reception?

ensure

If necessary, my friend and I will buy extra parts to ensure five-mile reception. However, if you feel that we cannot successfully operate the 56X in this area, please tell us what walkie-talkie to buy and whether you will accept the 56X in exchange. Ours was a cash purchase at $37.95, following your advertisement in the Chronicle.

I hope you can help us to get the 56X to operate at a distance of five miles or to suggest a walkie-talkie that will do so.

Sincerely yours,

Ralph Sherry

Ralph's answer came at once. The president of Mitsi apologized and thanked Ralph for calling the problem to the company's attention. He offered to send a new 56X set as soon as Ralph returned the original set by parcel post. What do you think the company would have done if Jack's letter had been mailed?

Shall we try one more problem? You have a three-year subscription to *Woods and Water*, which will not expire for one more year; yet you did not receive the May and July issues. You want to write to the company. This is the letter you send:

expire

```
Gentlemen:

My May and July issues of Woods and
Water did not arrive. I have a three-
year subscription to your magazine,
from January 1967 through December
1969. This is the first time I have
not received my copy on time.

Attached is the label I removed from
the June issue. This is the name and
address you have in your records, and
it is correct.

Will you please send me the May and
July copies of the magazine. I want
to have the complete series.

Thank you.

            Sincerely yours,
```

Remember, underscore or type in capitals the names of books, brochures, magazines, newspapers.

This is the way to get results: You identified the problem, you stated clearly just what your claim is, you were positive in offering a solution, and you were courteous.

SUMMARY

In developing personal-business letters, apply the same principles as you do for all other letter-writing. But, in addition to general principles, each type of letter has some guidelines you should follow.

Your order letter, for instance, should identify clearly the objects ordered, itemize costs and show the calculation, follow correct business procedures in the method of payment, and thank the company for processing the order.

When you write your letter of inquiry, you must list explicit questions, supply background information, and remember to say *please* and *thank you.*

Your letter of transmittal should identify the enclosure and call the reader's attention to specifics relating to the enclosure. While it is desirable to retain a copy of each letter you write, it is even more important here because you will have tangible evidence of your having sent the material along with the letter.

tangible

The good claim letter will assure you favorable treatment. Write in a calm frame of mind, identify your problem, describe the product, make positive suggestions for settling the claim, and be courteous.

[1] SPELLING

a. Proper pronunciation is often a great help in spelling. What spelling mistakes does correct pronunciation help you to find in these words?

unnecessry   porclain   registerar   sophmore   dicipher

b. Correct any misspelled words in the following paragraph:

The absense of a transmital notice caused an unfortunate delay in prosessing the shipment of merchandice. We did not want a disatisfied customer, but a reputible firm must take necessry precautions.

[2] VOCABULARY

a. Several of the words used in this chapter are financial terms. Can you define those listed below?

endowment   common stock   indemnified   dividends

b. Many words can be made into different parts of speech by the change of a few letters. For example, the noun *management* can become the adjective *manageable*; the verb *adopt*, when changed to *adopted*, can be used as an adjective (e.g., "an adopted child"). Change the following words into adjectives, and use each in a short sentence that illustrates its meaning.

proficiency   expire   itemize   audibly   ensure

c. What is a *concise* statement?

d. What does it mean to be *proficient* at something?

e. The two sentences below illustrate two meanings of the word *solvent*. In each case, tell what part of speech *solvent* is, and explain what it means.

Water is a very common solvent.
John claims that the company is solvent.

f.   What is the difference between *biannual* and *biennial*? Is there another word that means the same as *biannual*? (*Hint*: How would you say "twice a month" in one word?)

g.   Give a brief definition in your own words of each of the following:

waiver   imperious   solicited
irate   tangible

[3] SOUND ALIKES

Choose the correct word in each sentence.

a.   (~~Everyone~~, *Every one*) of the officers is responsible for his own report.

b.   (~~Their~~, ~~There~~, *They're*) certain that the bill was passed and signed.

c.   Mark takes more interest in his work now than he (~~formally~~, *formerly*) did.

d.   They read (*their*, ~~there, they're~~) assignments during the noon recess.

e.   The president (*formally*, ~~formerly~~) presented the new members of the faculty.

f.   (*Everyone*, ~~Every one~~) must meet with the dean at least once during the semester.

[4] PUNCTUATION: COMMA

RULE: *Use commas to set off nonessential clauses and nonessential phrases.* (A nonessential clause or phrase adds an additional thought to the sentence but is not essential to the meaning of the sentence.)

Mr. Wall, who has been around the world, spoke to the members of the Peace Corps.
The team, hoping for a victory, played to win.

RULE: *However, when a clause or phrase is necessary to the meaning of the sentence, commas are not used.*

All students who do not attend classes regularly must report to the office.
The men working on that contract will receive premium pay.

Punctuate these sentences according to these rules:

a.   All taxpayers who have refused to file returns will be penalized.

b.   The mayor, having completed his investigation, proposed a change in the charter.

c.   All factories that are declared unsafe must be demolished.

d.   Mr. Ruskin, who was trusted by both sides, came in to settle the dispute.

e.   The *Wealth of Nations*, written by Adam Smith, has become a classic.

f.   Employees, who wish to participate in the new pension plan, should report to the personnel division as soon as possible.

g.   All contestants who answer these questions correctly will win a trip to Paris.

h.   The Grand Hotel, located on Sunrise Road, is over a hundred years old.

i.   Every student who scores well on the examination will be graduated with honors.

j.   The new regulations, which are far more stringent than the old rules, go into effect on January 1.

[5]   CAPITALIZATION

Do you know which words to capitalize in titles of books, plays, musical compositions, book-length poems, paintings, ballets, newspapers, and so on? Here's the rule to follow:

> RULE: *Capitalize the first word in a title, and capitalize all other words except articles (a, an, the) and prepositions or conjunctions of fewer than five letters.*
>
> > *An Analysis of Consumer Purchases*
> > *The Kitten and the Falcon*
> > *Watching the Sails Go By*
> > *Thoughts Among Friends*

(Although titles in print are set in italics, when typing, remember to underscore them or to type them in all capitals.)

> RULE: *Capitalize parts of published works (chapters, poems within a book, articles, columns in newspapers or magazines, short stories) according to the rule for all titles.*

(Titles of parts of works are enclosed in quotes instead of being underscored. The same is true of unpublished works, such as internal company reports or unpublished theses.)

Now go to work on these sentences. Capitalize and punctuate as needed.

a. The Superintendent of Documents publishes the Statistical Abstract.

b. James Knox of the Bureau of Labor Statistics wrote a book called Employment Opportunities in the Middle West.

c. Professor Smith's new book a history of economic thought will be published in september.

d. Frank Sheldon from the Bureau of Internal Revenue spoke on the topic New Tax Regulations Affecting Business.

e. The Winged Victory is a famous statue in the Louvre in Paris —

f. Steel Builds for a New Era was a leading article in October's Fortune magazine.

[6] PRONOUNS

people   *things*

Relative pronouns — *who, whom, which,* and *that* — sometimes give us trouble. The following rules will give you some help:

> RULE: *The verb in a relative clause must agree in person and number with the antecedent of the relative pronoun that serves as the subject of the clause.*

> Have you spoken with the man who was waiting for you?

"Man" is the antecedent of the relative pronoun "who"; therefore, the verb must be third person and singular — "was."

> Where are the papers that were left on my desk?

The verb "were" agrees with "papers," the antecedent of "that."

> RULE: *If your sentence contains the phrase* one of the *or* one of those, *the antecedent of the relative pronoun is not the word* one *but the plural words that follow.*

> One of the letters that were on my desk has disappeared.

The relative pronoun "that" agrees with "letters"; therefore, the verb is "were." Remember, however, that the subject of the *main* clause ("one has disappeared") is "one" and takes a singular verb "has." It is only the verb of the *relative* clause ("that were on my desk") that agrees with "letters." Be sure you understand this distinction before you go on to the next rule!

RULE: *When the word* only *precedes* one *in this type of sentence,* one *is considered to be the antecedent of the relative pronoun.*

He is the only one of the men who is making the survey.

You will understand this rule if you think of what the sentence means. In the example for the second rule, there were "letters on the table." In this example, however, there are not "men making the survey"; there is only one man who is doing so. Therefore, the antecedent of "who" must be "one."

When you are certain you have mastered these rules, go to work on the following sentences. Choose the words that give correct agreement.

a. Secretaries who (*keeps, keep*) accurate files (*is, are*) valuable in any office.

b. One of the men who (*is, are*) attending the session (*is, are*) wanted on the telephone.

c. He presented a plan that, in our opinion, (*is, are*) the best of all the plans that (*was, were*) submitted.

d. One of the applicants who (*is, are*) eligible for a promotion (*is, are*) here now.

e. Marlene is the only one of the students who (*is, are*) receiving an award.

f. "It (*is, am, are*) I who (*is, am, are*) surprised," said the teacher.

[7] ORDER LETTERS

a. The following is an excerpt from a brochure from Maple Grove, Inc., 183 Main Street, St. Johnsbury, Vermont.

> Order your pure Vermont Maple Candy now! Maple Grove, Inc., produces the finest maple-sugar candies in the world. Five gallons of maple sap are boiled to make just one gallon of pure syrup. Then we "boil down" 2½ gallons of this pure maple syrup to make just one 8-ounce box of delicious candy, which sells for only $1.25 a box.
>
> If you are looking for a creamy, melt-in-your-mouth candy treat, order a good supply of Maple Sugar Candy now. Price of $1.25 per box includes shipping charges.

Order a box of Maple Sugar Candy for yourself and a box for a friend. You will pay with a postal money order.

b. Write a letter to order samples as suggested in this advertisement:

GREETING CARDS!

Make $25 dollars! Easy for you or your school or club to sell 100 boxes of designer Christmas cards. Send for samples on approval.
Carmine Cards, Box 1527, New York, New York   10001

c. You wish to have a good outline for a review of economics, and you decide on *Outline of Economics* by Chenault and Smith. Since your college bookstore doesn't have a copy, you must write to the publisher for a copy. You do not know the selling price of the book. Write the letter, using a fictitious name and address for the publisher.

d. Father's Day is coming shortly, and you wish to order a gold-plated tie clasp for your father. Write a letter to order the tie clasp advertised below.

LOG-DESIGN TIE CLASP

Our own exclusive design.

14K gold — $24.95
Sterling silver — $9.95
Gold plated — $3.50

CRAFTSMEN JEWELERS
41 Clapham Street
Brooklyn, New York

Mail orders accepted; no C.O.D.
Price includes federal tax. In New York,
add 5% sales tax; for shipment, add 25¢
postage and handling.

e. Comment on the following letter, which was received by Waxgiser Vitamin Supplies.

Dear Sirs:

I have been ordering my vitamins and prescription drugs from you for the passed 8 years. Due to the fact that you did not have the 100 mg. Vitamin C tablets the last time I wrote you I am now ordering them again.

Send me 300 mg. Vitamin C tablets. I will enclose my check for $4.75 and hope that theprice hasn't changed.

You did not send me my PartyBook stamps on my previous order for $11.25. Trusting that you will send them with the new order, I am,

                              Respectively yours,

[8] LETTERS OF INQUIRY

a.   Your bowling club is planning to hold its annual dinner at Lund's Restaurant on October 27. Arrangements must be made for no fewer than 25 and not more than 40 persons. Write a letter to Mr. J. K. Lawlor, manager of Lund's. Ask for sample menus as well as for prices. The dinner should be scheduled for 7:30 p.m., and your club will want the room until midnight.

b.   You have heard about a book called *They Signed for Us*. You know neither the author's name nor the publisher. The book tells the story of the signers of the Declaration of Independence. Write a letter to the Stern Bookstore in your town to find out if it is available and what its price is.

c.   You wish to open a charge account with Burchill's Department Store. Write a letter to ask if you are eligible for a charge account and how you should proceed.

d.   You are a member of a sewing club. At Christmas, the club members usually make dresses for the 50 girls at a nearby children's home. You have been asked to write to the X Corporation to see if they will donate material for this worthy project. What would you write?

e.   You have been shopping for a Finetone transistor radio. Write to the manufacturer in New York to ask for the name of a dealer in your area so that you can buy a Finetone.

[9] LETTERS OF TRANSMITTAL

a.   You have been assigned a term paper in your economics class. You have not completed your paper on the assigned date before the Christmas holiday, but Professor Nolan has agreed to let you mail it to him as soon as you have completed it. You mail the report on December 27. Write a covering message to enclose with your report.

b.   Assume that you have secured a reservation at Teepee Lodge for the Thanksgiving holidays. The Lodge has requested a deposit of $25. Write a letter of transmittal to send with your check covering the deposit.

c.   You have been clipping newspaper and magazine articles on the effects of automation on office employment. Now that you have five good articles, you wish to send them to your friend who is writing a paper on the subject. Write a letter to accompany the articles.

d.   Your club has drawn up its social calendar for the coming semester. You have written a brief article about it that you would like to have published in your school paper. Write a covering letter to send to the editor, asking him to publish your club news.

[10] CLAIM LETTERS

a.   Suppose that during the past two months you have been having problems with your mail deliveries. Mail for other people was often delivered to your home; your own mail was often delayed for no good reason. On one occasion a bill for $856 was not received, and you had to explain to the store why you hadn't paid the bill. Write a letter to your local postmaster, asking him to see that your postal service is corrected.

b.   You have joined a record club. The first shipment is made up of four records, specially priced as an introductory offer. You sent your check when you ordered the records. When the records arrive, you find that two records are badly damaged even though the package was wrapped correctly. You know that the damage must have taken place during shipping because you were very careful when you unpacked the records. What would you write to the company?

c.   You have ordered 100 sheets of stationery and matching envelopes with your name and address imprinted on them. You have received the package. Your address has been printed incorrectly on the stationery; it reads 105 Reed Avenue, but it should read 501 Reed Avenue. Write a claim letter to Thatcher Printing Company to ask them to replace the stationery.

d.   Rewrite the following letters to improve them.

> What kind of a packing department does your company
> have? I have just received my Book Club copy of "Let's
> Go West" but it is in terrible condition. The flimsy
> packing was torn open and the book was badly damaged.
>
> When I pay for books I want them to look like new books.
>
> When you send me another copy of "Let's Go West" plus
> allowance for postage, I will return the damaged book
> to you. If you do not send me a new copy, I will dis-
> continue my Book Club membership.

Sirs:

Last year I bought one dozen azalea bushes from your
nursery. You guaranteed that they would grow. I guess I
should have known better than to believe a newspaper advertisement because not one of those bushes is alive
and growing this year. Apparently you think that people
will not come back and ask for what they deserve.

I hereby demand that you send me one dozen azalea bushes
to replace those that did not grow. Trusting that you
will attend to this matter at once, I am,

Truly,

e. You have received an invoice from the Boro Appliance Company for
the purchase of a portable TV for $139.50 and an electric iron for
$20.50. You bought only the electric iron. Write a letter to accompany
your check for the correct amount.

8 | The Application Series

AMONG the most important communications you will ever write are those concerned with applying for a job:

> The letter of application and the data sheet.
> The thank you for the interview.
> The letter of acceptance or rejection of the job offer.

You have been gaining experience in writing business letters for personal reasons and have had a chance to learn to express yourself effectively. Many of the principles you have already learned can now be put to use in helping you get the job you want. You are now "selling" your working capacity to a prospective employer, so do two things: Put yourself in the reader's place, and plan your approach.

capacity; prospective

PHASE 1: DATA SHEET AND LETTER

Appearance Counts

No matter what the content of your materials, here, more than ever, appearance counts. Your letter presents a picture of you. Make its appearance say good things about you. Some letters are attractive and seem to ask to be read, while others cannot pass inspection. Neatness and carefulness are important in any job; if your letter's appearance doesn't reflect these qualities, your letter may never be read.

Hint for a good start.

The person to whom you are writing is a stranger, and your letter deals with a business matter. Therefore, avoid the use of hotel or social stationery, or paper embossed with your fraternity crest, or other special stationery.

embossed

Type your letter on white bond paper of good quality in the standard $8\frac{1}{2}$ x 11 size. Your envelope should match the stationery — its appearance counts, too. And the position of your letter on the sheet affects the reader's reaction. Allow enough space for margins.

Remember, of course, to place your return address in the upper right-hand corner along with the date and include your telephone number if you can be reached by phone. Type the prospective employer's name and address in the usual position for the inside address. If you are writing a letter of application in reply to a help-wanted advertisement, use the address given in the ad. If the ad gives a box number, type the box number as the first line of the inside address:

Remember to leave two spaces before the zip code.

```
Box 245
Los Angeles
California    90014
```

The salutation of such a letter should be "Gentlemen."

Follow the rules for breaking up the letter into paragraphs to improve its readability.

Be sure to sign your letter with your official signature, in longhand and in ink, directly above your typed signature. No one will mistake your name if it has been typed.

Take Time to Plan

preliminary

You know that your letter must pass an appearance test. Now you must do some preliminary planning so that the contents of the letter will match its attractive appearance.

A letter of application, to be complete and yet brief enough to get the reader to finish reading it, presents a difficult problem. Follow the modern practice of writing a short letter of application and attaching a data sheet, or résumé. This makes it easier for you to plan your letter and to use attractive display techniques in setting up the information on your background.

One of the first things to do is a little preliminary homework to learn something about the company where you are applying for a position — its main products and services, its position in its field, the number of its employees, its beginning salaries. If you are going to meet someone for the first time, you find it easier if you know a little something about him.

Keep the reader in mind.

Then do some thinking about your qualifications. Writing your letter of application and preparing your data sheet are very personal acts. The worst thing you can do is to copy a letter someone else wrote. You are selling yourself, and your letter should reflect you. Think in terms of what you have to offer. You may not have had much business experience, but you have an education. Get the exact dates of your high school and college career. List the specific courses you have taken that might be of value in the work for which you are applying. Jot down the names of the clubs you joined at school. Were you elected to an office? Did you work on committees to plan club activities? Be sure to mention that you were in the top quarter of your class (only if you were — otherwise forget it). Have you done volunteer work on charitable campaigns? Are you known in your community for your civic mindedness and assistance in community projects? If you have had business experience, tell a little about each job. With a little ingenuity, even that baby-sitting job can assume some importance.

then

charitable

ingenuity

Put down these facts one by one as they come to your mind. Then look them over and classify and organize them. Determine how you can present them in the most appealing way. Now you should be ready to prepare your data sheet.

The Personal Data Sheet

After one student completed his data sheet, he said:
"Here I am in compact, easy-to-read form!" That is
exactly what the data sheet is. It is a factual presentation of you — your personal history, education, extracurricular activities, work experience, honors and
awards, and references.

extracurricular

How should you begin? The usual way is to list
first your "vital statistics" — name (including middle
name), address, phone number, date of birth, height,
weight, state of health, marital status, and (for the men)
draft status.

Now you are ready to mention your background.
As you begin your career, education is your chief selling
point, so you will list the details of your education first.
(As a rule, lists, not sentences, are used in a data sheet.)
Make your entry complete by listing the names of the
educational institutions, their locations, and the dates of
your graduation or attendance. Omit data concerning
your elementary school if you have attended high school
and college.

attendance

In describing your educational background, you
should list courses that are relevant to the position for
which you are applying. You can mention four or five
major courses and several background courses. Always
list these courses by name rather than by a catalog
number, which would mean nothing to the prospective
employer.

Remember the reader!

Be sure to list activities during your school career
that would indicate your intellectual abilities, your
leadership qualities, your cooperativeness, and your
ability to get along with others. For example:

1. "A" average in college.
2. Dean's List, 1967, 1968.
3. Elected captain of basketball
   team.
4. Member of Phi Beta Lambda honor-
   ary business fraternity.
5. Member of Business and Economics
   Club, 1966-67, 1967-68. Elected
   secretary, 1967-68.
6. Member of college choir.

It is desirable to enter data relating to your education and experience in inverse chronological order, giving the most recent first. This is the logical approach, because most people like to see what you are doing now before seeing what you've done in the past.

desirable
inverse
chronological

Although your job experience may be quite limited, do not hesitate to take advantage of any entry you can make. If you have held part-time or summer jobs, you should include them. Even though these jobs may not relate to the position for which you are now applying, they tell something about you — that you have initiative and ambition, that you accept responsibility, that you have had some experience working. That summer job will show that you were dependable, for no employer would keep you for an entire summer if you were not.

initiative

Perhaps you have had some military experience. You may include this under work experience, or you may give it a separate heading, depending on its nature and its importance to the job you are seeking.

We have already noted that you should list extra-curricular activities. It is also well to list outside activities and organizations under the heading "Out-of-School Activities." These activities could include:

Outside sports programs — e.g., golf tournaments, baseball teams, bowling leagues, tennis clubs.
4-H Club membership.
Boy Scouting or Girl Scouting.
Junior Chamber of Commerce.
Travel experience.
Hobbies.

e.g.

Every good data sheet contains at least four references. Vary yours, selecting a teacher or professor who has known you well, a former employer if possible, and at least one character reference (i.e., someone who knows you well outside of business or school). Of course, you will never list a name as reference unless you have received permission in advance from the person to use his or her name. If the person named as a reference has an official title, include it; this adds importance to the recommendation. Above all, be certain

i.e.

Hint for good human relations.

recommendation

verified

Remember the amenities.

enhance

that all names are spelled correctly and that all addresses are verified — they must be accurate. If you should learn that one of the references has written a letter recommending you, write him a short note of thanks.

Now let's look at some things relating to the mechanics of the data sheet. Obviously you want your data sheet to make an excellent appearance. Therefore, you must arrange it for attractiveness and for easy reading. If you make effective use of display techniques, you will enhance the readability of your data sheet. Keep in mind the rule about using adequate margins to provide an attractive amount of white area on the sheet. Type your main headings in capital letters, either centered or at the left margin. Minor headings can then be underlined. You can experiment with different methods of display to see which would be most effective for your sheet.

Look over Thomas Hines' data sheet (Figure 8 – 1, pages 206 – 07) to see if it meets the standards you have been reading about. Thomas has seen this ad in the help-wanted section of the Sunday paper:

HELP WANTED

Junior Accountant. No experience required. Must like working with people. On-the-job training program. Retail Associates, 585 Oakland Drive, San Francisco, California   94105

Notice how Thomas set up his main headings so that his reader could pinpoint each item easily. His including his telephone area code was wise because he could very well live in a different area from the company's. Perhaps he could have left out his height and weight, which would probably be irrelevant for the accounting position. He used good judgment in listing the courses that would prove helpful in getting the job and extracurricular activities that showed him to be a leader.

Your Letter to Accompany the Data Sheet

When your data sheet is completed, you are ready to prepare an application letter. Its main function is as a letter of transmittal to accompany your data sheet.

RIGHT — AT THE START

Remember to arouse interest at the beginning. The first sentence is crucial; if it gets the attention of your reader, your letter has a chance to tell the rest of its story.

crucial

    Ideally, your first sentence should be direct — it should have the "you" attitude. Since you are selling yourself when you write the letter, however, you may use the first person pronoun. (Just be careful to avoid using "I" to begin each sentence or paragraph. A little careful planning will enable you to vary your sentences.)

    Try a one-sentence summary as a beginning sentence. Here are examples of sentences that have hit the target:

Opening-sentence summary.

> My three summers' experience as camp counselor qualify me for a position at Camp Cherokee this year.
>
> I am applying for the position of stenographer that you advertised in the Los Angeles <u>Times</u> on May 20.
>
> Now that I have had two years of office experience in addition to my formal education, I believe that I am prepared to fill the position of office assistant with United Supplies.

    If you have learned about a position through a person whose name commands respect, use his name in that first sentence. Of course, you must have his permission to do this. This name appeal is effective if the reader knows the person well and respects his judgment. Your opening sentence might read:

Or use a reference in the first sentence.

```
                    PERSONAL DATA SHEET


NAME        Thomas Joseph Hines

ADDRESS     999 Carson Drive
            Sacramento, California  95804

TELEPHONE NUMBER    (916) 351-7584


DATE OF BIRTH    March 17, 1948    MARITAL STATUS    Single

DRAFT STATUS    1S    COUNTRY OF BIRTH    United States

CITIZENSHIP    United States


HEIGHT    6 feet    WEIGHT    170 pounds    HEALTH    Excellent


EDUCATION
                                          Diploma
    Institution                Dates      Degree
    Castleton Junior College   1966-68    A.A.S.
    Castleton, California

    Central High School        1962-66    Commercial
    Buffalo, New York

    Scholastic Standing    3.2 (B+)

    Major    Accounting

    Courses                    Background Courses
    Elementary and Advanced    Psychology
      Accounting I, II, III, IV  English Composition
    Auditing                   Money and Banking
    Income Tax Procedures      Economic Analysis
    Business Law I, II         Marketing
    Business Management
```

Figure 8 – 1
A Personal Data Sheet

Thomas J. Hines
Personal Data Sheet
Page 2

EXTRACURRICULAR ACTIVITIES AND HONORS

    Accounting Club
      President (elective office) 1967-68
    College Glee Club 1967-68
    Phi Beta Lambda 1968
    Future Business Leaders of America 1965-66
    High-school valedictorian 1966

EXPERIENCE

Company	Dates	Job Duties
Bullock's Department Store Sacramento, California	9/66-6/68 (part-time)	Retail selling, men's furnishings
Lane's Buffalo, New York	6/65-9/65 6/66-9/66	Stock clerk

REFERENCES

Professor James Devine   Mr. Frank Naber
Economics Department   One Duane Terrace
Castleton Junior College   Buffalo, New York 14214
Castleton, California 95602

Mr. John Knight   Mrs. Frank Hastings
Lane's   758 Carson Drive
111 Main Street   Sacramento, California
Buffalo, New York 14213   95804

Figure 8 – 1
(Continued)

> Miss Anita Farrar in the vice presi-
> dent's office has told me that you
> will need a stenographer in June.
> Since I will be graduating at that
> time, I should like to apply for the
> position.
>
> Professor Thomas Cook, my finance in-
> structor, has suggested that I apply
> to you for the opening in your credit
> department.

Notice that it is good practice to mention the name of the specific position for which you are applying. It shows that you know what you are seeking, and it also helps the personnel staff if the firm has more than one position open.

Or try opening with a question.

A third method of attracting attention in your opening sentence is to ask a question. This approach carries with it the advantages of directness and simplicity; it places the applicant's qualities before the reader at once.

Here's how you can use the question technique:

> Do you wish to hire a stenographer
> who can take dictation at 140 words
> a minute and transcribe at 30 words a
> minute with 95 percent accuracy? I am
> the stenographer you want.

However, a word of caution if you use this question idea — be sure that your qualifications answer the questions you raise. How would you feel if the reader took you up on your statement and you could take only 100 words per minute and you made plenty of errors?

Other possible ways to use a question are:

> Will you call me when you need a man
> who is an expert tax accountant?
>
> Do you need a live-wire salesman?
> I hope I can fit your job require-
> ments.

THE MIDDLE PARAGRAPHS

Once you have had a good start, you will find it much easier to write the middle part of your letter. It is proper here to reemphasize some of the specific educational qualifications and work experiences that appear in your data sheet. Emphasize these as your central selling points. If you have had summer or part-time experience, be sure to mention it; for example:

Stress your strong points.

> My two summers at Lane's and my part-time work at Bullock's gave me some retail selling experience.

Call attention to any honors you have achieved:

> As you will see from my data sheet, I will be graduated from Harden College with an A.A.S. degree in June 1968. As a student, I also participated in extracurricular activities that further prepared me for a business position.

However, your letter should mention only briefly your most important qualifications; your data sheet gives the full information.

THE CLOSING PARAGRAPH

When you come to your closing paragraph, you want to secure the desired action — getting an interview. Make it easy for the employer to reach you and to schedule the interview: Give him the times you are available — such as, Friday after 1 p.m. and Thursday after 2 p.m. — and give him your telephone number. (Usually, of course, you will receive an answer by mail.)

Tell the employer how he can contact you.

These sentences show all that you need to include in your final paragraph:

> Will you please give me an interview? I am free on Friday afternoons.

May I come for an interview? My telephone number is 357-4389, and you may
reach me any morning.

Please suggest a time when you can
interview me for this position. You
can phone me at 598-7687 any day between noon and 4 p.m.

May I come to see you and bring samples of my work? I am available any
weekday during business hours.

Be positive.

Be sure to be definite in requesting your interview.
Endings such as the following do not hit the mark; they
are weak and colorless, and they show a lack of confidence:

I hope to hear from you soon.

If you feel that I can fill the position, allow me to come in for an interview.

Let's return to the advertisement we read for the
junior accountant's position with Retail Associates.
Thomas Hines prepared his data sheet; now let's see
the letter he wrote to accompany it:

                        999 Carson Drive
                        Sacramento, California   95804
                        July 1, 1968

            Retail Associates
            585 Oakland Drive
            San Francisco, California   94105

            Gentlemen:

Refer to the specific job.

            Please consider me for the position
            of junior accountant advertised in

the San Francisco <u>Gazette</u> of June
30.

My attached data sheet shows that I
have had extensive training in
accounting and business practice
in high school and college. And my
extracurricular activities while in
college included being president of
the Accounting Club for two successive years.

Mention important achievements.

successive

While your position does not require
business experience, my part-time and
summer jobs at Lane's and Bullock's
have given me an opportunity to deal
with people and to learn something
about the retail business.

Note any relevant experience.

May I come for an interview at your
convenience? You can reach me by
calling my home any time during the
day. My telephone number there is
351-7584.

Be positive, and make response easy.

Sincerely yours,

Thomas J. Hines

Enclosure
  Data Sheet

Do you agree that Thomas' letter was a good one?
What about the following letters sent in by job applicants? If you were an employer, would you interview
these two young ladies on the basis of their letters? The
letters were in answer to an advertisement for a stenographer with good skills and with a willingness to assume
responsibility.

123 Middle Avenue
Baltimore, Maryland   20782
May 15, 1968

The Kipling Company
1776 H Street, N.W.
Washington, D.C.   20006

Proper salutation?

Dear Sir:

"I" rather than "you" attitude.

When I was reading the Sunday paper yesterday, I noticed that you have advertised for a stenographer with good skills. I should like to be considered an applicant for the job.

"Some" is vague. Commas needed between independent clauses.

I had some business courses in high school and I continued to study business at college. I found my studies at school very interesting so I think I should enjoy a stenographer's job in business.

"I trust" is both old-fashioned and presumptuous.

I trust that you will grant me an interview so that we can talk about the job.

Proper closing?

Yours truly,

Marie Melinda

Marie Melinda

strive

Would Marie get an interview? Or could she have made her letter more effective? We suggest that Marie study her rules on the use of the comma and on letter mechanics and that she strive for a more modern, businesslike tone. Let's vitalize her letter.

First, let's scrap the opening sentence and replace it with:

Please consider me for the stenographic position you advertised in Sunday's <u>Gazette</u>.

Notice that Marie would be more direct in her approach with fewer words.

You will agree that Marie's second paragraph is vague, but that's easy to correct:

```
I had two years of stenography and
typewriting in high school and ma-
jored in the executive secretarial
program in college. The A.A.S. degree
included 32 credits of liberal-arts
courses and 30 credits of business-
background and career courses. My
educational background prepares me
for a position as a secretary.
```

For her final paragraph, Marie would have done better if she had ended something like this:

```
May I have an interview? You can call
me at my home at any time. My phone
number is 751-3227.
```

Marie made no mention of having prepared a data sheet. The omission of a data sheet could cost her the job.

A data sheet is essential.

Here is Francine's letter for the same job. She, too, seems to have forgotten a data sheet.

```
                454 Crane Avenue
                Baltimore, Maryland    20782
                May 15, 1968

The Kipling Company
1776 H Street, N.W.
Washington, D.C.    20006

Gentlemen:

You are looking for a highly-skilled
stenographer aren't you? I am willing
to work for you including the assum-
ing of responsibility that you men-
tioned in your advertisment.
```

Wordy.

Slang.

Negative.

Disorganized.

Presumptuous.

> My steno speed is 140 words per minute and that's no fooling. I can transcribe at 30 words per minute. You must admit that few of your employees can acheive those rates. I haven't had any business experience and I'm anxious to get started. I did work in the playgrounds during the summer, however.
>
> When I come in for an interview I will demonstrate my skills.
>
> Sincerely,
>
> Francine Simpson

wholesome

It looks as if Francine is hardly the bashful type! Couldn't she have toned down her letter to make herself sound more wholesome without losing sight of the fact that she has skills — at least speed. Did you notice the two misspelled words in her letter ("advertisement" and "achieve")? Did she punctuate correctly? (Look at both sentences in the first paragraph. Each sentence is missing a comma. Can you find three other such mistakes in the letter?) Francine needs something more than stenographic and typing speed.

Let's see what we can do with Francine's letter. We'll follow her idea of opening with a question.

> Are you looking for a stenographer who can take dictation at 140 words a minute and transcribe accurately at 30 words a minute? I have those skills, and I am eager to obtain the stenographic job you advertised in yesterday's <u>Gazette</u>.

My experience includes a vacation job
as playground supervisor, as you will
see on my enclosed data sheet. As
part of this job, I organized sports
events and tournaments.   tournaments

May I have an interview so that you
can go over my qualifications with
me? If you wish, you may call me at
my home, 761-1696, any time during
the day.

PHASE 2:   THE THANK-YOU LETTER

Did your letter of application get the interview? Will
you now wait to see what happens? Have you completed your letter-writing? One more short letter to
thank your prospective employer for the interview may
be the one that proves to be the clincher; it brings you   proves
back to his mind in clear focus. This little extra effort
puts you out in front.

The letter below is all that is needed:

999 Carson Drive
Sacramento, California   95804
July 8, 1968

Mr. Lester Barnes
Retail Associates
585 Oakland Drive
San Francisco, California   94105

Dear Mr. Barnes:

Thank you for granting me an inter-   *Be very brief and to*
view yesterday.   *the point.*

I am very much interested in the position of junior accountant with Re-

```
tail Associates. I appreciate the
careful consideration you are giving
my application.

                      Sincerely yours,

                      Thomas J. Hines

                      Thomas J. Hines
```

Taking note of names is important.

(Notice that Thomas was alert enough to remember the name of the man who conducted the interview.)

PHASE 3:   THE LETTER OF ACCEPTANCE OR REJECTION

Finally it came — the letter that said, "You are invited to join our staff." You have been waiting for this job offer, and you are ready to answer it immediately.

Respond promptly.

```
              108 East Washington Street
              Indianapolis, Indiana   46209
              July 15, 1968

Economy Finance Company
187 Capehart Drive
Indianapolis, Indiana   46207

Gentlemen:

I am happy to accept the position of
credit investigator at a weekly sal-
ary of $115.

As you requested, I will report to
Mr. Harold Ewen in the Personnel De-
partment on July 19 at 9 a.m.
```

Thank you for giving me this opportunity to work in your company.

Sincerely yours,

James Ball

James Ball

Suppose that when the letter offering you a position arrives, you have already accepted another job.
Will you disregard the offer you don't accept? Or will
you keep your good name by writing to say that you
cannot accept the position? It takes just a few minutes
to write:

Be courteous enough to inform the company of your refusal.

Thank you for offering me the position of credit investigator with
Economy Finance. Because I accepted a
position with another company yesterday, I must refuse your offer.

I am pleased that your firm considered me for the position.

SUMMARY

When you apply in writing for a position, you must plan
your approach to include a short letter of application
and a well-designed personal data sheet. In presenting
your materials, you must realize that no matter how
outstanding your qualifications may be, the appearance
of your letter and data sheet will either enhance or
detract from them.

Plan ahead while you are still in school. Collect
the information for your data sheet. When you apply

for your first job, you must be able to present a professionally typed, complete data sheet. It includes your name, address, telephone number (including area code), education, extracurricular activities, working experience, community activities, and names and addresses of the references whom you have asked to recommend you for the position.

Your brief letter of application that accompanies the data sheet should refer to your qualifications and to the specific position for which you are applying. In this letter, you should request an interview and list the times you are available for that interview.

Your writing a thank-you note for the interview may be the "little bit extra" that gets the job for you. And, because you are a professional person, you will write one additional letter – the acceptance or rejection of the job offer.

Each phase of your job application becomes part of your file. Each one contributes to your obtaining the position or strengthens the employer's evaluation of you.

8 | Exercises

[1] SPELLING

a. What is the missing letter in each of these words?

   desir__ble   whol__some   charit__ble   debat__ble

b. Correct the spelling in the following paragraph.

   John's recomendation is that we list the turnaments seperately in cronological order, but Richard disagrees. He thinks we must proove our capasity for analysis by using some other proceedure.

[2] VOCABULARY

a. Adding a word to your vocabulary not only means understanding its definition and learning how to spell it; you should also know how to make related words from the same root. For instance, from the word *plant*, you can make *implant*, *transplant*, and *plantation*, and so on. Use each of the words in parentheses below to form a new word that suits the blank left in the sentence.

   His suggestion was certainly an _____ (ingenuity) one.

   This was an _____ (inverse) of the usual order.

   He requested a _____ (verify) of the statistics.

   The supervisor wanted to _____ (initiative) a new system.

   There was great commotion and _____ (strive) when the news leaked out.

b. When is something *crucial*? *for example* *that is*

c. Do you know the difference between *e.g.* and *i.e.*? Explain.

d. Use each of these words in a sentence that illustrates its meaning:

   enhance   prospective   embossed   preliminary   successive

e. The prefix *extra* means, roughly, "outside of" or "beyond the scope of." What, then, does *extracurricular* mean? Think of two other words containing the prefix *extra*, and use each in a sentence.

219

[3] SOUND-ALIKES

Choose the correct words in each of these sentences:

a. His (*attendance, attendants*) at the meeting was compulsory.

b. The company reported higher earnings for this year (*than, then*) for 1967.

c. The (*passed, past*) quarter has been disappointing for the Acme Company.

d. Prepare your personal data sheet; (*than, then*) mail it to our personnel office.

e. The company's sales have long (*passed, past*) the billion-dollar mark.

f. We shall ask the (*attendance, attendants*) to record the number of people in (*attendance, attendants*) at the rally.

[4] PUNCTUATION: COMMA

RULE: *Place a comma before a short direct quotation.*

The supervisor said, "Type two copies of this letter."

RULE: *Use a comma to separate introductory words, such as* yes, no, *and* well, *from the rest of the sentence.*

Yes, your car should be at the garage tomorrow.
Well, you have finally completed the job.

RULE: *Use a comma to set off words in direct address.*

Mr. Smith, will you check these figures for us.
Yes, Mr. Perkins, we have received approval of your loan request.

Use these rules — and others you have learned — to help you punctuate these sentences correctly:

a. No we do not intend to change our methods

b. Mr Cerone asked "Have you filed your return"

c. Yes Mr Wise we have a subscription in your name

d. Do you plan to attend the conference in June Mr Peters

e. "Well we have reached our profit goal of $500000" he reported "and sooner than we'd anticipated"

[5] CAPITALIZATION

> RULE: *Capitalize the first word of a sentence within a sentence.*

Your letter of March 15 read, "We will send our check for $25 immediately."

This is our proposal: If you pay within five days, you may take the discount.

> RULE: *Capitalize points of the compass when they indicate specific geographical areas.*

When you have driven 3,000 miles west, you will be in the Far West.

Capitalize as needed in the sentences below.

a.   mr ansell said, "we expect to relocate our office in the south."

b.   members of the federal reserve board are studying banking conditions in the far east.

c.   frank smith pondered this question: how can we increase earnings by 20 percent?

d.   drive east for 25 miles, then north for 15 miles.

e.   "Have you read 'middle management and computers,' " mr. drew asked, "in this month's issue of *dun's review?*"

[6] PRONOUNS

Watch for ambiguous antecedents; they cause confusion in your reader's mind. These rules will help:

> RULE: *When a pronoun can refer to either of two antecedents, arrange your sentence so that it is clear which antecedent is meant. If necessary, replace the pronoun.*

John went to Paul's house to get his umbrella.

Whose umbrella? John's or Paul's? Rephrase this to read:

John went to get his umbrella at Paul's house.

Here's another example:

The professor told John that his writing was improving.

Whose writing was improving? To make this sentence clear, you must replace the pronoun with the appropriate noun.

The professor told John that John's writing was improving.

RULE: *Do not use forms of the same pronoun to refer to different antecedents.*

> Harry asked Mike to go to the movies, but he found that he had no money.

Who found that who had no money? This sentence could be rephrased in several ways, depending on what is meant.

> Harry asked Mike to go to the movies, but he found that Mike had no money.
> Harry asked Mike to go to the movies, but Mike had no money.
> After he asked Mike to go to the movies, Harry found himself without any money.

RULE: *Place your pronoun as close as possible to its antecedent.*

> A young man can always find a friend who is outgoing and cheerful.

This sentence would make better sense if it were reworded in this way:

> A young man who is outgoing and cheerful can always find a friend.

Wherever necessary, reword the following sentences to clear up any ambiguities. Where more than one meaning is possible, you need give only one.

a.   Place the letter in the file cabinet that was written yesterday.

b.   The president told the treasurer that he would have to make his report to the committee in March.

c.   She told the stenographer that she would be in her office until five o'clock.

d.   A lawyer can readily find a client who is capable.

e.   When he wrote to Mr. Jones, he told him that he was correct in his calculations.

f.   She told the student that his marks were high.

g.   The picture was hung on the wall that we bought last week.

[7] PROOFREADING

Your assistant has typed a letter that you composed. Since she is a beginning worker you feel it advisable to read the letter carefully before you sign it. Did she do a good job? List in order any errors you find and the way you would correct them.

June 1st, 1967

Mr. John Putnam, Esq.
125 E. 9th St.
Seattle, Wash.   98103

Dear Mr. Putman

Thank you for your order, which I received in todays
mail. Because our new production facilty in Springfeild,
Massachuesetts, have come ●on stream● reacently, your new
colour telivision set can be shiped immediately.

Your set will cost you $649 which reflects a an increase
of 5 precent over last years price. However, if you pay for
the set within forteen days from the reciept of your set,
you may deduct a cash discount of 2 percent.

When you uncrate your set, be sure to sign the gaurantee
card and mail it to us. It is your protection for a full
year of unlimited service.

Very Sincerly Yours,

Sales Dept.

vj.

[8] PROBLEMS

a. Analyze each of the following sentences, and see how you can improve
them.

1. In answer to your ad in today's *Times*, I know that you have been
looking for a super-salesman like me.

2. I have held many positions in the five years since my graduation
from college.

3. Hoping to hear from you at your earliest convenience for an interview, I am,

4. You are fortunate that I am available for the position of credit
manager with your distinguished firm.

5. Since I am the sole support of my aging parents, I need to have
a job very soon.

b. As a prospective employer, how would you react to these opening sentences? Make any changes you think would improve them.

1. Replying to your ad in the *Times* of March 1st for a bookkeeper, I wish to apply for the position.

2. When I was looking through the Sunday want ads, I noticed that you are looking for a bookkeeper.

3. I am writing to answer your ad for a bookkeeper in the *Times* of March 1.

4. This is to ask you to consider my qualifications as a bookkeeper with your valued company.

5. Please let me have the job of bookkeeper that you had advertised in the newspaper yesterday.

c. Your friend has told you about a position that will be open with her company in two months. Assume that this is the type of position you will be seeking at that time. Write a letter to apply for it, mentioning the name of the person who told you about it. Be sure to include your data sheet.

d. Assume that you have had an interview in answer to your letter in the preceding problem. The interviewer said he would let you know about the position. Write a follow-up letter to thank him for the interview.

e. After a week's wait, you have been offered the job for which you applied. In the meantime, you have received another offer by a dynamic new company. Write letters to each of the two companies accepting or rejecting its job offer.

f. Read the help-wanted ads in your Sunday paper. Find an ad that appeals to you and that refers to a position you can fill. Write your letter of application and your data sheet.

WRITING ON THE JOB

9 | The Interoffice Memorandum

YOUR developing career has recently led you to accept a full-time position as the head of the mail department in a small manufacturing plant. Three men work under you to effect the rapid delivery of the incoming mail and servicing of the outgoing mail of the departments in your division.

effect

THE MEMORANDUM
FOR THE RECURRING SITUATION

During that first week on the job, you formulated this breakdown of the duties involved in processing incoming mail: time-stamping and dating, checking the envelope for notations not listed on the letter, noting differences of date of letter and postmark date, confirming inclusion of all enclosures by checkmark on the letter, sorting, and delivery. You worked as a team; and it was, therefore, obvious to all of you that interruptions in the work flow prevented rapid delivery of the incoming mail. When Joe would say, "Another one!" it meant

formulated

that some piece of mail needed special attention, such as a note to a secretary explaining that the enclosure had not been included. With an average of 1,500 pieces of mail coming through the division weekly, it was not unusual for each of the team to leave the group to type a letter to a secretary more than once each morning. If

garrulous

friendly, garrulous Joe types the note, it takes some time for him to complete it.

                                                        January 28, 1968

Miss Rosemary Ramiriz
Secretary to Mr. John Breen
Accounting Department

Dear Miss Ramiriz:

I have checked the attached letter
again and again, but I cannot find
the enclosure. They must have forgotten to put it in the envelope.

*Incorrect use of pro-
noun "they"; no ante-
cedent is given.*

Perhaps they have already found it
and will mail it out immediately. As
soon as the next mail comes in, I
will see if this company has mailed
anything and open it right away. If
it is the check, I will deliver it to
you at once.

I am sorry this has happened and hope
that you will not have this trouble
again.

                        Sincerely yours,

                        Joseph Adams

                        Joseph Adams
                        Mail Room

When Miss Ramiriz read that note, she smiled; but she thought, "Joe must have a lot of extra time to write a note like this for a common error." She also mused: "What's the matter with the mail department? This is no way to handle this error."

Morton's cryptic note would have been more efficient if it had not become separated accidentally from the letter:

```
                          January 30, 1968

     Miss Aloise:

     Missing--the enclosure

               Morton Michaels
```

cryptic

Miss Aloise was annoyed when she found the 3 by 5 card unattached to a letter and without any reference information. Her remark typifies the reaction of business to errors or inefficiency: "What's going on in the mail department!" You notice that she did not question, "What's the matter with Morton Michaels?" As head of the department *you* must bear the responsibility for the procedures used in your department.

typifies

bear

To resolve the problem and to save time, you consider placing the word *Missing* in red next to the enclosure notation. But further marking the letters may bring objections from the addressee, so you decide to use a form. Since it will be addressed to another member of the company, you prepare an interoffice memorandum in which you can provide blank spaces for specific information.

Use blanks to make general form suitable for specific occasions.

Just as the notes of Joe and Morton represented not them but the department, so your note must show the efficiency of your department and its willingness to serve. What information is necessary? Three specifics must be referred to:

> The date of the letter.
> The name of the sender of the letter.
> The missing enclosure.

You prepare the following form and ask the duplicating department to run 500 copies for you:

```
              BUELL PRODUCTS CORPORATION
              Special Services Division


                                MAIL DEPARTMENT
                                Ext. 291

        DATE:

        TO:

        FROM:

        SUBJECT:

        The attached letter from_____

        _____, dated_____,

        did not contain the enclosure_____

        _____.
```

Length of blanks should suit information to be filled in.

Notice the difference from Joe's unprofessional letter. There is no reason to say that the letter was checked again and again. Are your procedures so inefficient that you could have lost the enclosure? Would you surmise that the sender had forgotten to put it in the envelope? Your objective is to give the necessary information. The department to which the letter is routed will handle the problem after that.

surmise

Your preparation of the memorandum form was a simple solution that kept your department running smoothly.

THE MEMORANDUM TO AVOID ERRORS

A few days later, the importance of writing instructions was forcefully brought to your attention by this news story:

The mail-room employee of Thewes and Company, a large brokerage house, was instructed by his supervisor to take the proxies of ABC Company from the Thewes mail room to the company's Shareowners' Relations Department — the unit responsible for relaying the proxies. On envelopes containing the proxies were the initials "SOR." Because of the initials the employee thought he had been told to take the material to the paper-shredding machine. The shredder made small pieces of the proxies in a few minutes.

Verbal instructions can be misunderstood.

With the loss of 2,800 proxies representing 400,000 shares of stock, Thewes and Company suffered considerable embarrassment and extra expense. The brokerage firm sent telegrams to the ABC shareholders asking them to call in their votes by phone and charge the phone bill to Thewes. The ABC shareholders' meeting was postponed indefinitely.

The mail-room employee resigned, but the major error was the lack of explicit written directions.

To prevent the occurrence of this type of error in your department, you immediately prepare a delivery slip in the form of an interoffice memorandum.

occurrence

```
      BUELL PRODUCTS CORPORATION
      Special Services Division


                  MAIL DEPARTMENT
                  Ext. 291

DATE:           TIME:

TO:

FROM:

SUBJECT:

Deliver to _____, Room _____.

Special instructions: _____

_____

                  Initials _____

Received by _____

Date _____  Time _____
```

Include all information. (Time is important in delivery.)

Initials place responsibility for the instructions.

Notice the receipt.

confirmation

Your memorandum provides short, simple, written directions that cannot be misunderstood and that can be referred to for confirmation.

THE DIRECTIVE

Your next problem is the effective servicing of the outgoing mail. No matter how many times you have mentioned to the secretaries and the office clerks that airmail letters would get much more rapid delivery if they were ready for the 2 p.m. mail pickup, the volume of airmail at the 4 p.m. pickup is still double that of the earlier one. Moreover, the secretaries, stenographers, and typists type the special mail services in different ways. Other annoying deterrents to rapid service — such as sealing the flaps, stuffing enclosures in the business-size envelope instead of using the legal-size envelope, or omitting the name of the sender at the top of the printed return address — interrupt the flow of operations. Following office procedure, you discuss the ways of handling the problem with the office manager, your

directive

immediate supervisor. He suggests that you send a directive to the employees of the Special Services Division, spelling out the exact procedures and requesting their cooperation.

You came to the office manager with a few problems. However, a directive must include *all* the regulations and procedures on outgoing mail. You plan to include these items:

> Mail-pickup service.
> Special mailing services.
> Bulk mailings.
> Typed envelopes.
> Enclosures.
> Mailing under separate cover.

Now that you have organized your thinking, let's work on the language you would use in writing a direc-

factual

tive. Your directive should be definite, factual. As its

name implies, it gives directions, and directions must be short and clearly stated so that no ambiguity can cloud the reader's understanding. For example, look at the following paragraph:

> Although it is sometimes possible to
> use the business-size envelope when
> you are enclosing small cards or
> forms, it is advisable to use the
> larger or legal-size envelope, re-
> ferred to as the No. 10 envelope,
> when making other enclosures. You will
> want to use the large manila envelope
> for bulkier enclosures.

Vague terms: "some-times," "other enclo-sures," "bulkier."
Passive: "it is advis-able."
Judgmental: "you will want."

Now see how a few improvements can clarify the instructions:

> Please use the No. 10 (legal size)
> envelope when enclosing five pages or
> fewer. Use the manila envelope for
> enclosures of more than five pages.
> To enclose small cards or half-sheet
> forms, you may use the No. 6 (busi-
> ness size) envelope.

There is no reason to write a directive if you allow exceptions to the stated procedures. Use an objective and impersonal tone in your directive, and make the language work for you. For example, the passive voice takes the burden off you and your department when you say:

> Outgoing mail will be picked up at
> 10:00 a.m., 11:30 a.m., 1:30 p.m.,
> and 4:30 p.m.

Use colon and cyphers ("10:00") when minutes appear in the list (as "11:30").

The clerical worker cannot ask you to pick up his mail at 10:15 a.m. or at 4:45 p.m. He must conform to the factual statement of procedure cited in the directive; it is impersonal and objective. You use this objective approach in the following directive:

conform
cited

BUELL PRODUCTS CORPORATION
Special Services Division

MAIL DEPARTMENT   Joseph DeNise
Ext. 291   Head

February 17, 1968

OUTGOING-MAIL PROCEDURES

Spell out numbers at the beginning of a sentence.
Hyphenate all numbers from twenty-one to ninety-nine.

<u>Organization</u>: Twenty-five pickup centers have been set up in all the departments of the Special Services Division. All outgoing and interoffice communications will be collected twice in the morning and twice in the afternoon at the following times:

<u>a.m.</u>	<u>p.m.</u>
10:00	1:30
11:30	4:30

respectively

The two morning pickups will be delivered to the post office at 11:30 a.m. and at 1:30 p.m. respectively, and the afternoon mail collections will reach the post office at 2:30 p.m. and 5:00 p.m. respectively.

Use headings for clarity.

<u>The Typed Envelope</u>: In order to facilitate work in the Mail Department, please use the following procedures in typing envelopes:

Notice parallel construction of this list — each item begins with a verb.

Give the complete address, including the zip code. (See form 105A, attached, for zip codes of the major cities in the United States.) Type the names of foreign countries in all capitals and underscore.

Note instructions for foreign addresses.

Type the name and department of the sender above the printed return address on the envelope. Metered mail must be charged to a department.

Type special mailing notations on
the right side of the envelope,
just below the position of the
stamps or meter indicia. These notations include: Airmail, Special
Delivery, Certified Mail, Registered Mail.

Leave the flap of the envelope
open. Let our stamping and sealing
machine do the work.

Type in all capitals a notation
for second-, third-, or fourth-
class mail below the place of the
stamps or meter indicia. If you
use a label for a package, place
the notation at the upper right of
the label.

*In a series of hyphen-
ated words with a com-
mon base, use a hyphen
after the first element
of each word, and write
the base after the last
word only.*

Special Services: Your Mail Department
will keep receipts for special services,
such as registered, insured, or certified
mail. "Return Receipt Requested" notices
will be sent to the individual department
requesting such service.

Bulk Mailings: Notify the Mail Department
at least five working days before the
mailing is to be sent out so that we can
prepare to give your mailing the attention
it requires.

PLEASE HELP US TO HELP YOU GET EFFICIENT
MAIL SERVICE!

*Remember the ameni-
ties.*

THE MEMORANDUM OF TRANSMITTAL

You cannot mail your directive without a coveriing
memorandum. To get the members of the Special
Services Division to follow the procedures outlined in
the directive, you must write a memo that will provoke
their interest in knowing what you have written and obtain their cooperation in following the procedures. To

Keep the reader in mind.

do so, your memo will have to show them how they benefit by these procedures.

How will you start? You consider three possible beginnings:

> Please read the attached directive carefully, and follow the procedures outlined there so that we may service your mail rapidly.

> The Mail Department needs your help!

> Does your airmail letter just miss the last post-office delivery to the terminal? Are you spending time need- lessly and delaying your letters by sealing envelopes? Your letters de- serve rapid delivery. The attached directive will tell you how to get them on their way.

You decide on the last approach, and you follow it with:

assure
"Assure you" is out- dated; use "give you."

The last two sentences do not fit into the man- aged whole; make them a postscript, or delete them.

> Please read this directive on Outgo- ing Mail Procedures. By following the procedures and meeting pickup dead- lines, you enable us to assure you of efficient mail service. Call us at any time for help with your special mailing problems. Our thanks for your cooperation.

approbation

worthwhile

You type the memorandum and the directive in good form for your supervisor's approval. That pat on the back and the smile of approbation make all the effort you put into this project worthwhile. The office manager predicts success for your department and you.

SUMMARY

In a business office, your communication does not represent only you — it represents your department, your division, your company. The error or inefficiency is not yours but your department's. The overly friendly, verbose letter detracts from the professional stature of the writer and the professional image of the department for which he works. The effectiveness of your communications redounds to your department's credit.

verbose

redounds

For the *recurring situation*, use a form that provides blanks for references to specifics. When these are to be used within the office, follow the style of the interoffice communication. Include: *Date, To, From,* and *Subject* in the heading.

To ensure *correct understanding and follow-through* on directions, the person issuing them should put them in writing. Remember the plight of the mailroom employee who misunderstood the directions for delivery of the proxies and brought them to the shredder.

ensure

When *general directions* are to be provided for a number of workers, the office or central agency providing the service issues a directive. The directive must be:

1. *Well organized.* Presentation, including major and minor headings and run-in headings, shows the whole picture. Tabulations are useful in listings.
2. *Complete.* All components of the operation must be included.
3. *Clearly stated.* Short, simple statements and exact words and phrases ensure correct follow-through of directions and avoid subjective interpretation by the reader.
4. *Objective.* Procedures are impersonal. The passive voice lends this tone to the directive.
5. *Polite.* The "please" may never be forgotten.

The directive is not addressed to any one individual, nor is it signed. Therefore, a *letter of transmittal* (in this case an interoffice memorandum) must accompany the directive to enlist the interest of the reader and his cooperation in following the procedures.

[1] SPELLING

Correct any misspellings in these sentences:

a. Its a difficult burden to bare, but the result is worth while.

b. His statement tipified the average soldier's attitude.

c. It was a normal occurence for him to recieve 30 letters a day.

d. The room was bare of furniture.

[2] VOCABULARY

a. In many cases, the meaning of a word can be altered significantly by a change of one letter. Choose the correct word in each of the following pairs:

> The improvements he has (*affected, effected*) will (*rebound, redound*) to his credit; but they only (*confirm, conform*) my opinion that (*further, farther*) changes are needed.

Now write a sentence or two in which you use correctly each of the words you did *not* choose above.

b. Give a short definition, in your own words, of each of the following:

cryptic	surmise	approbation
directive	factual	formulated

c. *Garrulous* and *verbose* both have to do with talking too much. How are the two words different?

[3] SOUND-ALIKES

Choose the appropriate word in each of these sentences:

a. He spoke (*respectively, respectfully*) about his superiors.

b. The engineers surveyed the (*cite, sight, site*) of the new building.

c. He (*ensured, assured*) her that it was correct.

d. If anyone disagrees with you, you may (*cite, sight, site*) the procedures outlined in the manual.

e. In order to (*assure, insure*) the watch, he had to (*ensure, assure*) the company of its value.

f. Meetings will be held with Mr. Jackson and with Mr. Brown (*respectively, respectfully*).

g. Please (*cite, sight, site*) him the clause in the contract that (*ensures, insures*) his protection.

h. You can (*cite, sight, site*) the parade from each building in turn.

[4] PUNCTUATION: SEMICOLON

The semicolon is a much stronger slowdown signal than the comma.

> RULE: *Use a semicolon to separate independent clauses of a compound sentence when these clauses are not joined by a coordinating conjunction.*
>
> > The game will be played this morning; the results will be known by noon. Many analysts worked on these figures; however, Mr. Jones received credit for the work.

See how easy it is to punctuate these sentences:

a. Register for your courses here then pay your fees at the business office.

b. The new engine is economical it is designed to use diesel fuel.

c. You must study thoughtfully otherwise you cannot succeed.

d. The date was July 10 1967 the place was Seattle Washington.

e. The books arrived on time but the bookstore was slow in displaying them.

f. Weather influences spending hence it affects our business.

[5] CAPITALIZATION

> RULE: *Capitalize a person's title when it precedes his name. Do not use capitals when the name precedes the title or when the title stands*

alone. (Exceptions to the latter rule are sometimes made in very formal writing, and a few titles are always capitalized — such as "the President of the United States.")

> Doctor Smith; President Cross; Chairman McManus; Senator Jones; Bureau Director Atkins
>
> James Ashmore, president of General Chambers; Albert Watson, the company doctor; the senator from Maine.

Note: Capitalize all titles, whether they precede or follow the name, when you type an inside address or an envelope.

> RULE: *Capitalize names of specific courses or departments, but do not capitalize fields of knowledge (except languages).*
>
> the Economics Department; Marketing 101; a course in French; studying geography and English history

> RULE: *Do not capitalize the names of the seasons.*

Apply our capitalization rules to correct these sentences:

a.   mr. raymond ewen, president of ewen electronics, will address the senior class during the spring semester.

b.   general george gates stated, "we shall fly to rome early friday morning."

c.   the secretary read the minutes of the fall meeting.

d.   john eggert, the mayor of springdale, spoke with secretary connors.

e.   marvin slade, president of the alpine ski club, has promoted winter sports.

f.   the professor said, "you should register for courses in economics, science, english, and history. I would recommend history 701 and economics 4 as a beginning."

g.   a purchasing department orders the supplies; the supply department only distributes them.

[6]   PRONOUNS

Watch the case of pronouns carefully. Take the pronoun *he,* for example. *He* is the nominative case and is used when the pronoun is the subject of a clause. *Him* is the objective case of this pronoun and is used when the pronoun is the object of a verb or a preposition. The third case is the possessive — *his* — and is used, of course, to show possession.

Most writers have little difficulty using the proper case of such pronouns as *he, she,* and *you.* But the case of the relative pronoun *who* is sometimes confused. *Who* is the nominative case; *whom* is the objective case; and *whose* is the possessive. Let's concentrate on the difference between *who* and *whom,* which usually gives the trouble.

RULE: *The case of a pronoun depends on its function in the clause.*

> Speak to the man who is at the desk.
> He is the student whom I met at the game.

In the first sentence, *who* is the subject of the clause "who is at the desk." In the second sentence, *whom* is the object of the verb *met* — "I met whom." Notice that in "I met whom" we have inverted the clause in order to place the subject (*I*) first, the verb (*met*) next, and the object (*whom*) last. Inverting the clause is an easy way to find out if your pronoun is a subject or an object.

The objective case is also used in this sentence:

> There is the boy to whom I gave the ticket.

Here the pronoun is the object of the preposition *to,* so we used the objective case, *whom.*

Now try your hand at picking the correct case in each of the sentences below. Remember to look for the subject and object of the clause — and don't be confused by intervening words or phrases.

a. Write letters to the many applicants (*who, whom*) we plan to interview on Saturday.

b. James Andrews is the man (*who, whom*) you may remember was chosen chairman of the committee last year.

c. Tell me if it is he (*who, whom*) the company should employ.

d. (*Who, Whom*) did you speak with when you telephoned the office yesterday?

e. Jack Moore is the man (*who, whom*) dreams up these singing commercials.

f. Here are several people to (*who, whom*) you can sell your product.

g. Have you spoken with the person (*who, whom*) they elected to the presidency?

h. Ignore businessmen (*who, whom*) you know are not truthful.

i.   The award goes to him (*who, whom*) works hard.

j.   (*Who, Whom*) do you wish to help?

[7] PROOFREADING

Mr. E. L. Jefferson, chairman of the Johnson and Marsh Company, has
written the following memorandum of transmittal to be given to all new
employees of the company. Because the girl who transcribed the memo is
a new employee, he asks you to check over her work to see that the memo
is written in correct form and that it contains no typographical or spelling
errors. Give the correct form of anything you find wrong. (List items in the
order in which they appear in the letter.)

JOHNSON AND MARSH COMPANY

Insurance Underwriters

To: New members of the staff of Johnson and March

From: E.L.Jefferson, chairman

Date: Oct. 10th, 1968

Subject: Welcome

Its my pleasure to welcome you, as a new employe, to the
staff of Johnson and Marsh. You will soon become aquainted
with many of fine men and woman who, over the years, have
found J&M a pleasent and rewarding place to work. I am
confident that thease experiencedsupervisers and co-workers
will make every effort to help you achieve a prompt and
happy adjustment to your new job.

To help you get off to a good start, we have prepared the
enclosed brochure giving you a brief history of the firm
and a description of the present scope and character of
our busness. The brochure is also a convient source of helpful information about our personal policies and facilities. I
hope you will read it carefully. If you should wish to get
additional information about any of the subjects discussed
I am sure that you immediate superviser will be glad to
help you-either by drawing on his own knowlege and expri-
ence or by referring you to the appropiate person within
our organization.

In closeing allow me to extend to you my sincere good
wishes for success and happiness in your new career at
Johnson and Marsh.

[8] PROBLEMS

a. Your supervisor has noticed that employees are taking an unusual
    amount of time during coffee breaks. Company policy allows a break
    of 15 minutes in the morning and a break of 15 minutes in the after-
    noon. Coffee and pastry are served at the employees' desks. Most of
    the employees are going from one desk to another and are taking
    about a half-hour on each coffee break. You are asked to write a direc-
    tive to be posted where all employees will be sure to see it. Restate
    the company policy — a 15-minute break at 10 a.m. and a 15-minute
    break at 3 p.m. Employees are to remain at their desks so that com-
    munications will not be disrupted during the coffee breaks.

b. Your employer had asked you to speak to the Accounting Club at the
    local junior college. You spoke about the courses you felt helped you
    when you went on your first job. Write a memorandum to your supe-
    rior to tell him what you spoke about at the meeting.

c. Andy Andersen, a long-time employee, has been transferred to the
    Milan office of your company. He is scheduled to leave for Milan on
    August 11. You feel that it would be appropriate for his coworkers to
    have a farewell dinner in his honor. Assume that you have gotten an
    estimate from the Peacock Club for a complete meal for $5.25, includ-
    ing gratuities. Write a memorandum to Andersen's coworkers inviting
    them to the dinner on August 1. The charge of $6.00 will include a
    gift for Mr. Andersen.

d. You have visited the local business-machine exposition, where you were
    favorably impressed with the RCS electric typewriter. You are using a
    15-year-old manual typewriter in your office. Write a memorandum to
    your superior to tell him of the advantages of using the electric type-
    writer.

e. Businessmen who call your company continually claim that they have
    difficulty in reaching the office they are calling. Since the telephone
    company has recently updated your telephone-communications system,
    the office manager feels that telephone privileges are being abused.
    The manager asks you to write a directive to be sent to all employees
    to restate the rules on telephone usage. He wants you to incorporate
    these ideas into your communication:

You will say that necessary local personal calls are allowed without charge. Personal long-distance calls are charged for, and the employee is expected to notify the operator when he makes such calls.

You will tell employees to keep personal calls to a minimum because they tie up the lines and interfere with the conduct of business. You will urge them to have personal calls come through either before 9:30 a.m. or after 4:30 p.m.

You will direct employees to dial their own numbers, to avoid asking the operator to look up numbers, to keep a list of frequently called business numbers on their desks.

f. Many employees have been working overtime at premium rates, and management has questioned the necessity for this expense. A careful investigation shows that people have been delaying some tasks until late in the day to earn overtime pay. You are asked to write a directive to make the rules on overtime work more stringent. You will incorporate these points into your directive:

The company will no longer permit an employee to work after office hours unless he secures approval in advance from the director of his department.

The company has set a 35-hour general workweek. Hourly employees who have approval to work overtime will receive the regular hourly rate up to 40 hours and the time-and-a-half rate after 40 hours. Under no circumstances may an employee work more than 45 hours a week.

g. Your office has recently moved to the outskirts of the city. Since the move took place, many employees have become careless about correct office attire — they have tended to become too casual. You are asked to compose a directive to be sent to all office employees to call their attention to correct office dress.

h. You are employed in the safety division of your company. There have been many accidents in the factory; several of them have been serious enough to have been reported in the local newspaper. The company has always taken pride in its safety record, and it has consistently been ahead of other companies in its field in installing the latest safety devices. Your superior feels that some of the foremen and supervisors have probably become negligent in enforcing safety regulations among their workers. You are asked to compose a memorandum to call all foremen and department heads to a meeting to be held on Friday, March 18, at 5 p.m., in the company cafeteria. Your superior wants to discuss the matter of safety with the foremen and department heads. You might ask them to be prepared to offer suggestions for improving the safety record.

i. Joe Blaine has been asked to write a memorandum to tell about the course in office management that he had taken at company expense. The company wanted to know about the course's content to see whether it would be advisable to send a group of employees to take the course. Here is Joe's memo. What do you think about it? Explain in detail; then rewrite the memorandum.

> I took the course in office management at State College during the semester from September to January. The course was offered at 6 p.m. until 7:15 p.m. on Tuesday nights. Because I felt it necessary to have a good dinner before attending class, I usually came in a little late but other students told me that I really didn't miss anything during the first quarter-hour or so. Because I had to rush to get to school, I couldn't pay as much attention to the lectures as I would have liked.
>
> Professor Jones lectured during most of the hour. Since the course was one in office management, he spoke about automation, correspondence techniques, filing, etc. It was a good course. I think that it would be good for the rest of our people to be able to take it.

10 | Claim and Adjustment Letters

AFTER a year as head of the Mail Department, you saw a classified advertisement describing an opening in the claims and adjustment department of a department store. Because you felt that the position offered opportunities and challenges, you applied. The job is yours.

THE PROBLEM

At your first orientation meeting, the manager identifies the two major objectives of the Claims and Adjustment Department: to build goodwill and to get repeat orders.

One way to build goodwill would be to give the customer what he demands whether or not his claim is justified. But every time you pay an unjustified claim, you add to the cost of the product or service of your company. This cost is ultimately reflected in higher prices, which will surely not bring repeat orders. Even the customer who was the recipient of the adjustment would quickly go to another department store to buy at lower prices. Not only are you asking your other

orientation

recipient

customers to pay for the mistakes of the customer who receives the adjustment, but you are projecting an image of weakness for your company. What respect do you receive from an individual who gets what he wants from you by deception or by unwarranted demands? Very little! The image you project for your company when you write that adjustment letter should be one of integrity and fair play.

What will you do with this claim?

unwarranted

```
Gentlemen:

I am returning this dress, priced at
$29.95, which was purchased two
months ago. The color has faded and
the fabric has shrunk so that the
dress does not fit. I am very dis-
pleased with this dress.

Please credit my account for $29.95.

               Yours truly,

               Mary James

               (Mrs.) Mary James
```

You know you must answer the letter speedily. The usual procedure in substantiating a claim of this type is to return the dress to the manufacturer for tests, which will take at least five days. In the meantime, how would you satisfy the customer? Would you send her this postcard?

substantiating

```
Your complaint has been received.
Your returned purchase has been sent
to the manufacturer for tests. You
will have to wait until the results
come in.
```

You can see that this communication violates the principles of good writing. What should you do instead?

Be positive: Avoid the use of the word "complaint."
Use clear, exact language: What returned purchase? What tests? When will the results be known?
Spotlight the reader: This communication implies that the testing is the important thing.
Enter the reader's world: You shouldn't be demanding **accept** that the reader accept your terms.

In addition, do not use a postcard; it detracts from the importance of the situation. This form of communication is used for general information, such as: "Your rug will be delivered on Friday, February 10." When you wish to develop rapport and understanding, when **rapport** you are discussing a difficult matter, as you are in the adjustment letter, give the courtesy of a letter, no matter how short it is. This note would give the customer an understanding of how you were handling her claim:

Dear Mrs. James:

We are sorry that you were displeased with the dress you bought from us.

The dress has been returned to the manufacturer, who will test the fabric for shrinkage and fading. The tests will take one week.

Thank you for telling us about your problem. You will hear from us as soon as we receive the manufacturer's report.

Sincerely yours,

When the report came back from the manufacturer, it read simply:

Shrinkage and fading were caused by
washing dress. Labeling instructions
warn against washing.

THE SOLUTION

guidance

Now you must answer Mrs. James and explain to her
satisfaction why you cannot accept her claim. You write
this letter and ask for guidance from the manager:

We cannot grant your request for a
credit of $29.95 for the dress you
returned to us on February 2. According to the manufacturer, you did not
follow directions for cleaning--you
washed the dress. This caused the
fading and shrinkage of the fabric.

Unfortunately, our company policy
does not permit us to make the adjustment when the customer is at
fault.

*Check for any way your
company might have
been at fault.*

conspicuous

The manager asks whether you checked with the
Dress Department to see if the "Dry Clean Only" label
was conspicuous enough on the dress. He points out
that if the label was not prominently displayed, the
Dress Department manager might agree to send Mrs.
James a new dress. That would make your letter much
easier to write.

Next, your manager asks you to reread your letter.
Does it build goodwill for the store? Will Mrs. James
want to buy there again? Or will your letter antagonize
her? You agree that your letter could be improved. Since
the Claims and Adjustment Department is giving a short,
in-service training program, the manager suggests that
you attend before rewriting your letter to Mrs. James.

A Positive Approach

At the first session, the speaker emphasizes the importance of keeping the customer satisfied. Whether you

accede to a claim or refuse to make an adjustment, he explains, you don't want· to lose the customer's good-will. Of course, you will be courteous and pleasant, but you should also be positive to minimize the unpleasant-ness of the situation.

accede
lose
(not "loose")

The speaker hands out the following list of nega-tive words and phrases that you should avoid:

> Your complaint; your error; you ne-glected; you say, state, or claim; you assert; we refuse; you have not followed directions; you misused.

Antagonistic.

> We are willing to allow you; we are at a loss to know; we are surprised to hear; we cannot understand; we are disappointed to hear; you failed to state; you would not want us to.

Belittling.

> It will never happen again; you can be sure; yours was the first com-plaint we ever had.

Doubtful.

When the Fault Is Yours

The second session of the training program deals with writing the letter to rectify a mistake your company made. When the fault is yours, you are told, be honest, and accept responsibility for your errors — don't try to deny them. Admit your mistake, and you will earn the customer's respect and understanding; try to cover up or shift the blame, and you will only irritate him.

rectify

THE BEGINNING

How should you begin? You remember from the previ-ous day's lesson that it is important to be positive. How can you write about your mistake, your defective product, or your deficient service so as to leave a positive impres-sion? When the group is asked to compare the follow-ing opening paragraphs, you can see the value of an apology.

deficient

We do not know how a mistake was made on your monthly statement.

Of course your monthly statement should be free of errors, and we are sorry that yours was not.

We have received your letter of June 8, in which you tell us that you received a damaged copy of Day's Long Summer.

A carefully packaged copy of Day's Long Summer is already on its way to you to replace your damaged copy. We're sorry that the back cover was crushed.

We have checked your allegation that the sales clerks in the camera department treated you rudely.

Thank you for telling us about your experience with the sales clerks in our camera department. Our apologies.

We cannot understand how there could be something wrong with your new Transo Radio.

We can understand how disappointed you must have been when your new Transo Radio did not work.

Because we have recently computerized our billing, your complaint about a bill being in error surprises us.

We're sorry. We have recently computerized our billing, but man-made errors still slip in.

Your claim that your mail doesn't arrive in time to enable you to take a discount is being looked into at once.

You have every reason to be disturbed about your bills' arriving late, especially when it affects your taking a discount.

It's hardly possible that your luggage could have been damaged on our New York to Lisbon flight, No. 136, on June 10.

Please accept our apology for the damage to your luggage on our New York to Lisbon flight, No. 136, on June 10.

An apology clears the air.

In each case, you see the advantage of admitting your mistake and expressing your regret. You yourself know that when someone says "I'm sorry" or "I apologize," the sting is taken out of your complaint. The speaker now turns to your next steps — to tell the customer what adjustment you will make and to explain the reasons for the error. These two steps, he says, may be interchanged, depending on the individual situation.

THE EXPLANATION

Be sure, the speaker cautions, to check carefully the reasons for your customer's complaint, since you must satisfy him with your explanation. Here are some ideas for explaining why something has gone wrong:

Much as we should like to do so, it is impractical for us to make a thorough inspection of every book that leaves our shipping room. We are glad to replace the ten copies.

A good explanation is logical and simple; it is not too elaborate, and it doesn't merely "make excuses."

Please excuse us during this transition period. Our computerized billing system will be straightened out this month. We know that you could not have placed 469 telephone calls a day from your home. Our computer must have confused you with a giant corporation. When human beings make mistakes, they can be serious; but when computers make them, they're astronomical.

Our new luggage-handling system has proved to be far more efficient than the system we had previously. But you know that it is impossible for any system to be 100 percent perfect. We have been working continuously to reduce the number of incidents in which damage occurs.

The reorganization of our local post office has caused some delays in handling outgoing mail. We hope conditions will improve shortly because they have inconvenienced us as well as our customers.

inconvenienced

During the rush season, many packages were handled by temporary employees. Although we paid the highest wage rates in the industry, we still found it difficult to get responsible employees in this tight labor market.

THE DECISION

You must tell your customer what adjustment you will make. You note this point: When the fault lies with you, the answer must be in the affirmative. Sentences such as these can be used to make the adjustment:

> You need not pay anything now. Just retain this statement until we send you a corrected bill.
>
> Please return the radio at our expense. When your new Transo Radio arrives, the Union Parcel delivery man will pick up the one you have.
>
> Please have your luggage repaired. Then send us your receipted bill, and you will receive reimbursement immediately.
>
> You are correct. The price of the No. 5 electric toaster is $21.95, not $24.95. Please disregard the original invoice, and pay $21.95 on the enclosed corrected invoice.
>
> Because the outgoing mail was behind schedule last month, we have extended the discount period two days. You will therefore be credited with the full discount.

invoice

THE CLOSING

As with all other letters that you write, you want your adjustment letter to come to a smooth finish. The speaker gives you these examples:

> Thank you for writing to us about your luggage. We appreciate our passengers' comments and suggestions, for this is the way we can improve our service to them. Please plan your future business and pleasure trips with TAW.

Please write us whenever you are not
satisfied with our accommodations. We
are here to serve you.

When our computer has been thoroughly
debugged, you will benefit from the
improved billing practices that automation makes possible.

thoroughly

Thank you for telling us about this
packaging problem. With our new procedures, including the required ten-
day training program, I am sure your
future orders, even during the rush
season, will be handled smoothly.

No matter how large our company becomes, we will never outgrow a personal interest in our customers'
problems.

When the Fault Is the Customer's

The subject of the third session of the training program
is the more difficult problem of answering a claim resulting from a customer's error. The speaker has the
following things to say:

A buyer may misunderstand the terms of a guarantee; he may take the wrong number from a catalog
when he places an order; he may take a cash discount
beyond the discount period; he may misuse the product. There are many other ways in which the buyer may
be at fault. Your watchword here is *tact*. You must do all
you can to retain the customer's business. Although each
case should stand on its own merits, you must not point
the finger of accusation at the buyer. Put yourself in his
place: How would you feel if you were to receive the
letter?

Above all, be tactful.

THE BEGINNING

The first sentence must be friendly; Don't come out
fighting. The best way to begin is to find an area of
agreement with your buyer. Here are some possibilities:

*Start with something
positive.*

We can readily appreciate your disappointment in not receiving your new
silk dress in time for Saturday's
wedding reception.

We are sorry that we sent you the
wrong book on your order of April 5.

We agree with you that you want color
when you buy a color TV.

Thank you for writing us so frankly
about our handling of your orders.

THE EXPLANATION

Take advantage of the passive voice.

minimize

Now get to the facts. An explanation of what has happened will then lead into an explanation of your decision. Use tact when you place responsibility. Here is a
place where the passive voice is helpful; it can be used
to minimize the personal aspect of the buyer's mistake.
"A mistake might have been made" sounds better than
"you made a mistake."

Compare these statements:

Harsh	Smoother
Evidently you did not read the terms of the contract.	Because it is possible that the terms of the contract were mis-understood, will you please re-read them carefully.
You must have read the catalog incorrectly when you copied the price.	The catalog may have been mis-read. The left column shows the price of one stamp, whereas the right column shows the price for the plate block that you ordered.
You mailed your order to us too late for us to get the dress to you on time.	Your order was received on Sat-urday. Thus, your dress could not go out until Monday morn-ing.

You didn't follow our advice to get a new color antenna when we originally installed the set. We did not guarantee good color reception under those circumstances.

If a color antenna had been installed when your set was delivered, reception would be excellent. I believe our serviceman recommended at that time that you change your antenna.

When you purchased your linoleum, we advised you to buy Tufguard because of your heavy traffic from outdoors.

As we mentioned, Tufguard is the only linoleum guaranteed to resist the heavy traffic of muddy and icy feet. Your linoleum can be protected, however, by "Hardiwaxing" once a week.

Our testing department reveals that you have washed the jacket in hot water, even though the label clearly reads "Dry Clean Only."

Our testing department reports that the jacket must have been washed in hot water. The cleaning-instructions tag and the label reading "Dry Clean Only" must have escaped your notice.

You didn't consider the size of your walk and garage when you ordered the snow thrower.

Yes, our No. 2 snow thrower takes care of the country estate of hundreds of feet, acres in fact. You will find our No. 15 more suitable for your 100-foot drive and walk. It is small enough to be stored next to your car in the garage.

THE DECISION

After you have explained to the customer why something has gone wrong, a question remains: Will you make an adjustment?

If the decision is yours to make, you must naturally consider the type of mistake the buyer has made. (At this point in the lecture, you remember Mrs. James' complaint. Did she just ignore the "Dry Clean Only" label, or was it so inconspicuous that she might reasonably have missed it?) You must also consider the kind of merchandise and its cost. (You might be willing to replace a $25 dress but not a $350 coat.) Another consideration is whether the claim seems to be honest or whether it is spurious and the buyer merely hopes to   **spurious**

take advantage of you. A favorable adjustment will keep
a buyer's goodwill; but, after weighing all the consider-
ations, you may have to take the more difficult path of
refusing to make the adjustment.

The favorable adjustment. When you act to grant
a claim, either wholly or partially, do it with a smile, not
a grudging attitude.

> Because you have not yet used your
> snow thrower, we will gladly exchange
> it for a smaller model that will bet-
> ter fit your needs. Just have it
> ready to return to our trucker when
> he delivers your new model No. 15.

alleviated

> Although we cannot replace your lino-
> leum, we are sending you a trial sam-
> ple of Hardiwax, which will give your
> floors a tough-as-iron finish. If you
> use Hardiwax according to instruc-
> tions, your problem should be allevi-
> ated.

> Although a color antenna costs $60 at
> any time other than when the TV set
> is delivered, we will install your
> color TV antenna for the low price of
> $45 if you want it. Then you'll get
> 100 percent color enjoyment.

ample

> Certainly, you may return the dress
> to us. We do not want you to keep a
> dress you cannot use. Instead, why
> not order something for spring. Our
> newest styles have just arrived. If
> you order now, you will have your
> spring clothes on hand in ample time
> for the new season.

Saying no. Sometimes you have to say no. It is
easy to say, "Company policy prevents us from allowing
your claim." But this makes your company an impersonal behemoth that does not consider the customer
as an individual. Make the customer feel that his complaint is important and that he has received an individ-

ual evaluation of his claim. Compare these ideas for refusals:

Your guarantee has expired, so we will not repair your clock without further charge.	Because the guarantee expired two years ago, we must charge for repairs on your clock.
You must mail us $5.80 or return the plate block at once.	If you wish to keep the plate block, please send us your check for $5.80 to cover the difference between what you have already paid and the actual cost.
Because the garment was not cleaned according to instructions, it is impossible to allow your claim.	We should like to send you a new jacket; but, since the cleaning instructions were written so clearly, we cannot do so.
Terms of sale read 2/10, n/30. Company policy dictates that we must adhere strictly to the terms; we cannot favor some customers at the expense of others.	In fairness to all our customers, we must maintain a consistent policy on discounts. Of course, we want you to take advantage of our discount policy, but we can grant a discount only when the invoice is paid within the discount period.

THE CLOSING

End your letter on a positive note. (Incidentally, if you have refused to make an adjustment, don't close by referring to the complaint. You don't want to leave your reader with that thought.) These statements assure an affirmative ending:

If you want a new color TV antenna, just mail the enclosed card. Our qualified serviceman will come to install your antenna whenever you wish.   qualified

Pack the dress carefully, and return it to us. When it arrives, we shall credit your account.

```
I am glad you wrote to us, because it
will avoid any future misunderstand-
ing about our discount policy.

We hope you will get many years of
excellent service from your Atlas
snow thrower.
```

When you give an honest, open explanation and a fair adjustment to a claim, you keep your customer's goodwill and his respect.

The "Preadjustment" Letter

The final session of the in-service training program opened with this question: Is there any way to prevent future claim letters? The speaker cited the case of a major utility that had increased its charges for electricity. This company took the precaution to enclose the following letter with each utility bill that was mailed. You might call this a "preadjustment" letter, because the company obviously hoped to forestall the receipt of thousands of telephone calls and complaint letters asking for an adjustment on the bill.

forestall

```
Dear Customer:

We would love to keep electricity
rates at the 1960 level, if somebody
would tell us where to buy copper
cable, trucks, iron pipe, switching
panels, rubber gloves, and the like
at 1960 prices.

And, while he's at it, he might also
find a way to roll back our taxes.
Today, Consumers Power is paying the
highest local and state taxes ever
imposed on a power company. For 1969,
these taxes will total some $155 mil-
lion on our electricity business
alone--an increase of $64 million
since 1960.
```

We realize that everybody has to pay
taxes. Taxes are part and parcel of
doing business these days. It's also
a fact that taxes, like any other operating expense, must be paid out of
the money we receive for our services. When taxes, along with practi-
cally all the other costs of providing electrical service, keep going
up, there comes a time when rates
have to go up, too.

So, recently, electricity rates were
moderately increased--an increase
that was absolutely necessary to ensure a continuation of the reliable
electrical service our customers must
have.

                          CONSUMERS POWER COMPANY

THE FINAL PRODUCT

Now that you have taken the training course, you feel
capable of rewriting that letter to Mrs. James. First, you
check with the Dress Department manager, who feels
that perhaps the label was not as visible as it should   **visible**
have been. He agrees to send Mrs. James a new dress
and says he plans to revise the department's labeling
policy.
      Then you write the following letter:

Dear Mrs. James:

The Glamour Dress Company found the
culprits--soap and water. Your dress   **culprits**
fabric must be dry cleaned only. Be-
cause of your experience, we are adding another label--a large blue one,
attached to the sleeve, that urges:

      "Please don't wash me. I
      can't stand soap and water!"

> Of course, we will continue to use in
> the neckline the label we have been
> using.
>
> While we cannot credit your account,
> we can send you a new dress. It is on
> its way to you; we hope you will en-
> joy it.
>
> We are sorry that you had this prob-
> lem with your dress. Thanks for writ-
> ing us about it.
>
>   Sincerely yours,

You are pleased with this letter — and so is your supervisor.

SUMMARY

When you write your adjustment letters in answer to
customers' claims, direct your efforts toward developing
goodwill. You expect to keep your customer satisfied
by granting the adjustment gracefully or by refusing it
tactfully.

Answer claim letters immediately. When the fault
is yours, admit the error, accept your responsibility for
the mistake, and apologize. Avoid those negative expressions that seem to convey your displeasure at being
taken to task by the customer. Naturally, your answer
to a justified claim letter is that you will gladly make the
adjustment for the customer.

Your problem in writing the adjustment letter is
more difficult to solve when the customer is at fault.
Your company's integrity must be maintained by refusing unwarranted demands, but the customer's demands

must be given serious consideration. Show the customer that your company has given his complaint a personal evaluation but that it cannot accede to his request. Fair and impartial decisions based on policy win your customer's respect for the company.

In all your adjustment letters, use forthright, positive language that tells your customer that you stand behind your product and your service.

[1] SPELLING

a. Correct end-of-line hyphenation is an important part of good letter mechanics. Can you divide these words into syllables?

recipient   minimize   inconvenience   deficient

b. Correct the spelling in this paragraph:

Helen requires your guidence. She wants to forstall any complaints by writing a letter that covers throughly all the recomendations that have been made. In the prosess, she'd like to emphasize the visable improvements that have all ready been made.

[2] VOCABULARY

a. What does the italicized word mean in each of these sentences?

He was not *qualified* for the position.
He *qualified* his original statement.

Can you *alleviate* their distress?
Can you *rectify* their error?
Can you *assuage* their feelings?

b. Give a synonym for each of these words:

invoice   ample   substantiate   conspicuous   spurious

c. Use each of the words listed below in a sentence that illustrates the word's meaning.

rapport   orientation   culprit   accede

[3] SOUND-ALIKES

Choose the correct word in each of these sentences:

a. Please (*accept, except*) my apology for sending you the wrong package.

b. After the label became (*lose, loose*), it must have dropped to the floor.

c. You may expect to (*lose, loose*) the respect of your customers when you do not write honestly.

d. It became an (*accepted, excepted*) way to handle such complaints.

e. All members of the sales team (*accept, except*) the sales manager are expected to attend the meeting.

f. He left instructions to set the dogs (*lose, loose*), but John was afraid he'd (*lose, loose*) track of them.

[4] PUNCTUATION: SEMICOLON

> RULE: *Use a semicolon in place of the usual comma before the co-ordinating conjunction in a compound sentence when the clauses are long or already contain commas.*

> > Professor Allen taught marketing, statistics, and finance; but his specialty was monetary theory.

> RULE: *Use semicolons between items in a series when one or more of the items contains commas.*

> > Our club speakers were John Evans, a former student; Ronald Duggan, a financial analyst; and Sylvia Lerner, a fashion designer.
> > While on the tour, they learned something about shipbuilding; studied the lumber, fur, and copper trade of the region; and attended an industrial-planning meeting.

Note: Use a semicolon only between equivalent items — to separate clauses from clauses, for example, or phrases from phrases. A semicolon should *not* be used to separate a clause from a phrase or an independent clause from a dependent one, even if the items are long or contain commas.

Correct the punctuation of the following sentences. (You may have to change some punctuation as well as to add further punctuation.)

a. There were two members from Chicago, Illinois, four from Boston,

      Massachusetts, twelve from Spokane, Washington, and one from Anchorage, Alaska.

b.   Mr. Edgar can teach French, Spanish and Italian and Mr. Burke can teach history, economics and economic geography.

c.   The first meeting of our club will be held on Monday January 8, and the second meeting will be held on Thursday July 1.

d.   Rule your paper, write your name at the top, number the lines from one to ten.

e.   Although we went to the brunch, the rally, and the game; we were still going strong in the evening.

f.   Sally was reading, Babs was playing the piano, and Joan was taking a nap.

g.   The situation is serious, therefore we shall appropriate funds.

h.   Marty handles a bat well; is an excellent skier; and plays tournament tennis.

[5] PRONOUNS

Remember our discussion of cases in Chapter 9? Here are two more rules about the correct use of case:

> RULE: *Use the nominative case of a pronoun when it is used as a predicate pronoun.*
>
>> It is he who will make the decisions.
>> It is she at the door.

Note: Although usage has made it acceptable to use "it's me," "it's him," and so on in speaking, you should always use the nominative case in writing.

> RULE: *Use the possessive case of a pronoun when it modifies a gerund.* (A gerund is the *ing* form of a verb when it is used as a noun.)
>
>> I oppose your accepting the blame for something you did not do.
>> His paying the bill restored his credit standing.

Use your knowledge of case to make the necessary corrections in these sentences:

a.   Before we can go ahead, your approval of us signing the paper will be needed.

b.   The president says that it is you who are to blame.

c.   The winner of the award was probably Mr. Baker or me.

d.   There can be no agreement between him and me.

e.   Type two copies for the president, whom I know will need them.

f.   There is no possibility of me changing my mind.

g.   Do you object to us working on the project with you?

h.   There's the man who saw the whole thing.

i.   Since it is him who has made the mistake, no one will object.

j.   The project was submitted by the committee members — by he, she, and I.

[6] NUMBERS

Rules for handling numbers vary with the type of writing you are doing. If you pick up three or four books, you will probably find that their number styles differ. However, in any particular piece of writing, the treatment of numbers must be consistent. The rules we have been giving you in the marginal notations of this book are those generally followed in business correspondence, and you should learn to use them.

RULE: *Spell out numbers one through ten; write numbers larger than ten in figures.*

There are ten men on the squad.
He spoke for 45 minutes.

RULE: *All numbers in a group should be expressed in figures. But, if a sentence contains two series of numbers running concurrently, express one series in words and the other in numbers for clarity.*

Order 28 chairs, 6 tables, and 5 lamps.
Two players scored 3 runs; three players scored 2 runs; and one player scored 1 run.

RULE: *If your sentence begins with a number, write out the number.*

Sixty courses are offered in this department, and no other department offers more than 35.

Note: If the number is complex, it is better to reword the sentence than to have to write out that number. "There are 365 days in a year" is better than "Three hundred sixty-five days make a year."

Apply these rules to the sentences that follow, writing the correct forms.

a.   47 salesmen attended the 3 meetings.

b.   The Appliance Department sold 30 radios in April, 25 in May, and only six in June.

c.   After you have read these 10 letters, will you make some suggestions?

d.   We shall open our new Hartford store in twenty-five days.

e.   Five firms employed 15 clerks, and 3 firms are willing to employ 12 more.

[7] **PROBLEMS**

a.   Revise these adjustment letters:

```
We are surprised to receive your letter of complaint of
January 12. While you had requested Gemex tires on your new
car, your dealer gave you Royax tires because all cars of
that model come factory equipped with Royax tires--the best
that money can buy.

Now for your specific complaint about Royax tires. Because
you had your mind made up for another brand, you probably
looked for weaknesses in Royax tires. You claim that they
cause a thumping action when you reach a speed of 60 miles
an hour. Are you sure that your wheels are balanced cor-
rectly? Are you sure that the tires are inflated properly?

We are willing to make some concessions to you. Instead of
going to your car dealer, drive to James Kent, your nearest
Royax dealer. He will check your tires thoroughly. If there
is something wrong with the tires, he will give you a pro
rata allowance toward the purchase of a set of new tires.
In other words, you will pay only for the mileage you al-
ready have on your tires.

If you follow Mr. Kent's instructions, you will never have
to write another letter of complaint to us.
```

```
We cannot understand your claim that an Adma Model X824,
for which you paid $649, is sold for $588 in Lord's Appli-
ance Shop.

As you know, we pride ourselves on the fact that we will
not be undersold. In cases where people claim that another
```

store sells at a lower price, we immediately send our com-
parison shopper to see whether the complaints are true.
This is what we have done in your case.

You ought to be glad to know that we are allowing you the
difference in price just as we say in our advertisements.
We value your patronage and want you to continue to buy
with us.

Your check for $61 is herewith enclosed.

———————

Your complaint of April 15 was received and turned over to
me for my attention.

Re your statement that the sweater you purchased is not
colorfast, I am sorry to advise that our testing department
informs me that some strong bleachlike solution must have
been used for cleaning. No colored material, regardless of
cost, can be subjected to bleaches without destroying the
color.

Under the circumstances as stated above, we cannot send you
a new sweater; nor can we grant you credit for same.

I am sorry to have to refuse your request, but you are
clearly in error in this case.

b.   Rewrite these opening sentences:

1.   We are sorry that we cannot accept the return of the blouse that
     you bought on August 5.

2.   You are certainly being unfair to us when you insinuate that we
     tried to put something over on you by sending you a defective
     lamp.

3.   We cannot understand how your records could have been broken
     as you claim in your letter of March 10.

4.   We are surprised to learn that you are already having trouble with
     your Cine movie projector.

5.   In answer to your letter expressing dissatisfaction with your dic-
     tating machine, I wish to state that we stand behind anything
     we sell.

6. Your complaint that the woolen fabrics we sold you are defective is under consideration.

7. It's too bad that you didn't receive anything that you had ordered on June 5.

8. Your misreading of the instructions is probably the reason for your not being able to assemble the table about which you complain.

9. Your letter complaining about Stakleen is the first one we have ever received attacking this fine product.

c. Revise these statements granting or refusing adjustments:

1. Although we are not at fault, we are willing to accept return of the lamp shade.

2. It is simply impossible for us to grant your request. Everyone gets the same fair treatment at Gordon's.

3. Since the delay in delivery was not our fault, we cannot accept the responsibility for your loss.

4. We shall be willing to exchange the machine in order to retain you as a valued customer.

5. We will make this concession to you, even though it is much more than should be expected under the circumstances.

6. Since we advised you to be home to accept the delivery, you must pay the additional delivery fee or face suit.

d. You are employed at Harris Sporting Shop. It is April 1. Mr. Jones, a steady mail-order customer, has written to tell you that a casting reel he bought in January has no spool. He had not opened the package when he purchased the reel because he planned to keep it packaged until the end of March, when the trout season was to open. Naturally, he was disappointed that he could not use his new spinning reel. Write an adjustment letter to solve this problem. Your letter might tell Mr. Jones that you are sending a spinning reel by special delivery. Be sure to tell him how sorry you are about his misfortune.

e. You are employed by Peers Camera Company. A customer in another city ordered 50 inexpensive cameras, which you sent out by freight — your usual method of shipping. The customer has written a letter to complain that he did not receive the cameras in time for a giveaway he had planned for his special sale days. He had not told you anything about wanting faster shipment or about a date when he needed the cameras. How would you handle his complaint?

f.   A mail-order customer ordered an "as is" coat from a Grassman's ad. She now writes that she wants to return the coat because it has a slight defect. You must refuse her request. Write the letter to tell Grassman's part of the story, but try to keep her goodwill.

g.   You are employed by Colorlabs, which processes film. You have received several complaints from Mr. Ritter about the way in which his films have been processed. He asks for new film because of your poor work. On two previous occasions you have told Mr. Ritter that his camera must be defective. You ask him again to have it checked. You might say that you do not wish him to send more film for processing unless he has his camera checked, because he is really wasting his money.

h.   You work for Colonial Printers. You have received a letter from a customer asking for a corrected rerun of stationery on which an error has been made in his address. The stationery read "105 Read Avenue," when it should have been "105 Reade Avenue." What type of adjustment would you make? When you have decided what your solution should be, write a letter to the customer.

 i.   Kurt Fleming has a subscription to *Great Speeches* magazine that expires in December. He paid for a reduced-rate renewal in May. He received two copies of the magazine in June and two copies in July, at which time he wrote to clear up the misunderstanding. In August, he received two copies of the magazine with an invoice for the subscription. He wrote another letter. You check with the subscription department and uncover a clerical error that has caused the problem. Write to Mr. Fleming to apologize for the trouble he has been caused. Naturally, he will not pay for the duplicate magazines.

j.   You have received a letter threatening legal proceedings because the customer has found a small piece of metal in a can of White Crest pears. He says that he could have broken a tooth or swallowed the metal if he had not seen it. Write a letter to handle this adjustment.

11 | The Sales Letter

YOU HAVE been with the TRK Textile Company for six months and are considered a permanent employee. As part of management's policy of maintaining flexibility of personnel, you are assigned to a training program, which will take you to a different department every two weeks for the next two months. Your first assignment is to the Advertising Department.

flexibility

In your preliminary meeting with the manager, you glean these facts: The department utilizes the usual communications media — television, telephone, radio, newspapers, magazines — in its sales campaigns. It also relies on bulk mailings of sales letters.

glean
media

KNOW YOUR MARKET

You are quick to ask the manager how he decides which method to use, and he explains that the most important criterion is what audience the company wants to reach. To sell a product through advertising, you must know your market — your customers. If, for example, the objective of a sales campaign is to attract new textile retailers for the company's wholesale division, an ad in one of the trade magazines would be a good choice. On the other hand, a newspaper or radio advertisement would probably be the most effective and least costly way to inform the general public of a sale in the company's department store. But, to reach a specific group of individuals, TRK often uses the personal touch of the sales letter. For example, charge customers are usu-

prior

ally given prior notice of certain sales in department stores; for that purpose a written communication to each person on the list will bring a greater response than would an ad in the newspaper.

TRK is currently working on a campaign to attract new charge customers. After some consideration, the Advertising Department decided to use the sales-letter technique, on the premise that the personal touch of

premise

an individual letter would help to bring new customers to the company.

In showing you how this program is being developed, the manager explains some of the fundamentals of bulk mailing. Here, too, the key requirement is knowing the market. For example, if you were trying to sell jewelry priced at $5,000 or more, it would be senseless to send a direct-mail piece to everybody in the city directory, since the great majority of people couldn't afford such expensive merchandise.

potential

For TRK's present mailing program, a list of potential customers has been obtained from a company that supplies such lists, but an important clerical operation is needed before the list is used. The names of persons who already have charge accounts with TRK must be eliminated. Think how quickly you would puncture a customer's ego if you sent him a form letter inviting him to open a charge account when he had had one for years!

Meanwhile, the manager's assistant, Mr. Jaspers, is at work composing the sales letter. This is the heart of the campaign, and it requires careful thought. You are now turned over to Mr. Jaspers, who will explain to you how he goes about writing such a letter.

THE TRUTH SELLS BEST

To sell a product, he begins, you must really know its
attributes and write about them truthfully. If you ask a   **attributes**
novice what the objective of a sales letter is, he may
tell you: "To sell the largest amount possible." Many
companies are willing to settle for this inadequate con-   **inadequate**
cept, which takes the customer out of the picture and
substitutes a dollar sign with the product under it. After
buying a product, have you ever said, "That's the last
time I'll ever buy that!" The product did not live up to
the promises of the advertisers. When your sales letter
presents a false picture, it will not only lose customers;
it will destroy the company's name as a reputable business. True, you may make a one-time "killing," to use
the jargon of the trade; but your company cannot live
on past successes. The sales letter that ultimately makes   **ultimately**
money for a business is the letter that builds repeat
sales. Its objectives are:

> To create customer interest in, and a predilection for,   **predilection**
>   the product.
> To get action.
> To develop continuing customer demand for the product.

You want a customer to say:

> I always go to Atman's for my rugs.   *Quotations of three*
> Everything they say about their rugs   *lines or more are single*
> is true--they do grow in beauty, and   *spaced and indented*
> they show no wear after years of   *from each margin; quo-*
> service.   *tation marks are omit-*
>   *ted.*

Not only will she always patronize Atman's, but she will   **patronize**
convince her daughter and daughter-in-law to rely on
the judgment of the company's rug department.

WILL YOUR LETTER BE READ?

Keeping in mind that ultimate purpose of the sales letter
— to build repeat sales — you are now ready to tackle
the first problem: how to get a prospective customer

to read your sales letter. You receive many letters trying to get you to buy something. Why do some of these letters get a positive response from you?

Appeal to the Customer

excerpts

Mr. Jaspers asks you to look at some excerpts from successful sales letters:

> Will you be one of the 25 skiers who
> will win the Swiss skis at Snow Peak
> this Sunday, February 27? Return this
> card, and come to see the skiing
> demonstration at three o'clock. If
> you are there and your number is
> called, the Swiss Speed Skis are
> yours.

> Please listen to this record. You
> will hear some of the most beauti-
> fully read passages in the literary
> world.

> Here are four rugs for you to see in
> their full color and beauty. Just
> place each slide in the enclosed pro-
> jector, hold it up to the light, and
> you will see each rug in the comfort
> and convenience of your own home.

chrome

> Please put this 10 cents toward your
> purchase of Tru-Blu Chrome Cleaner.

You can see that these paragraphs make the customer the center of attention; they talk about the product's advantages for *him*. These are the letters that are read, Mr. Jaspers tells you. And, when you compare the following paragraphs, you can readily see that customer appeal is much more effective than product appeal.

Product appeal	Customer appeal
We are enclosing a sample of our long-lasting cold-relief pill.	Here is your long-lasting re-lief from cold miseries.

We wish to announce the opening of our new suburban store on October 10, in ample time for your Christmas shopping.

Your Christmas shopping this year will be easier than ever in our new store, which opens on October 10. Please join us for the opening.

We are hereby notifying you that there are spare-time employment opportunities at TRK Textile Company, located in your town.

Are you an experienced clerical worker tired of traveling, tired of fighting crowds? Are you looking for extra money? Apply at TRK Textile for a part-time clerical position.

The All-Important Opening

Spotlighting the reader makes him receptive to your communication, but you realize that your opening sentence must first have enough punch to get his attention. Mr. Jaspers is just getting to that; he illustrates a few techniques that the department uses:

Ask a question. Your question must interest the reader in getting an answer. Some letters that use the question approach begin like this:

> Planning to buy a new color television?

> Can you afford not to read The Weekly Review?

Remember to underline magazine titles.

> Do you want your living-room furniture to look like new?

> When was the last time you checked the tread of your tires? Have you traveled 15,000, 20,000, 25,000 miles on them?

Here are some good examples of this technique that arrived in the incoming mail this week:

> Where do you want to spend your vacation?

Can your chief file clerk leave without your being worried about your
files?

Do you want your employees to stand
out at the next convention?

What are you doing to provide for
your family's future security?

fulfills

enlivened

Open with a direct statement. This method arouses interest if it solves a problem, fulfills a need, or satisfies some desire of your reader. It is one of the easiest openings for a sales letter. But use that "you" in the beginning sentence. Note how the colorless openings on the left can be enlivened by appealing to the reader's interest, as in the sentences on the right.

Colorless	Appealing to reader's interests
We are having a year-end sale on all merchandise in our bargain basement.	Now you can save more than ever in our bargain basement at our year-end sale.
Our magazine keeps you in touch with current events for only a few pennies a day.	For only 4 cents a day, you can keep in touch with what is happening in the world today.
We want to take a few minutes to describe the perfect gift for the busy student.	Give us a couple of minutes to tell you about the perfect gift for the busy student you know.

Mr. Jaspers pulls three letters from the incoming mail and shows you how he would rewrite their opening sentences.

We want to tell you how you can get the new books you want at the greatest savings anywhere.	You will find the TRK Book Club the way to get the new books you want at the greatest possible savings.

Many business firms are victimized by fire every day, and
most of them are seriously handicapped because they lose
their records.

Every 56 minutes, 14 or more
firms are victimized by fire.
And 13 of these victims are
seriously handicapped because
they lose their records. It's
14 to 1 you, too, are inviting
this tragedy.

We are writing to tell you how
you can improve your filing
system.

Put your records at your fin-
gertips with Martax.

Use a courteous command. But make it positive,
not negative.

Negative	Positive
Do not fail to take advantage of this money-saving offer.	Take advantage of this money-saving offer.
Don't forget to have your car checked thoroughly before you take that long summer trip.	Have your car checked thoroughly before you take that long summer trip.
Avoid waiting any longer to plan that round-the-world trip.	Plan ahead for that round-the-world trip.
Don't drive on tires that should be replaced.	For safety's sake, replace those worn tires today.
Don't postpone paying your taxes because you have no money.	Pay your taxes on time. Get your tax loan at United.

Use a testimonial or a quotation from an eminent   **eminent**
person. Be sure, though, that the person is someone
your reader will know about.

"My trip with Arrow Tours," writes
Dr. Martin Dunn, well-known neuro-
surgeon, "was sheer pleasure all the
way. My every need was provided for."

"Thank you for your assistance in
helping us to make our 1968 spring
campaign such a success," writes Mr.
Rickenbacker, president of the Life
Insurance Company of Alabama.

Last year's winner of the Emons
Award, Miss Anne Poppins, stays at
the Hall Hotel whenever she visits
Portland.

After 24 leading bankers looked over
all makes of typewriters, they chose
Fastwrite.

*(To encourage member-
ship in a professional
organization.)*

Charles **Dickens** once wrote: "It is
well for a man to respect his own vocation whatever it is, and to think
himself bound to uphold it, and to
claim for it the respect it deserves."

topical

Use a topical reference.

School opens soon. Come in for your
back-to-school wardrobe.

Earn your tuition for your senior
year. Apply at TRK for a summer job.

Easter arrives early this year. Is it
too soon to talk about an outdoor
pool?

Use the headline or two-line idea. Although the
advertising division had not used this technique lately,
these copies of incoming mail showed its effectiveness:

HURRY
Deposit money before the tenth of the
month to earn interest from the
first.

You asked for it . . .
     Now pack up and go . . .

```
What are you doing in New York??
You could have flown to Paris
this morning!

Here's a challenge . . .
Read how First American squeezes
6-1/2% interest out of a 10-year,          Banks usually use the %
5% savings bond.                           sign for percents.
```

SELLING THE PRODUCT

Develop a Desire
for the Product or Service

You have caught the attention of your reader with that
first sentence. Now — sell your product. Create a desire
for that product, a preference for it over other items   preference
the reader may want and need, by showing him how he
will benefit from your offering. Mr. Jaspers illustrates by
making the following revisions in some letters received
last week:

Original	Revision
We can give you the type of engraving service that will satisfy all your needs.	Do you want invitations engraved? Artistic personal letterheads? Specially designed cocktail- or dinner-party invitations? Embossed calling cards?
Our hand-made shoes are beyond comparison for comfort and style.	You can walk a mile or stand on your feet for hours in style and in comfort you have never known! You owe it to yourself to try our hand-made, specially fitted shoes. Remember your two feet are the only ones you'll ever have.
<u>Contemporary American Economics</u> boasts of broad coverage of major issues by leading economists and financiers of the nation.	Let the leading economists and financiers of the nation discuss the major economic and monetary issues of our nation with you. Just let us deliver <u>Contemporary American Economics</u> to you each month.

Our Mary Ellen Couturier Salon
is known as the most exclusive
salon in this area. Of course,
we make only one of a kind.

When you want an elegant original that is yours alone, come
to the Mary Ellen Couturier
Salon at TRK.

As you read your mail that evening, you decide
to try to improve an advertisement that you received:

Original

Our Super jets fly at the rate
of 600 miles an hour at an al-
titude of 35,000 feet. They
will take off from JFK Airport
and land in London in five
hours. We serve excellent cui-
sine and entertain with the
finest and newest films. Our
service includes hotel and
theater reservations if you
wish.

Revision

You can be in London in five
hours, flying through the
stratosphere at 600 miles per
hour. You will enjoy a gourmet
dinner and, if you wish, see
one of the newest films. And
when we set down in London, you
will be taken directly to the
hotel room we have reserved for
you. Do you want tickets for
the theater? We will be glad to
have them waiting for you.

Enable the Prospective Customer to Come to a Decision

entails

The decision to buy a product entails more than bring-
ing the customer to the point of saying, "I want that
product." He must go one step farther and say, "I am
willing to pay the price asked for this product or service." Because this is an individual judgment, Mr. Jaspers
points out, you should give your customer the facts,

unique

describe the unique attributes of your product or service, and tell him why it is worth the asking price. Show
your respect for his judgment by letting him evaluate
the facts.

Several methods may drive home the answer to
the question: "Why should I buy the product?"

Present testimonials from satisfied users. How
often do you ask your friend what he thinks about a
product before you buy it? It is a natural way to get a
firsthand reaction from someone you know. The sales
letter can use that technique. Here's how a seller of

power mowers used a testimonial from a satisfied
customer:

> One of your neighbors, Morris London,
> writes to us: "I have just acquired
> my Scout Lawn Mower and must say that
> it is a real pleasure. I just roll it
> out, and 'away we go.' Imagine, no
> more wasting time trying to get a
> balky engine started."

The producer of a lawn builder uses this testimonial:

> Alley Pond Nurseries, the largest
> landscaper in Mansfield, writes: "We
> have acquired more customers through
> using your Super-Grow Lawn Builder
> than anything else we have done."

Another company, which markets electronic tape re-
corders, says:

> Standard Petrol Company has purchased
> 124 of our transistorized tape re-
> corders so that each field engineer
> may record his observations on the
> spot.

A sporting-goods company uses the testimonials of top
athletic stars to promote its products:

> Jesse Lyons, winner of the World Ten-
> nis Championship, says: "The light
> weight and perfect balance of my Mal-
> lory tennis racquet helped me to win
> in a breeze."

*Offer your reader a sample, a trial use, a money-
back guarantee, or some other inducement* to show him   **inducement**
that he really is not taking a chance when he buys your
product. You thus give him an opportunity to know
more about the product before he commits himself.
Such an appeal often pays for itself by enabling the
prospect to make a quick decision.

The trial drive has been a popular method employed by some automobile dealers. The dealer may write to his selected list:

> Come in to prove to yourself that the
> 1969 Master Eight handles and behaves
> like a luxury car at only a fraction
> of the price. Spend a day at the
> wheel of this superb car. Test its
> perfect steering, its Powermaster
> brakes, its rapid response to your
> every action. Be our guest.

A letter enclosing an advertisement for men's shirts includes samples of the materials from which the purchaser may choose:

> Examine these samples of the material
> that goes into our superior shirts.
> Note the fine quality of the cloth,
> the rich color selection, and the
> wrinkleproof feature of the material.
> Here is quality merchandise offered
> at special sale prices.

The book club offers a free trial:

> As an introduction, choose any 4 of
> the 98 best sellers or reference
> works listed in the enclosed bulle-
> tin. If you are not completely satis-
> fied, you may return them within ten
> days without any cost or obligation
> on your part.

Take care in wording the guarantee.

When you give a guarantee in your letter, it becomes part of the contract of sale, so you must be definite and careful in your statements:

> Niteguard guarantees your automatic
> night light for a period of one year
> from the date of purchase against all
> defects of workmanship, unless the
> unit has been subjected to mishan-
> dling or negligence. If you find any

> problems with your night light, you
> get your money back with no questions
> asked.

*Present facts based on experience with the prod-
uct.* But be brief; resist the temptation to reproduce
charts and tables in the letter. (If such figures are necessary, include a separate sheet.)

*Don't burden the reader
with too much data.*

> In the 1968 Nobel Gas Run, the Su-
> preme averaged 24 miles to a gallon.

> In 1967, we sold 285 Warner air con-
> ditioners; we had only one minor com-
> plaint.

> Carton labeling is so easy with
> Speedy Marking Systems. Anyone can
> produce 150 labels per minute and can
> save up to 75 percent of his labeling
> costs.

You recall the reason you bank at First Savings
was that letter stating:

> First Savings has never missed a
> quarterly interest payment in its
> 125-year history. Our depositors have
> had perfect safety through six wars
> and ten depressions.

And this data presented by Smythe and Norten,
Stockbrokers, has you saving money for them to invest
for you:

> Of the 50 stocks we recommended in
> 1967, one declined slightly, five re-
> mained at the same level, and the
> rest showed price increases. Can any
> other service match that record?

But your data must be complete. After all, this
is an offer, and an acceptance binds as a contract of
sale. The seller, as well as the buyer, has a right to

*The facts must be com-
plete.*

know all the terms. The TRK Theater Club, which operates out of the Book Department, sent this letter. It required two revisions before all the information was included.

How would you like to have two tickets reserved for you for a performance of the newest top shows within one month after opening night? You choose the night, the type of seat (orchestra, loge, balcony), and we do the rest. You also choose the shows you prefer from reviews you will receive every three months.

Spell out numbers from one to ten, but use figures for money and percents.

How many shows will you be expected to attend each year? Just four. And the cost of only $5 a year makes you a full member of the Club. Your membership will give you 50 percent off the ticket price of from four to ten shows each year. You may order only two tickets for each show.

Please complete the attached card, and enclose your check in the self-addressed stamped envelope for this year's membership. If you act quickly, you will receive a review this week and can be enjoying your first theater party as a member of the TRK Theater Club next week.

You are giving the facts to the reader for him to make a decision. Is this service worth the cost of membership?

CLINCHING THE SALE

If you have written well, by now you have the customer agreeing that he would like to accept your offer. Will you now assure a sale by making it easy for him to do so? The customer who is just barely convinced will be lost if you do not.

Mr. Jaspers asks you to look closely at the last paragraph of the Theater Club letter. It does some important things: It tells the reader what to do next, it urges him to do so right away, and the action it suggests is a simple one.

Urging Immediate Action

You want immediate action. Once the reader puts the letter down, he must overcome the usual inertia in taking up the matter again. How can you urge him to "do it now." You have heard of many of these persuaders:

inertia

```
The first 25 to buy this stove will
receive a set of copper-bottom pots
to go with it.
```
The treat or reward.

```
Open an account with us tomorrow, and
choose one of the 50 gifts on display
in the lobby.
```

```
There are only 50 of these sets left.
Be sure you get one of them by making
your purchase tomorrow.
```
The short supply.

```
Our membership is limited to 99 mem-
bers. Will you be one of them? Hurry!
```

```
Will yours be one of the first motels
in your area to install an indoor
pool?
```
The "be first" appeal.

```
Yours can be the first hotel in the
state to own its own helicopter.
```

```
There are only 50 of these hearing
aids in the country. We will hold one
for you.
```
The "save money" approach.

```
This is a one-day sale. Don't miss
the savings we offer.
```

```
This rug would sell anywhere else for
$200 more. Buy it before someone else
does.
```

You can't afford to miss this opportunity to buy a new Itcan Washing
Machine.

By putting in your order for a new
car this month, you will receive the
dealer's discount of $125.

*The "prestige" per-
suader.*

You will be proud of your appearance
in a Walt Richman suit. Make an appointment today.

Only the most successful professional
men drive an Empire.

Suggesting What to Do
and How to Do It

expend

*Prescribe definite ac-
tion.*

The reader is now ready to act, but the sales letter that
does not tell him what his next step should be may
still lose him. He may not feel that your product is
worth the time and energy he must expend to get it.
Therefore, you should provide a definite course of action for him. Mr. Jaspers proves his point with these
paragraphs:

Indefinite	Definite action
Our electric heater will give your porch a warm even heat. Visit our Appliance Department tomorrow.	Will you complete the enclosed postcard by checking one of the following: ____ Send the No. 112 heater for a three-day free trial. ____ Send a representative to demonstrate the No. 112. ____ Make an appointment for me to see a representative at the store at ____ on ____.
TRK Fashions will be modeled at Farseers on Friday, March 27, from 6 to 9 p.m. Please join us in the Dress Salon on the third floor.	Please return the enclosed card in the envelope provided before March 15, so that we may reserve a special place for you at our fashion show on March 27. You will receive your admission ticket on March 18.

Let us help you develop the
successful investment portfolio. We have the information
you need to make the right investment at the right time. Try
us and see.

Let us know if you're coming to
the Bahamas again this year.

Call us at 971-9000 to tell us
you are interested in developing an investment portfolio.
We'll do the rest for you. Or,
if you wish, drop in to one of
our many offices, listed below.

Just write across the enclosed
self-sealing letter already
addressed and stamped:

Yes, I am coming.

Check the type of reservation
you want--you have first
choice. You will get your confirmation within a week, assuring you of another delightful
vacation next May.

Furthermore, he continues, the action you prescribe should be as simple as the situation permits. You
yourself know how easy it is to tear off a flyer at the
bottom of a letter and enclose it in an envelope or to
complete a postcard and drop it in the mail. Both are
much easier than writing a letter, and both are much
more likely to result in an acceptance. Here are some
ideas for using reply enclosures:

Make the action easy.

Just take your pencil and check your
four choices on the enclosed card
. . . with the understanding that you
are placed under no obligation whatever. Your books will reach you in a
few days.

Now that you have examined the samples, fill in your selection on the
handy order blank. Place the blank
into the stamped and addressed envelope, and drop it into your nearest
mailbox.

You need send no money now. Just fill
in your name and address on the special enclosed order card (postage
free), and mail it to us. We'll start

your subscription immediately and
bill you only $2.

Use the enclosed card and reply envelope to get your free book and six
months of <u>Current Times</u> for only $1.
Mailing the card right now is really
the only way to be certain that it
will be done.

In anticipation of your continued
NYFP membership, we have enclosed
your combination membership card and
your 1969 dues bill.

prudent

Act at once. Mail the order form NOW
--before it slips your mind! It could
prove one of the most prudent acts of
your life.

Simply check the program in which
you are most interested, and we will
send you a valuable free booklet describing the opportunities in that
field.

Join the thousands of smart people
who save at First American. Fill in
the enclosed deposit slip, and bring
it to First American.

THE FOLLOW-UP

You think you have now heard the end of Mr. Jaspers'
story, but he has one more question for you: What happens if the reader puts aside the letter and forgets, or
if he hasn't made up his mind to buy, or if he simply
procrastinates? You contact him again, reactivating his
interest, redeveloping his preference for the product.
Your main objective in the follow-up letter is to urge
action. Mr. Jaspers shows you an example from his files
and one from his incoming mail.

Before we open our private sale to
the public, we want each of our

charge customers who is interested to
view the antique and modern sale
pieces. If you haven't had a chance
to come in yet, please do so before
Monday, March 1, the first day of the
regular public sale.

Has your secretary enjoyed using the
Speedwrite? We hope so. However, the
time has come to place this demon-
stration machine in another office.
Complete the order form attached so
that we may deliver your own brand
new machine when we pick up the one
you have.

Your own mail provides other examples of the follow-up
sales letter.

You will receive only two more issues
of the weekly magazine Week's News.
Then your subscription will expire.
To prevent any interruption in your
news coverage, please complete the   coverage
enclosed card, which lists a special
rate for renewals.

We are holding a room on the ocean
just for you. Before you put this
letter aside, please tell us whether
or not you can be with us again in
May this year.

Because people are known to procrastinate, your
department plans follow-up sales letters as a matter of
policy. These give the customer a second chance to
say yes.

SUMMARY

The sales letter is written to sell a product or service to
a specific individual or group of individuals and to

develop a continuing customer demand for that product or service. In order to accomplish these objectives, the writer centers all action on the prospective customer from the first sentence to the last.

The all-important first sentence attracts the customer's interest by such techniques as asking a question of the reader; making a direct statement that solves one of his problems, fulfills one of his needs, or satisfies one of his desires; using a courteous command that resolves an issue or urges care; quoting an eminent person that will make the offer attractive by association; or using a topical reference or a headline or two-line idea to snare the reader's attention.

Of course, the product or service is important — but only as it serves the reader. After you have created a preference for your product over other items, you can use several methods to bring your prospective customer to a decision to buy: presenting testimonials from satisfied users; offering samples, or trial uses, or money-back guarantees; or presenting pointed factual information.

Once the reader has made a decision that he wants the product enough to pay the price you are asking, you must clinch the sale by getting immediate action. Make it easy to act by giving simple directions, and prove it is worthwhile to "do it now" by one of these persuaders: the promise of a treat or reward, the threat of a short supply, the "be first" appeal, the "save money" approach, the "prestige persuader."

Finally, you must plan follow-up sales letters for the procrastinator. You give this customer a second chance to say yes, a second chance to benefit from the product or service the sales letter offers.

11 | Exercises

[1] SPELLING

a. What letter is missing in each of these words?

    flex___bility   inadequ___te   c___rome

b. Correct any misspellings in this paragraph:

Irv was trying to gleen some information prier to his interview. He wanted to ascertain weather he could fullfill the requirements for either job. His preferrance was for the selling job, which seemed to have greater potenshal and would give him a chance for total covrage of a territory.

[2] VOCABULARY

a. Use each of the following words in a sentence. Be sure the context shows that you understand the meaning of each word.

    ultimately   entails   inducement
      enlivened   excerpts   procrastinate

b. Is the word *unique* used correctly in the following sentence?

Hers was a very unique and interesting idea.

If so, what does it mean? If not, why not?

c. What does *eminent* mean? How, if at all, does it differ from *imminent*? from *immanent*?

d. Explain how the meaning of the italicized word differs in these two sentences:

I enjoyed *patronizing* the Spanish restaurant.
His attitude toward Jenny was very *patronizing*.

Do the same for the italicized words in these pairs of sentences:

The play had many fine *attributes*.
He *attributes* their success to high-quality merchandise.

293

Guarding the *premises* was a vicious dog.
An erroneous conclusion is often the result of faulty *premises*.

e.   Define briefly each of the words below.

predilection   inertia   media   topical   prudent

[3] PUNCTUATION: COLON, DASH, AND PARENTHESES

The colon, dash, and parentheses are more emphatic pauses in a sentence than the comma or semicolon. Your most frequent use of the colon in business writing will be following the salutation of a letter. You will also use it between the hour and minutes in writing the time — as, 3:30 p.m. Now let's check some other uses of the colon.

RULE: *Use a colon following an independent clause to separate it from a series or list.* (Notice that, as the second example shows, a colon is usually not used when the series or list is necessary to complete the sentence.)

Here are some traits the successful worker must possess: responsibility, loyalty, initiative, and good judgment.
Some traits the successful worker must possess are responsibility, loyalty, initiative, and good judgment.

RULE: *The colon is used to introduce a long, formal quotation — usually one that is indented and not enclosed in quotes* (see notation on p. 275).

The Declaration of Independence reads:

When in the course of human events . . .

Many times, a word, phrase, or clause breaks into the main thought of a sentence. Usually, such parenthetical expressions are set off from the sentence by commas. However, when a more abrupt break is in order, dashes are used instead.

RULE: *Use dashes to show a sudden change in a sentence or to show emphasis.*

This letter is about an important matter — your credit.
We are asking you — as we have before — to send your check at once.

Dashes are formed in typing by using two hyphens without spacing before, between, or after them.

RULE: *Use parentheses to enclose words, phrases, or clauses that are explanations or asides in a sentence but are not of major importance. Use parentheses also to enclose an entire sentence that is secondary to the logical flow of a paragraph.*

> During the late afternoon hours (from 4 p.m. to 6 p.m.), Mr. Green will assist the trainees.

Apply these rules to the sentences below. Be sure, also, to add any other necessary punctuation.

a. We are again demonstrating as we did on several occasions some fine new products that have high customer appeal

b. Five important cities where we have offices are New York Chicago Los Angeles Boston and Seattle

c. The following officers have been elected for the coming term President Bill Nally treasurer Ralph Hicks secretary Irene Furman

d. Everything seems to favor his proposal the plant is operating the market is available people are ready to spend

e. Peter Roget 1779 – 1869 published the first edition of his Thesaurus in 1852

f. One of the distinctive features of the film a feature that appeals to many viewers is its excellent sound recording

g. My office has just purchased a typewriter a used one by the way that is the best I've ever used

[4] NUMBERS

Here are some more rules for the correct use of numbers:

RULE: *When one number immediately follows another, spell out the first number and write the second in figures. If the second number is simpler than the first, you may spell it out and write the first in figures instead.*

> Put on four 5-inch handles.
> He had to adjust thirty 26-inch tires.
> They ordered 352 ten-foot extensions.

RULE: *Write out approximate numbers.*

> About three hundred students attended the pre-game rally.

RULE: *Express in figures numbered items, including page numbers, chapter and book numbers, policy numbers, and highway numbers.*

Now apply the rules:

a.   The trucker drove about 40 miles to deliver 269 ~~5~~ *five*-gallon cans of roofing tar.

b.   If you will read page 2 carefully, you will see that we ordered ~~5~~ *five* 9 nine-inch rollers.

c.   About ~~300~~ *three hundred* students analyzed the paragraph on page ~~six~~ 6 correctly.

d.   125 different calculations ~~can be performed by this amazing device.~~

e.   Drive ~~sixty-five~~ 65 miles north on Interstate ~~nine~~ 9, then ~~five~~ 5 miles east on the Ribbington Road.

[5]   MISPLACED MODIFIERS

High on a list of sentence errors is the misplaced modifier. Words, phrases, or clauses that are misplaced may confuse or amuse your reader.

RULE: *Place modifiers as close as possible to the words they modify.*

> *Not:* We saw the car walking on the road.
> *But:* As we were walking along the road, we saw the car.
> *Not:* Mr. Edgar has resigned from the presidency after having served four years to the regret of the members.
> *But:* After serving four years, Mr. Edgar resigned from the presidency, to the regret of the members.

Certain adverbs are often misplaced, changing or obscuring completely the meaning of a sentence.

RULE: *Use special care in placing the modifiers only, almost, nearly, also, quite, merely, actually, and hardly as close as possible to the word they modify.*

> *Not:* The case can only be settled by the court.
> *But:* The case can be settled only by the court.
> *Not:* We lost money almost when we did not figure costs accurately.
> *But:* We almost lost money when we did not figure costs accurately.
> *Not:* The company nearly sold its entire stock of furniture during the sale.
> *But:* The company sold nearly its entire stock of furniture during the sale.

Rewrite these sentences to make them correct:

a. The Acme Company advertised for salesmen to market its radios that have cars.

b. The products have been carefully packaged in plastic food wrap that you eat.

c. Mr. Prout wrote his speech while he was flying to New York on a scrap of paper.

d. The dealer nearly makes $200 on the sale of each car.

e. The president is responsible alone for making the final decision.

f. We saw the holiday parade passing through our store window.

g. The tax statements are only due on the first of the month.

h. After you have made this payment, you will have almost paid the entire price of the equipment.

i. Place your holiday order now, as we only have limited supplies on hand.

[6] PROOFREADING

Proofread this letter, listing in order all the corrections you make:

Oct. 16th, 1968

Mr. Bruce Smallpeice
Box 9744
  Saint Paul, Minnesota   55177

Dear Mister Smallpiece

You may try our new Shiny-Brite Car Wax at no expence to
you.

Heres all you do. Go to you nearest Shiney-Brite dealer.
Preasent the inclosed coupon to him to receive your free sample of Shiny Brite. This free sample contains enough wax to
give your car the most perfect shine it has ever had--one
that will last for month's through all kinds of wether.

After you have used Shiny-Brite this one time, you will use
it again and again.

All we ask in return for the free Sample, Mr. Smallpeace is
this. When you freinds ask how you manage to keep your car

so beautifuly waxed tell them that Shiney-Brite did the job
and that they can get that same glossy finish if they buy
Shiny-Brite for only $.98.

Sincerely,

A. R. Albrecht
Sales Dept.

[7] PROBLEMS

a. You have a favorite magazine. Since you probably know the magazine
quite well, write a sales letter to a group of teenagers to get them to
subscribe to it.

b. You are the manager of the Noranda Camp for boys. The proprietor
asks you to write a sales letter to the boys who had spent the preceding
summer at the camp. He wants them to return this year. You should
mention that the camp will have a new Olympic-size swimming pool
and a new recreation hall.

c. The boys in your neighborhood have been canvassing door to door to
sell subscriptions to the daily newspaper in your town. As supervisor of
the delivery boys, write a sales letter to try to convince those people
in the neighborhood who didn't subscribe.

d. Write a sales letter to go to owners of home freezers. You want to
sell them See-Safe plastic food bags, which are used to preserve frozen
foods. You might mention that the bags come in various sizes and that
they can be used for meats, poultry, fruits, vegetables, and bakery
goods. They are guaranteed to seal in flavor. They require no heat
sealing.

e. You have been supervising a team of demonstrators of the Kelsey
electric vacuum cleaner in their door-to-door selling of these vacuums.
You have decided to follow up the demonstrations by sending a sales
letter to give added weight to the salesman's visit. Write the letter.

f. As an insurance salesman, you visit prospects to discuss their life-
insurance programs. Because you know that people do not remember
figures — and because they often say later on that they really didn't

know what they were buying — you write a letter pointing out what their insurance objectives should be and how much the insurance will cost.

g. You are secretary of the Fish and Game Club. You want to increase membership in the club. From your local sporting-goods store, you have gotten a list of names of people who have fishing and hunting licenses. Write a letter to encourage them to join the Fish and Game Club.

h. You are employed by a charter-bus company. Write a letter to be sent to ski enthusiasts to get them to sign up for trips to the ski country on weekends during the ski season. You will offer them a low rate for the bus transportation as well as two nights at the Avalanche Ski Lodge for $20.

i. It is early in October. Write a sales letter to be sent by the local garage and repair shop to encourage car owners to come there for their winterizing.

j. Revise these sales-letter beginnings to give them more reader appeal. You may use any method of gaining attention in the opening sentence.

   1. We are conducting an intensive sales campaign to get the public to know about the Book Club.

   2. November 5 was a night of darkness for millions of people in the East. There was a power failure that lasted for several hours.

   3. Can't you remember the fun you had at Lake Joy last summer?

   4. The Mayfair Washing Machine is now available for sale at local stores.

   5. The quality of the paper you use will affect your reader's reaction to your message.

   6. We believe that the *Current Review* is a winner.

   7. We have the machine for the man who has everything but time — the Empire portable dictating machine.

k. Change these negative introductions to make them affirmative:

   1. You don't want to waste your money when you buy tires.

   2. Stickem was developed to prevent your plastic floor tiles from buckling and curling. You will never have to worry about unsightly playroom floors again.

3. Don't you remember last December 26? Were you prepared to
    cope with the record snowfall? Weren't you huffing and puffing
    with your snow shovel while your neighbors guided their snow
    blowers along their walks?

I. Read the sales letters which follow. Identify (1) the attention-getting
    device, (2) the place where the reader's desire was aroused, (3) the
    section where the writer tried to convince his reader, (4) the final
    action in these letters. The first letter went out to commercial bankers
    to sell them paper for their checking accounts.

> Is your check paper in the rough?
>   Or smooth as a putting green?
>
> There's almost that much difference in check papers.
> Starting with the worst, full of hills and valleys, you
> can progress right up to Johnson's Safeguard--the lead-
> ing "pro" in safety papers.
>
> Safeguard has a smooth, level surface, where magnetic
> inks dry fast. Safeguard always plays the course at par,
> going through your reader-sorters without a missed
> stroke. You won't get rejects due to faulty paper--and
> rejects can cost you 40 cents each.
>
> Safeguard is the safety paper that comes in white and
> seven colors, in your own selection of design.
>
> Send the enclosed coupon to your bank stationer for
> samples of Safeguard. Examine the quality and perform-
> ance of this fine check paper yourself. It's the only
> fair way.

Here's a letter to the office manager:

> You're the boss. But could you ever demand that desks
> be kept clear of clutter? Where would your employees
> put all the things that clutter their desk tops and make
> your offices messy looking?
>
> Look at the work stations in the attached picture. All
> the things that permanently clutter other desk tops are
> in the drawers; letter trays, binder racks, form racks,
> card trays are inside.

Thatcher Clear-Deck Desks make it easier to eliminate
messy desk tops, improve work habits, and ensure greater
accuracy throughout the office. Ingenious drawer facilities separate all paperwork and working tools into
definite, easy-to-find groups, positioned for the great-
est convenience of the user.

There's a "right" Clear-Deck Desk for every office job.
Each basic model can be expanded, converted, or re-
arranged to fit any degree of job specialization.
Ask us to show you.

How? Phone your local Thatcher dealer; or fill in the
enclosed postage-paid card, and mail it to us.

The tour operator sends this type of letter:

June in January? Yes, now is the time to plan ahead for
that summer tour of Europe. Begin immediately on the
enclosed planning kit.

Our tours provide all the essentials required by Ameri-
cans traveling abroad: first-class hotels; a private
bath guaranteed every night of the tour; fully air-
conditioned motorcoaches; the services of a multilingual
tour director, who is on hand every minute of the day
and night. You will travel in true American-style com-
fort, in the manner to which you are accustomed back
home.

But Storey Luxury Tours provide the one feature that
other tours of Europe lack--leisure. On a Storey tour,
much of the travel in Europe is by air and first-class
rail. You do not sit for interminable hours in a motor-
coach. The result is more time for sightseeing, shopping,
exploring, or just relaxing. And we have added evening
entertainment and other thoughtful extras to your tour
at no extra cost. A Storey tour is a true vacation.

I very much hope that we may see you on one of our tours
in 1969. We promise you an experience in leisurely
travel that you'll never forget. But please remember
that the best policy is to reserve early.

The automobile dealer may write to a group like this:

Caravel--the logical step in any success story.

For years Caravel has been the overwhelming luxury-car
choice of successful professional and businessmen--men
who recognize quality and value and interpret it in
terms of sound investment.

Ownership of a Caravel provides a sense of satisfaction
matched by no other car--the reward of owning the finest
that motoring has to offer.

Never has this been as true as it is for 1968. Caravel's
completely new styling is complemented by smoother,
quieter, more agile performance. Its comforts are more
luxurious than ever. And, as you would expect, its
safety features are unsurpassed.

With its famed long life and high resale value, Caravel
represents the world's soundest automobile investment
--from both a personal and a professional standpoint.
Cunningham stands ready to show you how well a Caravel
accompanies accomplishment.

Call Cunningham today. We will drive a new Caravel to
your home and give you the opportunity to spend a day
at the wheel of this great car. No obligation, of course.

12

The Credit Letter

YOUR assignment for the next two weeks takes you to the Credit Department. On your way to work that first morning, your friend Ralph says, "I spent all last night paying bills. I had to send out 25 checks to settle monthly accounts for telephone, gas, electricity, drugs, milk, groceries, department-store purchases, gasoline, and . . . and. . . ." Ralph and his wife had made many purchases on credit during the month. Because they were good risks, they had a good credit standing. Businessmen were willing to supply them with many goods and services and to wait until the end of the month for payment.

Credit cards and charge accounts are familiar services of business. They enable customers — both individuals and businesses — to "buy now and pay later." Although this requires more record-keeping and clerical work for the seller, it enables his customers to buy more and higher quality merchandise. Actually, therefore, he sells more and makes more profit.

The value of credit.

How does the businessman know that a customer is a good risk? How does he know that he will receive

Who gets credit?

303

payment at the end of the month? Does everyone who wants a charge account get one? When you walk into the office that day, you have a number of questions you would like answered. One of the first is: How does a credit manager decide to accept or reject an application for a charge account?

THE INITIAL LETTER

When the Account Can Be Opened

Your immediate supervisor for these two weeks is the assistant credit manager for the manufacturing division, Mr. Wood. You work with him and his secretary. This order awaits the approval of the Credit Department before the goods can be shipped:

```
TRK Textile Company
356 Fifth Avenue
New York, New York   10002

Attention Order Department

Gentlemen:

Please ship me the following items
from your brochure, No. 5704:
```

Cat. No.	Units	Description	Unit Price	Ext.
35X	2 bolts	Long fiber cotton, white	$ 40.00	$ 80.00
15W	3 bolts	Italian silk, pink	120.00	360.00
18W	2 bolts	Chambray, navy blue	80.00	160.00
				$600.00

"Open account" means granting of credit without requiring security or collateral.

```
Will you please fill this order on
open account according to your regu-
lar trade terms.
```

For credit information, you may refer to:

    Millgert Textiles
    548 Fifth Avenue
    New York, New York   10016

    Millis Mills, Inc.
    364 River Road
    Pawtucket, Rhode Island   04218

    Burling Mills, Inc.
    101 Travis Boulevard
    Raleigh, North Carolina   27609

    Factory Point Bank
    28 Main Street
    Middlebury, Vermont   05753

Also, here is an audited copy of our latest financial statement for your consideration. We can report our Dun & Bradstreet rating as C+ 1.

audited

We would like to stock your textiles for our regular retail trade.

           Sincerely yours,

           John S. Kilduff

           John S. Kilduff
           President

What does Mr. Kilduff include in his letter to make the processing of his order an easy job?

    Specific order — catalog number, units, description, unit
       price, total price.
    Names and addresses of references, including his bank.
    His latest financial statement.
    The company's Dun & Bradstreet rating.

(Dun & Bradstreet, an outstanding credit-rating organization, publishes credit ratings of businesses that have been evaluated. The C+ 1 rating means that Kilduff's estimated financial strength is between $125,000 and $200,000 and that he is reliable and quick in paying his bills. Many companies are willing to grant credit solely on the basis of a favorable D & B rating.)

solely

In making a judgment as to the reliability of this company, Mr. Wood looks at the D & B rating. His secretary checks the current volume of D & B to be sure that Kilduff's statement is accurate. Although Mr. Wood will check Kilduff's references and financial statement later, he has sufficient information to open an account for the Kilduff Fabric Center in the interim. So he tells you to see that the order is filled and to write a letter in his name to Mr. Kilduff.

interim

What will the letter contain? You make this list:

> A welcome to Mr. Kilduff as a credit customer.
> An explanation of the terms of sale — 2/10, n/30 — encouraging prompt payment.
> A thank you.
> An offer of continued service.
> An invitation for future orders.

Here is the letter you write, and here, too, are Mr. Wood's marginal comments:

Avoid passive.

Use specific date.

```
The fabrics that you ordered--as
listed on the enclosed invoice--have
been shipped by Railway Express. They
should reach you by Saturday.
```

Use active voice to establish relationship.

```
The amount of the bill, $600, has
been charged to your account with TRK.
```

Don't make assumptions.

"Good integrity" is redundant.

```
While we have yet to check the credit
references you gave us, we have
rushed your order to you because of
your fine credit rating with Dun &
Bradstreet. We know that your suppli-
ers will assure us of your good in-
tegrity.
```

```
It is our policy to offer the regular
trade terms of 2/10, n/30. These
```

terms apply to all orders including your present order. Therefore, you can save $12 if you pay your account in full by February 10; the full amount of the invoice will be due by March 2.

Long-winded and redundant.

Insulting (reader can figure this out.)

You will be delighted with the excellent service our company offers its dealers. Orders are filled promptly and efficiently. You and your customers are never kept waiting if it should be necessary for you to send a special order.

Unnecessary boasting; omit this paragraph.

Our sales representative will visit you regularly. Now that he is on the road in New England, we shall ask him to call on you. He will be able to offer you many excellent ideas for promoting TRK fabrics.

Be specific: When will he visit? What is his name?

Mr. Wood has also noticed a major oversight: You did not welcome Mr. Kilduff as a new customer.

You must rewrite your letter to incorporate these comments, reorganize the ideas to achieve a smooth, flowing communication. Figure 12 – 1 shows the letter you finally submit for Mr. Wood's signature.

When Further Information Is Needed

Another order arrived at the office that day, from Bleak & Company. The writer did not mention credit references, nor did he enclose his financial statement. Mr. Wood would not extend credit immediately — he was unwilling to take the risk of sending an order to an unknown buyer. Bleak & Company may become one of TRK's best customers, but only if you answer that order letter tactfully and intelligently. What must you tell Mr. Bleak?

Remember your tact.

Conditions under which you can ship immediately. Company terms.

(212) 475-1125

T R K

Manufacturers and Distributors of Fine Fabrics

356 Fifth Avenue, New York, New York 10002

February 1, 1968

Mr. John S. Kilduff
President
Kilduff Fabric Center
111 Marcher Street
Cambridge, Massachusetts 02138

Dear Mr. Kilduff:

Your order for our fabrics will reach you on Monday, February 5, via Railway Express. We have charged your bill for $600 to your new open account with us. Our trade terms are 2/10, n/30.

Thank you for including your references and your Dun & Bradstreet rating.

Our sales representative for the New England district, Mr. Kenneth Miller, will visit you every three months. Now that he is in Boston, we shall ask him to call on you. Let him help you with the free TRK displays for your window.

Thank you for ordering TRK fabrics. You will be the first to offer these fine imports in Cambridge.

Sincerely yours,

James T. Wood

James T. Wood
Assistant Credit Manager
Manufacturing Division

sbt

Figure 12 – 1
A Preliminary Granting
of Credit

Request for credit references, financial statement, bank reference.
Statement of goodwill.

Here is your first draft:

Thank you for your letter of January 26, in which you order $200 worth of TRK fabrics.

Can you see what's wrong with this letter?

Our regular credit terms are 2/10, n/30. These terms apply on all orders after you have had a credit clearance. As an astute businessman, you will appreciate the value of paying your bills within the discount period.

astute

Since we have not done business with you previouly, it will be necessary for you to send us credit references. Don't forget to list the names and addresses on the enclosed credit application form. You also neglected to send us a copy of your latest financial statement.

The only way we can service your order would be to send it C.O.D. As you know, it will take a long time to check your credit references after we receive them.

"C.O.D." ("cash on delivery") is typed in capitals with periods but no space between initials.

If you wish us to send the fabrics immediately, let us know. We can't ship them until we hear from you.

You decide that the letter is too wordy, doesn't get to the point immediately, and is negative and somewhat patronizing. You rewrite it as follows:

Dear Mr. Bleak:

Your TRK fabrics can be sent immediately if you will allow us to send

partial

them C.O.D. Please call us collect,
and we will ship that day. If you
would prefer to receive only a partial shipment now, we'll hold the
balance of your order until your account can be opened.

Please complete the enclosed credit
application form so that we can evaluate your account quickly. This is
part of our routine credit procedure.

Thank you for your order. We hope
that by next month you will be one of
our credit customers.

                          Sincerely yours,

*It is wise to mention
that your credit check
is routine and not a
questioning of this cus-
tomer's reliability.*

THE THREE C'S OF CREDIT

After receiving your letter, Mr. Bleak returned his credit-
application form. You are now asked to write to the
references he listed, while another member of the
department assesses Bleak's financial statement. What
information will you need from these references? And
what does the department hope to learn from the financial statement?

assesses

Remember, on your first day in this office, you
were wondering: How does a credit manager decide to
accept or reject an application for a charge account?
Mr. Wood now introduces you to the "three C's of
credit" — character, capital, capacity. They determine
whether credit will be granted.

Character

He explains that although you will check all three C's,
character is the most important element, the one that
money cannot buy. No matter how much capital or
capacity an individual may have, they are as nothing if

he lacks honesty and a sense of fairness. You remember when your friend Jim Harris asked you to lend him $10 until the following week. You knew that Jim had a very small allowance and had never saved any money. But you knew, too, that Jim was a man of his word and could be relied upon under any conditions. So you gave the loan to your trustworthy friend.

Capital

The second item, capital, Mr. Wood continues, concerns how much money the firm has and how that money is being used. For instance, what is the extent of Bleak & Company's indebtedness? Does it have money **indebtedness** readily available to meet its day-to-day and month-to-month needs? Does it make efficient use of its money through investment and expansion? Is the company making a profit? Is it in a growing industry?

One of the first steps in assessing a firm's financial position is to contact its bank. (If you have ever filled out an application for a charge account or some other type of credit, you remember that the form asked for the name of your bank.) Although a bank will not normally reveal how much money is in a customer's account, it will give the credit office its estimate of the customer's credit reliability and will specify whether **reliability; specify** the account is one of long standing. And the existence of a bank account is itself some (though not sufficient) evidence that the customer has money on hand to pay for his purchases.

A second source of information about Mr. Bleak's capital is his references. They, too, will be asked to give their evaluation of the firm's position.

However, the credit office will obtain most of its capital information from Bleak & Company's financial statement. When Mr. Wood assigns one of his assistants to study it, he will expect answers to such questions as these:

What are Bleak & Company's assets? (What does the **assets** company own? What is the monetary value of those possessions?)

liabilities

What are the company's liabilities? (How much does Bleak & Company owe? To whom?)

Which are short-term debts? (How much will have to be paid in the next year?) And which are long-term ones?

equity

What is the owner's equity in the business? (How much is left for the owner after the company's liabilities are subtracted from its assets — that is, after all its debts are paid?)

liquid

How liquid are the company's assets? (How much of its assets can be turned into cash quickly to pay its bills?)

curious

Mr. Wood has just used a number of terms that are new to you. You are curious to learn more, so you ask him to show you Bleak's financial statement and to tell you a little about it.

He is pleased by your interest and begins by explaining that businesses have two major financial statements; first, the income statement, which presents a summary of revenues and expenses of the business for a specified accounting period; second, the balance sheet (what you are interested in now), which presents a picture of a company's position at a given time.

What balances on a balance sheet?

On the balance sheet (Figure 12 – 2) assets are listed on the left side, liabilities and the owner's equity on the right. The statement is called a "balance sheet" because the two sides must always be equal. In other words, everything that the business owns must equal the debts it owes *plus* what the owner has invested or retained in the business. (The owner here is Mr. Bleak; the owners of a corporation are its stockholders.)

Remember, from the list above, what "liquid" means?

The assets are normally listed in order of decreasing liquidity — that is, first cash, next items (such as inventory) that are easily turned into cash, and last those items (such as plant and equipment) that are difficult to turn into cash. Similarly, on the liabilities side, current (or short-term) liabilities — those that will require cash for payment soonest — are listed first, and longer-term debts are listed next. Since the owner can claim his money only after other debts have been paid, his claims are listed last.

```
                    Statement of Financial Condition
                           December 31, 1967

            Assets                            Liabilities

Cash                    $ 9,276    Accounts payable          $12,022
Accounts Receivable      11,721    Reserve for taxes           3,041
Inventory                48,294
                                   Current liabilities        15,063
   Current assets       $69,291
                                   Long-term bank loan        18,500
Plant and equipment
  after reserves for                  Total liabilities       33,563
  depreciation           21,481
Goodwill                      1    Owner's equity
                                   William Bleak               57,210
   Total assets         $90,773
                                      Total liabilities
                                      and owner's
                                      equity                  $90,773
```

Figure 12 – 2
Bleak & Company's
Balance Sheet

TRK will apply a wide variety of tests to Bleak & Company's financial statement, Mr. Wood explains. And his staff had to take a special course in analyzing financial statements and evaluating the results. The aim of this analysis, of course, is to learn enough about Bleak's position to determine if his business is financially sound.

Capacity

This brings Mr. Wood to the third of the three C's of credit — capacity. The critical question for him is: Will Bleak & Company be a healthy, profitable firm in the years ahead? To find that answer, he must take account, not only of Mr. Bleak's character and his company's financial situation, but of his capacity — his business sense. Does he manage his business well? Is his an expanding company in an expanding industry? Do his past judgments augur well for the future? And so on.

  In evaluating Mr. Bleak's capacity, Mr. Wood will be helped by the answers from Bleak's references and

critical

augur

by his own staff's research on the customers, location, and history of Bleak & Company.

THE LETTER FOR CREDIT REFERENCE

You now turn to your job of writing to check Mr. Bleak's references with a good idea of what you want to know from them. Before you begin, you jot down these ideas:

What to ask the reference.

How long have you known Mr. Bleak?
What is your opinion of his character and reliability?
Have you ever granted him credit, and, if so, what was your experience with him?
Do you have any information about his financial condition?
Would you rely on his business judgment?

To make it easy for the references to answer your questions and for the credit officer at TRK to organize their replies, you decide to draw up a form to enclose with your letter:

Remember — in form letters, leave space after questions in accordance with the probable length of the answer.

Credit Reference Form

Name: Bleak & Company
Address: 1010 Orchard Street
               St. Louis, Missouri

1. How many years have you done business with this firm? ____

2. Have you extended them credit? _____ If so, on what terms? _____

3. What is the highest credit you have extended this company?

_____

4. What amount do they currently owe? _____

5. What is their usual speed of payment?

   Within discount   Within net
   period ____   period ____
              Number of
              months ____

6. Please give your estimate of the company's reliability.

7. What is your opinion of the owner's character and ability?

8. Can you provide any information about the firm's present financial status and its prospects?

Submitted by: _____

Now you turn to the letter:

Please give us your opinion of Bleak & Company, 1010 Orchard Street, St. Louis, Missouri. Mr. William Bleak has given us your name as a credit reference.

We at TRK would like to extend credit to this company. By filling out the enclosed form, you will give us the

Note: Letter is brief, to the point, and courteous.

information we need to do so. We have
included a stamped, self-addressed
envelope for your convenience. Of
course, we will consider your reply
completely confidential. Our thanks
for your help.

In looking over your work, you are satisfied that
the letter is courteous and to the point and that the
form requests all the information the Credit Department
will need.

THE LETTER TO REFUSE CREDIT

We must be realistic — all references do not send favorable replies, and all analyses of financial statements are
not favorable. Sometimes it is necessary to refuse credit.

abruptly

What does Mr. Wood do in such circumstances?
Does he turn away the business abruptly? Does he say
no and leave it at that? The company does not want to
lose a sale; if possible, it wants to keep the customer's
business although on a cash basis. How does Mr. Wood
try to accomplish this?

He explains the following: It is always difficult to
accept a refusal. Therefore, the credit officer must be
persuasive and tactful. It helps to soften the negative

*Be as positive as pos-
sible.*

answer with some positive suggestion — perhaps that
the order can be shipped C.O.D. or that credit may be
extended when the customer's financial situation improves. An explanation of the reasons for refusal is also
imperative, and it should be as complete and specific
as it can be. Whenever possible, this explanation should
mention the favorable aspects of the credit investigation
before proceeding to the unsatisfactory ones. If such
information is confidential, the letter must convince the
customer that his application was given full and serious
consideration and that the decision was not taken
lightly.

Mr. Wood gives you the file of Gordon Shoppes,
Inc. Mr. Gordon had sent in an order and had requested

credit. An investigation of his references and financial statement had resulted in a decision not to grant him credit. Your job is to inform him of this decision.

First, you review the file, noting that Mr. Gordon's references are very complimentary but that the application was turned down because of a poor capital situation. After some thought, you write:

Dear Mr. Gordon:

Thank you for your order and for your consideration in enclosing credit information.

Positive opening.

Your references vouch for your fine character and business acumen. But the current ratio of your company--1:1--does not permit us to extend credit now. Your order--or a smaller one--can be filled immediately, however, if you will accept C.O.D. shipment. Just telephone us collect.

vouch
acumen

Good qualities mentioned first; followed by specific explanation and positive suggestion.

We hope that improved business conditions this spring will enable you to increase your company's liquidity. Please apply again when your current ratio improves.

We look forward to the time when we can open an account for you. Meanwhile, please allow us to serve you as a cash or C.O.D. customer.

Tactful effort to persuade customer to accept cash terms.

Sincerely yours,

OTHER CREDIT LETTERS

During the past few days, you have seen several letters requesting credit, you have observed how these applications are handled, and you have even had the opportunity to write some acceptances, some refusals, and some requests for references.

Mr. Wood now mentions several other types of credit letter, among them the letter to attract new credit customers, the letter of thanks to paying customers, and the letter granting or refusing credit to a retail customer.

Credit for the Consumer

Extending individual credit, he explains, involves substantially the same procedures and problems as granting credit to business firms. There are differences, however, because you are evaluating an individual and not a company. For instance, an individual does not provide a balance sheet, but he is often requested to list any large debts he may have — such as a bank loan. And he must **divulge** his source of income — where he works and what job he holds there. Sometimes he is asked to put down his salary. Reference letters also differ for the individual, but only slightly.

divulge

The similarities and differences between granting credit to businesses and extending it to individuals are brought home to you the following day. You arrive at Nayles Hardware Store, where you sometimes help out on Saturdays, to find Mr. Nayles **scrutinizing** a credit application from a new customer — Mr. John Stillwell. Since you have now had a little experience with credit letters, you offer to write to Mr. Stillwell's references. Here is your letter:

scrutinizing

Can you see how this letter differs from the reference request on a business firm? Compare it to the reference form and letter on pages 314 – 15.

Please give us a credit reference on Mr. John Stillwell of 56 Frost Pond Street, Great Neck, New York. He has listed your name as a reference.

Your answers to the questions below will enable us to decide upon Mr. Stillwell's application for an account. A return envelope is enclosed for your convenience.

Of course, any information you give us will be strictly confidential.

1. For how long a period has he had an account with you?

   _____

2. How extensive is his business with you? _____

3. What is the highest credit you extended to him? _____

4. How promptly does he usually pay his bills? _____

5. Does he owe anything now?

   _____

6. What is your estimate of his character and reliability?

Thank you for your cooperation. We shall be happy to reciprocate at any time.

reciprocate

Simple as the letter is, it will elicit information that will give Mr. Nayles a basis for accepting or rejecting Mr. Stillwell's request for credit. After Mr. Nayles receives favorable replies concerning Mr. Stillwell's credit history, he quickly sends this communication:

Mr. Stillwell . . .

   We welcome your credit business.

   Please come in tomorrow and charge your purchases.

Encouraging Credit Relations

influx

Mr. Nayles has noticed that there are many new home-owners in Great Neck as a result of an influx of new industry. He feels that these residents are responsible people whom he would like to have as customers, and he has obtained a list of their names and addresses. To encourage greater use of his credit facilities, he asks you to compose a form letter welcoming them to the community and, of course, to Nayles Hardware Store. Your letter encourages them to buy at Nayles:

Your letter should in-clude:

Please come to Nayles Hardware Store when you need lawn seed, paints, tools, nails, barbecue equipment, or any of the hundreds of other things large and small that we keep in ready supply for your new home.

How the customer can be served.

What special services are available.

Our rush delivery service is an additional convenience. If you need any item in a great hurry, just telephone, and we'll deliver it within the hour.

A welcome to get acquainted.

As one of our newest residents, you are especially welcome. Come in, if only to visit us and get acquainted with our helpful store personnel.

An easy way to open an account.

If you will fill in the enclosed application blank, we can arrange a charge account for you within the week. That will make your shopping more convenient and enjoyable.

Please stop in to see us soon.

A Note of Thanks

promptly

Continuing to apply what you learned at TRK, you suggest to Mr. Nayles that he make use of one more type of letter — the note of thanks. Nearly all people who have credit cards or charge accounts pay their bills promptly. In too many cases, they are the forgotten ones. Such reliable people should occasionally receive a note of appreciation from the company that has issued credit. This type of letter adds to the company's image; it does not really have to be written, but it serves to develop and maintain goodwill. The individual who neglects to pay his debts receives attention; the person who pays should receive at least an occasional thank you.

There are many ways to remember the amenities.

Mr. Nayles likes your idea and makes a list of his good customers, to whom you send this brief note:

> Thank you for making such good use of your Nayles charge account. It is a pleasure to do business with someone who pays his bills so promptly.
>
> Customers like you are an asset to any company, and we want to let you know that we appreciate you.

SUMMARY

The widespread use of credit in today's business affairs cannot be ignored. Therefore, let your correspondence with prospective credit customers help attract a greater volume of business rather than deflect it to your competitors.

deflect

When you first grant credit to a buyer of your product, be sure to extend a welcome to him. Explain the terms of sale, offer quick and efficient service for now and for future business, and thank him for buying from you. When a new customer wishes to buy on credit but has neglected to supply you with names of references or with financial data, you must handle him tactfully. Thank him for his order, suggest that he pay cash until his account can be opened, and ask him to complete an application for credit so he may be entitled to an account — being sure to make it clear that this is routine procedure.

Letters written to credit references should be accompanied by easy-to-complete forms that pinpoint the specific information you want. In your letter, tell the reader that you will keep the information confidential.

If you must refuse credit, try to be positive. Offer some suggestions so that the customer will be willing to be a cash customer until he is qualified to receive credit.

reciprocity

Consumer credit is playing an ever greater role in business. Usually you must write to banks and other references to see whether the individual is a good credit risk. Here, too, provide an easy form. Also, offer reciprocity and emphasize the confidential nature of the information. Positive attempts to attract consumer accounts are frequently employed. In such cases, write to ask potential customers to apply for credit. (Although you may make it seem easy to open an account, the final decision, of course, will depend upon the character, capital and capacity of the individual or business involved.)

Be sure also, from time to time, to write the letter that gives words of praise and thanks to those customers who avail themselves of credit and who make their payments regularly.

12 | Exercises

[1] SPELLING

a. Make a noun from each of the following words.

    curious   reliable   indebted   reciprocal

b. Correct any spelling errors in this paragraph:

    John insisted that the error was partialy his fault, since he had failed to specify the terms. But Mr. Winckler answered abruply that the responsability was soley his. It was his, Mr. Winckler's, job to assess the referrences of each firm and to do so promply.

[2] VOCABULARY

a. In this chapter, you were introduced to several terms relating to financial statements. These terms are listed below. Give a brief explanation of each.

    balance sheet   assets   liabilities   equity   liquidity

b. Use the word *interim* correctly as a noun and then as an adjective.

c. Explain briefly the difference in the meaning of *critical* as it is used in these two sentences:

    He was highly critical of the governor's program.
    This matter is of critical importance.

d. What does it mean to *divulge* something? to *vouch* for something? to *augur* well?

e. Would it be correct to say that an *astute* man had *acumen*? Why or why not?

f. Use each of these words correctly in a sentence that illustrates its meaning:

scrutinize   reciprocate   influx   deflect

[3] PUNCTUATION: QUOTATION MARKS

RULE: *Use quotation marks to enclose a direct quotation (but see marginal notation on p. 000); to set off words and phrases used in a special sense; to enclose titles of chapters, poems, magazine articles, and works of art.*

Mr. North said, "There will be a staff meeting at noon."
Your letter said, "I will mail my check on November 1."
The blind man could "see" the child's face with his fingers.
This selection is taken from an article entitled "How to Win."

RULE: *Place quotation marks after periods and commas and before colons and semicolons. If a question mark or exclamation point punctuates only the quotation, it precedes the quotation marks; if it punctuates an entire sentence that includes more than the quotation, it follows the quotation marks.*

"I believe," said Charles, "that Mr. Andrews is right."
Mrs. Phillips asked, "Have you read my latest book?"
What did you mean when you said, "This is some problem"?
She said, "It's okay to proceed"; he repeated, "Okay to proceed."

RULE: *Use single quotation marks for quoted material that falls within material already enclosed by quotation marks.*

"In my article 'Mountains to Climb,' " said Mr. White, "I have written about my experiences in the Alps."

Punctuate the following sentences correctly.

a. Knowledge of correct usage is an asset to anyones writing said Miss Knox

b. Professor Edgar asked Have you read the chapter Applying for Consumer Credit

c. The new spring fashions said the designer will appeal to the young people

d. Da Vincis great painting Mona Lisa is priceless

e. Buy now and pay later is a slogan frequently used in soliciting credit accounts

f. Look out shouted the driver

g. He said One good turn deserves another; he himself did not follow that principle

h. Which one of those articles said The economy has hit a new high

[4] NUMBERS

Writing would be simpler if all handbooks agreed on correct usage of numbers where percents and money are concerned. Whichever handbook you use, be consistent. Here is how we feel about it.

RULE: *Use figures for percentages, regardless of the amount.*

6 percent; 25 percent; 4^1/$_2$ percent

Note: Although financial institutions usually use the percent sign (%), the word *percent* is written out in most business correspondence.

RULE: *Generally use figures for money, regardless of the amount. Be consistent within a single context.*

When cents only are used, write:

5 cents; 92 cents

When dollars only are used, do not use decimal point and cyphers:

$2; $265; $2,000

When dollars and cents are used, write:

$.15; $2.00; $4.78; $249.24

When all amounts are in millions or billions, write:

$10 million; $1 billion; $3^1/$_2$ billion; $9.7 million

Isolated small or round numbers may be written out, as:

I wouldn't give two cents for that idea.
There are a hundred reasons for the change.

Use the number rules you have learned to correct these sentences:

a. Interest of four percent would yield forty dollars on a principal of $1,000.00.

b. Mail $.75 in coin to the Superintendent of Documents for the 5 pamphlets.

c. Here is twenty-five cents for the purchase of the five five-cent stamps.

d. Sales of Magna Corporation have declined from $2,500,000 in 1967 to $2,000,000 in 1968.

e. He paid $6 for the paper, $4.31 for the envelopes, and $10 for the stamps.

f. There was more than a thousand dollars in that safe.

g. The company's net profit was over 4 million dollars.

[5] MISPLACED MODIFIERS

One of the most common errors in writing is the dangling verbal phrase. (A verbal phrase is one containing a gerund, participle, or infinitive.)

> RULE: *A verbal phrase occurring at the beginning of a sentence must be followed immediately by the subject of the sentence.* (A verbal phrase at the beginning of a sentence *always* modifies the subject of that sentence; so be sure you choose the right subject!)

Not: Being sure of your answer, the ticket is enclosed.
But: Being sure of your answer, we are enclosing the ticket.

(The *ticket* isn't sure of the answer; *we* are.)

There are several ways to avoid a dangling phrase. You can change the position of the phrase so that it will be near the word it should modify. (Notice that it no longer modifies the subject of the sentence.)

Not: To become well informed, the habit of reading good newspapers and magazines will help you.
But: The habit of reading good newspapers and magazines will help you to become well informed.

You can also change the sentence so that the word that the phrase modifies becomes the subject of the sentence.

> To become well informed, you should develop the habit of reading good newspapers and magazines.

A third way is to change the phrase into a subordinate clause:

> If you wish to become well informed, the habit of reading good newspapers and magazines will help you.

Revise these sentences to eliminate dangling phrases:

a.   Before rejecting these designs, we suggest that you compare them with other plans.

b.   Relying on his ability to react quickly in emergencies, the car picked up speed.

c.   Already filled with students, the visitors could find no place in the auditorium.

d.   Referring to your letter of March 13, your complaint was ill advised.

e.   Having sent the incorrect invoice to you, be assured that we will adjust it at once.

f.   Lying on the desk, you will find a copy of the employee-evaluation chart.

g.   After discussing the proposal, a vote was taken.

h.   Having had five years of experience with Jones & Smith, you will find that I know auditing procedures very well.

i.   To get to the stadium, the left fork is the one we should take.

[6] PROOFREADING

List any corrections you make in proofreading this letter:

Aug. 1st, 1968

Jones & Hicks
65 Woodland Ave.
Hartford, Conneticut   14756

Attention Mr. R. G. Heseltine

Dear Mr. Heseltine:

We have now recieved from the Eastern Division the lay-out drawings to completed the set which is allready in the hands of the F.I.A.. We are enclosing 3 copies of Drawing E-16-7 and 4 copies of Drawing C-16-4 for the office lay-out. Drawing # 2 has been superceded by Drawing #6.

The writer understands from the Eastern Division that the

men in Boston, have been in contact with F.I.A. and that
progress have been made.

> Very truly yours
>
> *[signature: Irwin Wrede]*
>
> I. A. Wrede
> Treas.

agd

[7] PROBLEMS

✱ a. Here is the body of a letter your company has received from a prospective credit customer:

> Please enter my order for 1 dozen Delta Lights, Number
> 23-a, which I believe cost $8.56 each plus freight.
> Charge the lights to an account that I want to open with
> you.
>
> Please ship the lights as soon as possible, as I want to
> open my new business in two weeks.

Write the letter you feel would be necessary to handle this situation.

b. You are the assistant credit manager of Raynhem's Grocery Supplies. You are asked to check the references that have been given you by Frank Seewalk's Super Market, which wishes to purchase supplies from you on credit. Mr. Seewalk has recently moved his business from the city to the suburbs. His references are Delgardo Wholesale Grocers, Inc., and Union National Bank. Supply addresses and other necessary details, and set up your letters.

c. You are employed in the main office of the Heaslip Fuel Oil Company, which has been expanding rapidly in its marketing area. The officers of the company have a list of homeowners who heat by oil. They want to get a bigger share of the oil-heating business by capturing it from a major oil dealer. They ask you to compose a letter to offer a charge account to the homeowner who purchases from them. As an added incentive, you can mention that the company gives trading stamps, which will amount to a discount of 5 percent on all purchases. Whenever a buyer has stamps from $100 in purchases, he may turn them in for a $5 reduction on his next oil bill. You might also stress the 24-hour emergency service Heaslip offers.

d. As a follow-up to the preceding problem, compose a form letter that can be sent to those who open accounts with Heaslip Fuel Oil Company. Express your appreciation for the business. Mention that a statement is sent at the end of the month; payment may be made at any time during the following month. Mention once again the 5 percent value of the trading stamps.

e. Read and correct the following letters, rewriting when necessary. Watch for all types of errors — and be sure to proofread your own retyped letter.

> Please except my very deepest appreciation for your kind offer to let me open a charge account at your establishment. I will be glad to take advantage of this kind offer.
>
> I have filled in the application blank you inclosed with you letter to the best of my ability. The only references I could give was those of my friends and relatives because I have no charge cards or business connections. I do have a savings account with the Security Trust Co. for $75 which is the name of the bank listed on the blank.
>
> Hopeing to recieve my credit card in the very near future and thanking you in advance, I am

---

> Your application for opening a charge account at Granby's Dept. Store has been received with pleasure. Your application has been checked thoroughly because we do not want a charge account to be opened and then turn out to be a mistake.
>
> I am sure that you will be pleased to know that after the careful consideration given to your application, you have been excepted as a credit customer of our good store. We know that you will not default on your bills.
>
> After the instruction sheet about the use of your credit has been read carefully, than begin your credit shopping at Granby's. A statement will be sent at the end of each month to prove how much has been purchased during

the month. Be sure to pay the bill as soon as possible
because we will have to charge interest on any bills
that are not paid within the following 30 days. Furthermore, if the bill is not paid within 60 days, the right
to take away your credit privelege will be reserved.

You will enjoy buying on credit at Granby's and it will
be a profit to us also. Looking forward to seeing you,

We are sorry to inform you that it will be impossible
to grant you credit. Apparently you thought that we
would not check your references and would open an account for you without question. As a business man, don't
you realize that when it takes you six or seven months
to pay bills that it will effect your reputation as a
credit risk? We would be naive to grant credit under
such conditions.

Naturally we have no objection to you buying for cash.
Inclose your check with all orders and as soon as the
check has cleared banking channels, the order will be
shipped. It will pay you to buy from us because our
merchandise is a profitable line for anyone to carry.

f. The owner of a local department store wishes to write a letter to
    thank those credit customers who have an excellent paying record. He
    asks your help with this letter. Make any changes or corrections you
    feel will make his letter flow more smoothly.

Dear Sir or Madam:

It is a pleasure to observe that the 4 of Febuary will
mark the tenth anniversary of the opening of your charge
account with our good store.

We wish to express our apreciation for the confidence
in our management, evidenced by this relationship and
assure you that we anticipate serving you for many more
years.

With kind regards,

Truly yours,

Amelia Padula

Amelia Padula
Credit manager

13 | The Collection Series

YOUR fourth assignment in the TRK training program is to the Collection Department. TRK takes a calculated risk when it sends $500 or $10,000 worth of fabrics to a customer on credit. In times of economic stress for the individual or of recession in the economy, those bills may not be paid. The Collection Department tries to obtain payment as soon as possible and at the same time to keep the customer's goodwill.

When TRK sells goods on credit, it loses the use of the money those goods represent until they are paid for. If they are not paid for by the end of the month, TRK will not have the money to pay its own bills and salaries. Even more important, it will not be able to buy new merchandise to sell to its customers the following month. TRK, like all companies, cannot continue to do business unless its dollars are constantly working for it; and every dollar that isn't collected is a dollar that does no work for TRK.

There is another reason that companies strive hard to get prompt payment from their customers. When you

Why is prompt payment important to the creditor?

Keeping money working.

owe someone money or a phone call or a thank you, you avoid meeting him because you feel guilty. The customer who owes money will keep his account dormant until he pays his bill, and an inactive account holds profits down.

dormant

Keeping accounts active.

Despite the importance of prompt collections, businessmen are concerned with keeping their customers' goodwill. In an effort to do so, a company may send its credit customers monthly statements for two or even three months without mentioning lack of payment. Usually, a customer makes full payment within that time, and the embarrassment that has been avoided makes up for the time that the money has not been used.

Keeping goodwill may overbalance the need for prompt collections — to a point.

There are several possible reasons for failure to pay on time.

Some customers, however, do not pay their bills within a reasonable time. Some have perhaps forgotten; others may be in financial difficulty; still others may really be trying to avoid payment. Most companies, therefore, set up a procedure for handling collection problems. During your time in the Collection Department at TRK, you learn the following things about your company's collection procedure:

THE BASIC PROGRESSION

A series of collection letters advances from gentle reminders, to appeals to fair play and conscience, to insistent urgings and threats of action, and, finally, to legal action. Although the order of steps in the collection process is predetermined, the progression from one step to the next is flexible. For instance, a customer who has always paid promptly in the past might receive several gentle reminders before he is sent an appeal to fair play and conscience. But a customer who has been a problem before might receive one gentle reminder; then a strong appeal to his pride in his business might follow directly, without an intervening appeal to fair play.

flexible

The Reminders

THE GENTLE REMINDER

Anyone can overlook an obligation. In fact, many people simply forget to pay a bill. You write your first letter as a gentle reminder that a specific sum of money is due. Here is an example of such a reminder:

> In the rush and confusion of the holiday season, have you forgotten to send us your check for $55.70, which was due on November 30?

Assume a simple oversight.

Since you are assuming, at this stage, that the only problem is one of forgetfulness, you might emphasize your confidence in the customer by suggesting that he consider some new merchandise you have to offer. For instance:

> Perhaps you have forgotten us. This reminder comes to ask you for your check for $72.48, which was due on March 1. A return envelope is enclosed for your convenience.
>
> We have also included some samples of our new line of imported worsteds, which we think you'll want to have on hand for the fall. Orders will be filled any time after April 30.

THE STRONGER REMINDER

Should it be necessary to send a second reminder, your wording will be a little stronger, and you will, of course, omit mention of any new merchandise. But you must still assume that failure to pay is just an oversight. You might send the following note:

The second reminder is stronger, but still friendly.

> Apparently you have forgotten your balance of $55.70, which was due on November 30. Please bring your ac-

```
count up to date by placing your
check in the enclosed envelope and
mailing it to us today.
```

The Appeals

Your best appeal is the one that puts human nature to work for you.

The reminders are based on a fact of human nature — people forget. The appeals, too, are directed to human nature — to the sense of fair play and the desire for a good reputation. If the reminders have not brought a response, you should still assume that the debtor is not dishonest but is only delaying — perhaps because he is in some financial trouble, or because he is very short of office personnel, or even because he is **habitually** late in paying his bills. The purpose of the appeal is to convince him of the importance of seeing that your bill gets paid. There are several tacks you can take.

THE CREDIT-STANDING APPEAL

The first appeal might be little stronger than a reminder, including only an additional mention of the debtor's credit standing. Here's one example:

```
Please send us your check for
$271.04. As your statement shows,
this amount is now three months past
due.

You have always had a superior credit
standing at TRK. We hope you will
maintain this fine rating by mailing
us your check today.
```

THE PLEA FOR FAIR PLAY

A slightly stronger approach is to make the debtor feel he should give you the same treatment he would expect from his own charge customers. You have extended credit to him because you felt he could be relied upon; you have shipped merchandise immediately to cooperate with him. Therefore, he should treat you just as fairly. Your letter might read:

As you know, you still owe us $178.90
on your March account. Yet you have
not responded to our reminders, and
the account is three months overdue.

We must continue to pay our bills on
time, or our credit rating will be
impaired. You expect your customers   **impaired**
to meet their obligations each month,
and we count on ours to do so, too.

Please send us your check, and return
your account to its usual fine status.

THE APPEAL TO GOOD FAITH

American business is run on credit, and American customers pay their bills. The low percentage of bad debts
in the United States shows that businessmen, as well as
individuals, accept the responsibility for paying what
they owe.

When the plea for fair play does not bring results, your next step is to stir the conscience of your
customer still further. When he makes a purchase, he
enters into a contract enforceable at law. However, you   **enforceable**
do not yet want to threaten legal action. Your approach
is to appeal to the customer's code of business ethics,
which should insist on his paying his debts. This letter
might bring the desired results:

Won't you please fulfill your part of
our contract by paying your account
of $750, which is now four months
past due?

We firmly believe that a contract is
an agreement that must be kept by
both sides. We have performed our
part by shipping your order as soon
as we received it.

Please take the time right now to do
your part. Send us your check for
$750. Your payment will complete our
contract and restore our faith in
you.

THE CALL FOR AN EXPLANATION

Very often in business, the delinquent customer is not just reluctant. He has run into a financial problem that *precludes* the outlay of cash. The straightforward debtor volunteers an explanation before he receives any letters asking for payment of his account. However, a debtor may be reluctant to admit to you, his creditor, that his business is suffering a setback; so he ignores your initial letters.

precludes

In disregarding routine notices, he is leaving himself and his business open for criticism and loss of faith. But you must give him every chance before you assume the worst. You need your money; if you get a reply from the debtor, perhaps a payment plan can be worked out. And, if temporary financial stress is the cause of the problem, you want the customer's future business. So you do your best to open the lines of communication, to obtain an explanation.

Opening the lines of communication is the biggest step.

You might write one or more appeals before resorting to this approach, or you might include it in your first appeal. Here's one way to do it:

> Your shining record is about to be dimmed by its first overdue account. Will you please tell us why?
>
> After a perfect payment record of 20 years, you must be unhappy with this unpaid balance of $1,500, which is now four months past due.

Remember to suit the letter to the reader and the situation.

> Please take us, your business associates over these many years, into your confidence. If you will just explain the trouble, we can work out a schedule for meeting your commitment that will be convenient for you. This is all we ask.

Of course, you can use one or more of these approaches at the appeal stage of the collection series. If you write more than one appeal letter, each should be stronger than the preceding one.

THE INSISTENT URGING

If the appeals have brought no answer, you must become insistent. Before you threaten legal action, however, you see if milder threats bring a response.

The customer is undoubtedly concerned with his business. But he has jeopardized its standing by his actions (or, rather, lack of action). You bring this to his attention, using a more forceful tone than in the appeals letters. Your letter can read:

jeopardized

> Your business has built a reputation
> for service in this community. It has
> also earned an excellent credit rat-
> ing. It seems incredible that you
> should risk the loss of this stand-
> ing.
>
> We cannot decide what to do. We have
> written you four times to ask you to
> pay your account of $2,300 or to
> write us to arrange terms for pay-
> ment. Since you have not replied, we
> can only feel that you do not wish to
> cooperate with us. Therefore, unless
> you send us your check now, we will
> have to place your account on a cash
> basis.
>
> Retain your good name in the commu-
> nity and with us. Send your check
> today.

incredible

THE THREAT OF LEGAL ACTION

How unpleasant it is to write this type of letter! You have finally come to the stage where legal action seems inevitable, but you will try once more.

inevitable

You threaten the debtor with the loss of prestige and the other difficulties that will ensue if you are forced to turn over his account to a collection agency or to an attorney. His loss of credit standing is publicized immediately by the major credit services, and it becomes impossible for him to purchase on credit. In addition, he may face legal action to collect his debt.

untenable

Always be polite.

Your letter should give him a true picture of his untenable position. You are no longer interested in retaining his business; you want to collect what is owed you. This case calls for clear and strong language. But the language should not be abusive; no purpose is served by a show of anger. Here is one letter you might write:

By using this service, you are assured that Mr. Griffin has received the notice.

adverse

lies

Note cold closing.

```
                                 July 10, 1968

Certified Mail

Mr. Walter Griffin
123 River Street
Dubuque, Iowa    52001

Dear Mr. Griffin:

You have had five letters asking for
payment of the $985.67 that you have
owed us since January. Not one re-
sponse has come from you.

We want very much to have this ac-
count settled without involving an
outside agency, but you leave us no
choice. On the twentieth of this
month, just ten days from now, we
must turn over your account to a col-
lection agency. You know, of course,
the adverse effect this will have on
your credit standing.

Please do not force us to take this
unpleasant action. You can prevent it
--and its unfortunate consequences--
by sending us partial payment of $400
and an explanation of how you will
handle the balance. Your check must
be in our hands by July 20.

The choice lies with you.

                        Yours truly,
```

THE INTRANSIGENT DEBTOR

If your threat of legal action brings no reply, you must follow through by turning the case over to your collection agency. In a succinct note, you inform the debtor that his intransigence has forced you to take this step.

succinct

intransigence

Dear Mr. Griffin:

We have turned over your account for $985.67 to our collection agency. Since you have not responded to our letters to you, we had no alternative.

You will hear from the agency before the end of this week.

We are sorry that you have forced us to take this action.

            Yours truly,

Note that the tone remains polite.

This customer is, of course, lost to your firm. But a debt must be paid. In fairness to all your customers, you must take every step to see that payment is received from those few debtors who refuse to pay voluntarily.

As you have by now learned, the collection process goes from the simple reminder to the demand for payment and the legal action that finally results from nonpayment. Throughout the series, it is important to make the letters persuasive — to inject the element of self-interest by convincing the debtor that he is the one who benefits most by paying promptly.

Although the language of collection letters becomes more forceful and more demanding as the series progresses, the maintenance of politeness at all stages is important. Your aim is to get the customer to pay his bill, not to antagonize him. At each stage, you want to give him the benefit of the doubt insofar as your previous letters allow.

maintenance

WHEN THE CUSTOMER EXPLAINS

straitened

indulgence

Few customers require the entire collection series. A few reminders for the forgetful debtor or an appeal or two to the businessman in straitened circumstances almost always bring about positive action. The usual answer is quick payment, for which no reply is required. But the customer who needs your indulgence in an emergency must receive a sympathetic reply when he writes:

```
I need your help.

Will you please extend my credit for
the $1,500 I owe on my January ac-
count.

The usual cold weather this spring
has kept our sales to a minimum. Added
to this, our own charge accounts have
been very sluggish, leaving us with
insufficient cash to meet current ac-
counts.

If you will bear with us, we shall
make complete payment by April 15.
```

You are pleased that the customer has defined the problem and has offered a solution. You want to accept this solution and to thank him:

```
Dear Mr. Webster:

Thank you for suggesting a solution
to the problem of your overdue ac-
count. Yes, we will be glad to extend
your credit to April 15.

We understand that your sales have
been adversely affected by the unsea-
sonable weather and hope that by
```

unseasonable

April 15 your sales curve will have
turned upward.

Your account with us is open. Please
use it.

Sincerely yours,

This is another way to say thanks to a good customer.

THE COLLECTION SERIES IN ACTION

Your friend, the proprietor of Nayles Hardware Store, has had some difficulty with some of his charge customers. He lays the problem in your hands and asks you to draw up a series of collection letters that he can send to his customers when their accounts are overdue. You apply the principle of progressing gradually from the simple reminder to the last resort of turning over the account to a collection agency or an attorney.

lays

Here is the first letter, which Mr. Nayles can send after the statement has become overdue and a duplicate statement has been sent without obtaining a reaction from the debtor:

Just in case you have forgotten to
pay the $78.50 due on your statement
of January 31, may we remind you that
your check is already more than a
month overdue.

Please use the enclosed envelope to
send us your check. And come in to
see the new buffer attachment we have
just received for the Model 621
Sander you purchased last summer.

Since many of Mr. Nayles's customers are busy people who might well misplace or forget a bill, you

Keep the customer in mind.

feel that another gentle reminder is a good idea. So
you write this note:

> Did you forget? Nayles Hardware needs
> that $78.50. Please bring your ac-
> count up to date by sending us your
> check today.

In your third letter, you decide to appeal to the
customer's sense of fair play — "Do for me what you
would want others to do for you." You hope that this
appeal will stir him out of his lethargy.

lethargy

> How would you feel if you did not re-
> ceive your salary check on time?
> Would you say nothing and assume that
> you would get your money sometime? Or
> would you do something about it?
>
> It's the same with us. We need the
> money you owe us as much as you need
> your money.
>
> Please avoid the annoyance of receiv-
> ing further correspondence by sending
> us your check for $78.50, which is
> now three months overdue. A return
> envelope is enclosed.

In your fourth letter, you feel it is time to try to
elicit the debtor's reason for delaying payment.

*Assume the best, not
the worst.*

> When it is necessary to remind a cus-
> tomer for the fourth time that his
> account is overdue, there must be
> some valid reason for his delay.
>
> You know that you have owed us $78.50
> since January 31. If you will tell us
> why you cannot pay all or part of
> this debt now, we will try to work

out a plan that is convenient for
you.

Your credit record with us has always
been excellent. Why not keep it that
way? Please send us your check today,
or give us an explanation and let us
work out a payment schedule.

You decide not to go beyond five letters in your
series for Nayles Hardware. In your fifth letter, then, you
must threaten action, even though you still hope to
persuade.

Why haven't we heard from you? You
have owed us $78.50 since January 31
--five months ago--and you have not
answered any of our correspondence to
let us know why your account is still
unpaid.

We seldom need to pass an account on
to our attorney. However, if your account is not paid within 30 days, or
if no explanation is forthcoming
within that time, we shall have to
take that unpleasant step.

Once again, we have enclosed a
stamped, self-addressed envelope for
your check. Please use it. Do not
force us to take drastic action that
will be detrimental to your credit   detrimental
standing and reputation.

IN CLOSING

Looking back over this collection series, you can see
the benefits of the training program you have just completed. In addition to improving your knowledge of the
business, it has sharpened your organizational ability,
increased your efficiency, and developed your sense of

responsibility. It has taught you to focus upon the purpose of your job and to consider the reactions of those your work will affect. The results of the course are apparent in the growing ease with which you can express yourself and in the sharp, vital, modern communication you are now able to produce.

SUMMARY

Extending credit carries with it the burden of maintaining a careful watch over the payment of outstanding accounts. To the collection department falls the task of obtaining payment of bills as quickly as possible, while retaining the goodwill of the slow-paying customer.

Although specific collection procedures vary from company to company, there is a basic progression in the collection process. After the normal routine of sending monthly statements, you write friendly reminders to the customer to persuade him to pay. When necessary, a stronger appeal follows to remind the customer that his credit standing with you and with other companies may be affected by his delaying payment. Your next step is to call for fair play on the part of the debtor.

You continue to strengthen your case when you write to remind your customer of his contractual obligation. If he cannot fulfill his contract, he is asked to explain his reasons so that you could perhaps extend the term of the debt or reschedule his payments.

As the need for stronger measures becomes evident, you must begin to threaten him with the possibility of reporting his delinquency to a credit bureau and, finally, with turning over his account to an agency for collection.

Regardless of the anger you may feel toward non-payers, you must show restraint in your writing. Throughout your collection series, you assume that the customer intends to pay; you treat him politely; you try to persuade him; you appeal to his self-interest. Remember, though, that each customer is an individual. Consider his case in the light of your experience with him. Allow sufficient flexibility in your procedures to provide for individual cases. Don't use the same letter for the first offender as you do for the consistently negligent debtor. In each case, the individual must receive your genuine concern. Your objective is to collect and also to retain the customer's goodwill up to the final step.

[1] SPELLING

a. What letter is missing in each of these words?

incred___ble   inevit___ble   unseason___ble   flex___ble

b. Correct any misspellings in the paragraph below.

John had a firm committment to the law. As an attorney he felt responsable for the maintainance of the legal system, which permited a proceedure for the peaceful settlement of disputes. This morning, he was faced with a problem — an unenforcible law. Whatever decision he made would jepardize the system.

[2] VOCABULARY

a. Do you know the difference between *lie* and *lay*? Choose the correct words in the following sentences.

As he (*lay, lie*) on the narrow bunk, he thought of how he might have to (*lay, lie*) down his life for the cause.
(*Lay, Lie*) down!
(*Lay, Lie*) it down on the table.
This morning, the jacket was (*laying, lying*) across the bannister.

b. Give a synonym for each of these words:

lethargy   detrimental   succinct

c. What is the difference between *adverse* and *averse*? between *straitened* and *straightened*?

d. Use each of the words listed below in a sentence that illustrates its meaning. (You may change the part of speech of any of the words.)

dormant   precludes   intransigence
habitually   untenable   indulgence
impaired

[3] NUMBERS

Let's bring together some miscellaneous rules about writing numbers.

RULE: *Fractions used alone are spelled out.*

a one-fourth share; was two-thirds finished

RULE: *Write mixed numbers in figures.*

5$\frac{1}{2}$ bushels; 7$\frac{5}{8}$ gallons

RULE: *Measurements are usually written in figures. (Show the unit of measurement only with the last figure of a series.)*

5 by 9 by 14 feet; 8 x 10 inches

RULE: *Time is designated by figures when the exact time is given with* a.m. *or* p.m. *With o'clock, time is usually written out.*

1 p.m.; 2:30 a.m.; 12 noon; 12 midnight; four o'clock

RULE: *When the date follows the month, use figures; when it precedes the month, use words or figures. (Remember that when the month is given first, use the cardinal, not the ordinal, form.)*

May 1; the 1st of May; the first of May

Now correct any mistakes in these sentences, remembering all the number rules you have learned:

a. He has willed $\frac{3}{4}$ of his estate to his wife and the rest to his daughter.

b. The stock of United Motors sold for five and $\frac{1}{2}$, which was a drop of one and $\frac{1}{2}$ points.

c. Please order fifty-five reams of letterhead stationery eight by ten inches.

d. According to this letter of June 10th, you have an appointment with Mr. Carswell at 8:00 o'clock.

e. The rug, which measures 10 feet by 14 feet, costs $50.00 and can be delivered between eight a.m. and four p.m.

[4] DOUBLE NEGATIVES

RULE: *Use only one negative word in a sentence to express a single negative idea.*

Not: I don't want none.
But: I don't want any.
Or: I want none.

Notice, however, that more than one negative word may be used if more than one negative idea is to be expressed.

He neither agreed nor disagreed.
Nobody wanted to go, so nothing happened.

Sometimes the double-negative error is made because the writer doesn't recognize one of the negative words for what it is. Remember that these words convey a negative idea by themselves:

never	scarcely	none
nothing	nobody	nowhere
barely	hardly	neither
no one		

Rewrite these sentences to eliminate all double negatives:

a. Didn't you hear nothing from the personnel manager about your promotion?

b. The problems had arisen so unexpectedly that scarcely nobody in the office knew what to do.

c. Plan your vacation trip now. Don't plan to go nowhere this summer.

d. That cannot be done no longer by any member of the tax department.

e. None of us didn't go.

f. There is hardly nowhere to go.

g. Isn't there nobody who will volunteer?

[5] REDUNDANCIES

Many writers, through carelessness, say the same thing twice — that is, they allow redundancies to creep into their writing. For example, there is no point in saying "6 a.m. in the morning," since "a.m." means "in the morning." See if you can eliminate the redundancies from these sentences:

a. Since a substantial segment of our population is moving to the suburbs of the city, we have arrived at the conclusion that new shopping centers should be erected in these areas.

b.   There is another alternative that you may choose.

c.   John Blake has recently completed a biography of the life of Adam Smith.

d.   Because of the difficulty of obtaining credit at the present time, we suggest that you postpone your building program until later.

e.   We hope to regain again the place we occupied among the ten first corporations in the United States.

f.   If you will refer back to our letter of March 1, you will see that we explained our position quite accurately.

g.   The consensus of opinion among each and every branch manager is that the machine has a serious defect.

h.   We shall replace your radio with one that is exactly identical to it.

i.   We agree with the committee that no one company should have a complete monopoly in marketing the new film.

j.   The supervisory personnel will assemble together in the meeting room on the fourth floor.

[6] PROOFREADING EXERCISE

Proofread this letter, and list any corrections you find it necessary to make.

Augut 15th, 1968

Dear reader:

Saving money is, to a large estent, knowing how to spent it wisely.

     Some times its as simple as buying summer close in September or keeping a small night-light on to prevent dangerous and costly accident.

Other times, though, it can get pretty involved. For instants, computing true interest rates, understanding the difference between strait life and term insurance or, perhaps, knowing how to treat you lawn.

Today you must place emphasize on cautious money management. The cost of hireing such management is self defeating to all accept those who subscribe to MONEY SAVER MAGAZINE.

```
Use teh inclosed card to subscribe to MONEY SAVER MAGAZINE
for 6 months for only $2. If you pay in advance, deduct a
discount of 2 percent, and send only $1.94.

Thank you for you interest.

                              Sincerly,
```

Brian Morse
Vice president

el

[7] PROBLEMS

a.   Mrs. Jane Blackwell has an account with the Hall Department Store. She has had the account for six years, during which time she has been prompt in meeting all obligations. On December 15, she spent $97.50, which she charged to her account. The bill was due on January 31. On February 20, the collection manager asks you to write to Mrs. Blackwell about her overdue account. What would you write?

b.   The Standard Tire Company has a credit policy of 2/10, n/30. Upon looking over his accounts on October 15, the collection manager notices that George Boyle owes $66.55 that should have been paid on August 31. He asks you to write a letter to Mr. Boyle to remind him to pay his bill.

c.   Standard Tire Company has not heard anything from Mr. Boyle about his account. On November 15, you write another letter to him to try to collect.

d.   By December 31, patience is wearing thin. You write to Mr. Boyle again. You might remind him that he had been slow at paying in the past and that you had always given him time to pay. However, his previous delays in paying were not so long as this. Try to be considerate but firm.

e.   On March 1, you write to tell Mr. Boyle that his account will be turned over to a collection agency if he does not pay by March 20.

f.   On April 1, you write your last letter to Mr. Boyle. He has not replied to any of your correspondence, so you have placed his account in the hands of Smith and French for collection.

g. The following letter was written by one of your customers who found himself in financial difficulty. Mr. Ryder, your collection manager, asks you to write an answer to the letter. Mr. Ryder tells you that Mr. Splain has been a good customer for ten years and has never been behind in his payments.

> Thank you for filling our order for 12 Fyr Fiter alarms so quickly. We have your invoice Number 6783 dated January 31 for $276.50.
>
> In the ten years that we have had our account with you, we have always made payments on schedule or even within the discount period. Right now, however, we find ourselves in serious financial difficulties because we had to close our store for five days when our heating system failed. The most we can pay on account now is $100. We hope that we can pay the rest of the bill by March 15.
>
> Will you bear with us for a short time? We just want you to know why we cannot send you a check in full payment.

h. Correct and retype the following letters:

> We are disappointed that you have neglected to send your check for the $98.07 due on our account No. 358, dated July 1. It would seem to us that you are unreasonable, and we must insist that you comply with the terms of credit so graciously extended to you by us.
>
> You cannot expect us to grant you special concessions when you as a businessman probably would not do the same thing for your own credit customers.
>
> We expect payment in full at once. We are even enclosing a self-addressed envelope in which you can enclose same.

> This missive is just a short note to let you know that the writer wishes to thank you for your esteemed account, which has been handled so judiciously during the past nine years.
>
> It is hoped that you will continue to favor us with your valued patronage for many years to come. Accounts like yours are a pleasure to have on our books. They enable

you to buy on credit and at the same time help us to
increase our profits through the greater volume of business that can be done this way.

Assuring you of our continued cooperation with you,
I am,

We duly appreciate your fine charge account, which you
opened with us recently. So that there will be no mis-
understandings, we want to tell you what your responsi-
bilities are when you have an account.

You will receive your statement at the end of each
month. This statement will list your purchases during
the month and the final balance. If you make payment on
said balance within ten days after receipt of the statement, you may deduct a discount of 2 percent. Be sure
that you do not deduct the discount if you pay at any
time after the ten days. The full amount of said balance is due by the end of the month following the date
of the invoice.

INDEX

A page number in italics refers to an illustration.

A

Q

T

transitional, 102–03
  See also Vocabulary
Writer of letter, impression given by, 95–99
Written communication vs. verbal, 4, 5, 7, 231, 237

Z

ZIP code, spacing before, 25, 28

D
E   2
F   3
G   4
H   5
I   6
J   7